M000012945

Practice-Building 2.0

for

Mental Health Professionals

Strategies for Success
in the Digital Age

TRACY TODD

W. W. NORTON & CO.

New York • London

Copyright © 2009 by Tracy Todd

All rights reserved
Printed in the United States of America
First Edition

For information about permission to reproduce selections from
this book, write to Permissions, W. W. Norton & Company, Inc.,
500 Fifth Avenue, New York, NY 10110

Manufacturing by Quebecor World, Fairfield Graphics
Book design by Gilda Hannah
Production Manager: Leeann Graham

Library of Congress Cataloging-in-Publication Data

Todd, Tracy, 1962 –
    Practice-building 2.0 for mental health professionals : strate-
gies for success in the digital age / Tracy Todd. — 1st ed.
        p. cm.
    "A Norton Professional Book."
    Includes bibliographical references and index.
    ISBN 978-0-393-70562-1 (pbk.)
    1. Psychotherapy—Practice. 2. Mental health counseling—
Practice. 3. Mental health services—Marketing. 4. Mental health
services—Internet marketing. I. Title.
    RC465.5.T63 2009
    616.89'140068—dc22
                                                    2009030965

W. W. Norton & Company, Inc.
500 Fifth Avenue, New York, N.Y. 10110
www.wwnorton.com

W. W. Norton & Company Ltd.
Castle House, 75/76 Wells St.
London W1T 3QT

1 3 5 7 9 0 8 6 4 2

This book is dedicated to those full-time private practice owners working long hours and attempting to keep their business profitable, while significantly contributing to household income. May their spirit of entrepreneurship continue perpetuating innovations in all aspects of mental health service delivery.

Contents

Acknowledgments

There are many to thank, but none more than my business partner and dearest friend Tracey Ayers. She encompasses the definition of success, both personal and professional. Tracey's creativity, business acumen, and perseverance prevailed during the most challenging times of building our business. She provided a solid foundation through success and failure, and her unwavering support of my endeavors continues to astound.

I would like to thank my parents, Ted and Wilma, and sister, Kim, for always encouraging me and never questioning my career or choices. Thanks to my nieces Nicole and Marissa, who are totally delightful and keep my spirits young.

My genuine and warmest thoughts go to Renae and Elizabeth for providing so many years of stability, sense of family, and care. Without them, I shudder to think how things would be different in such a negative way.

Thank you to Mark and Scott for such long, prosperous, and amazing friendship. Thank you to Cathy for coming to my rescue when I needed rescuing, for the encouragement, and for the phone calls keeping me on task during the last, long stretches of this project.

Thank you to Shelley Green, Frank Thomas, James Morris, Joe Strano, and Bruce Kuehl. Many years ago, this group instilled the importance of creativity, determination, and resilience. There has never been, and probably never will be, a set of professional colleagues of which I am so proud to be part.

Thank you to Deborah Malmud and Kristen Holt-Browning, for their kindness with comments and perseverance throughout this project.

Finally, I would like to thank the American Association for Marriage and Family Therapy for providing me with opportunities and challenges. Without the mentoring and guidance present in AAMFT, I would never have lived to the potential others recognized in me. Thank you to Mike Bowers and Karen Gautney for accommodating and persevering through my transition from business owner/therapist to colleague.

Disclosures

Throughout this book I use examples of practices with stories of success and failure. I keep names confidential out of respect for their efforts. Similar to clients, no one likes to read about themselves, especially regarding failed strategies. Although changing identifying information, I retained the accuracy of the story.

It is important that with any practice-building, self-help strategy you publish on your Web site the necessary legalese providing the appropriate forewarning that self-help strategies do not replace psychotherapy, and that any thoughts of harm to self or others should result in an immediate call to the police or a trip to a hospital. Include what is legally sound and gives you comfort.

Although I am confident that the tools and strategies will help your practice grow, I cannot make any such guarantees. Practice growth is dependent on many factors and you may or may not achieve the same level of success described.

The History Behind This Book

As a naïve young professional having the distinct advantage of ignorance of historical practice-building patterns, I opened the Brief Therapy Institute of Denver in 1993. Operating in a market dominated by managed care and having statistically seven times more therapists than the population could support, like many other therapists I struggled to make ends meet. However, I soon had the good fortune of great business partners (Elaine Penny and then Tracey Ayers) with vision and exceptional adaptation skills. We navigated the challenges associated with a city ranked as "one of the best places to live," resulting in substantial increases in personal and business expenses while managed care was cutting rates. Surviving the conditions, I was asked to write, "Surviving and Thriving in a Managed Mental Healthcare Marketplace."

Through all the challenges, the Brief Therapy Institute of Denver Inc. (BTID) has maintained a high degree of integrity with referral sources, third-party payers, and the psychotherapy community. Our reputation within the community is solid, and clinicians associated with the BTID are regularly invited to participate on quality assurance committees, give presentations, teach, and consult. The BTID continues to have challenges like any other small business but perseveres and succeeds while others fail.

Adapting to and overcoming extreme market conditions has resulted in numerous awards:

2000 Practice Award, American Association for Marriage and Family Therapy. A national award for innovation and practice development.

1997 Innovation Award, Behavioral Health Centura Link. A national award for innovation.

1996 Best Practice Award given by consortium of managed care organizations. A local award for innovation and quality services.

1993 Outstanding Service Award given by Colorado Association for Marriage and Family Therapy.

Awards, publications, and high-quality services resulted in numerous interviews with such media as *Psychotherapy Finances*, *Family Therapy Magazine*, *Best Life*, the *Wall Street Journal*, *Glamour Magazine*, *Ladies Home Journal*, *CBS Market Watch*, and *Parenting Magazine*, to name a few.

As I was completing this project, I received a telephone call from Michael Bowers, executive director of the American Association for Marriage and Family Therapy, inviting me to apply for the position of director of professional and public affairs. Believing in my abilities to build and manage in the world of private practice, he strongly encouraged me to consider how I might positively impact therapists and the profession on a grander scale. After a few sleepless nights, long conversations with family and friends, and the blessing from Tracey, I applied and was eventually hired for the position. The many years of challenges, innovations, awards, media attention, and seminars delivered culminated in *Practice-Building 2.0*. Feeling, and believing, that I was going out at the top of my game, the decision was right.

PART ONE

Conceptual Shifts
in
Practice-Building 2.0

Introduction

Practice-building gurus, consultants, and publications generally emphasize that building a practice requires networking, getting on panels, creating a new niche or specialty, public speaking, and belonging to business groups such as a Chamber of Commerce. The phrase *practice building* is synonymously used with referral development. It also seems an accepted fact that practice building requires marketing, advertising, and some form of exposure to people and agencies unfamiliar with practice services (Myths 1, 3, 4, and 6–9, discussed in another section of this chapter). There are many myths about practice building because virtually every strategy is about gaining referrals, not actually establishing and *building* a business in mental health service delivery. Operating a private practice is owning a small business requiring attention to such challenges as market trends, infrastructure efficiencies, changing demographic populations, reimbursement systems, and technological advances that alter practice patterns.

Personal Reflections

Although having a business mindset is mentioned, rarely do practice-building consultants actually discuss business infrastructure technology that leads to an efficient service delivery system, thereby increasing profit margins (Chapter 5). Infrastructure technology is the internal technology of a business used in day-to-day operations. Lacking are discussions about how such internal technologies as contact management systems and electronic forms documentation increase revenue by reducing labor and office management costs. Psychotherapists tend to avoid training dealing with the boring business components that result in referral and revenue increases. Admittedly, I find it intriguing when a practice-building trainer promises "10 easy steps to cash pay clients" or "increase your referrals now." These are alluring presentations, and they presuppose that therapists deliver high-quality clinical and customer services. *Practice Building 2.0* is significantly more comprehensive toward building a thriving practice than simply "getting more referrals" or "having a cash pay practice."

It does not take much foresight to see how technology and communications have fundamentally altered virtually every business, psychotherapy included. A psychotherapy business owner needs technological efficiencies that reduce labor costs and increase revenue streams. Owning a business means monitoring business trends, adapting to new technologies, developing business efficiencies that increase profit margins, and conducting customer satisfaction surveys to determine what customers think of both clinical and customer services. Practice building is about owning and operating all aspects of a business, allowing the capitalization on trends and technologies.

There are many myths and misunderstandings about the implementation of technology in private practice. Technology, for many, is a great struggle. Intimidation often paralyzes therapists from implementing changes, thereby creating another barrier to effective practice building. Therapists, rather than learning and integrating technology, will rely on familiar but outdated methods of practice building. Networking may create some distress but is perceived as easier to do than creating an interactive Web site. Today's technology is easy to implement and extremely affordable.

Giving practice-building seminars exposes me to a diverse range of stories about therapist success and failure. Of concern are those stories of clinicians diligently following an instructor's referral development strategies such as networking, advertising, developing a niche, or pursuing specialty training and subsequently realizing a small payoff. For example, realizing a minimal return on her investment, Sherry discontinued practice-building efforts following 18 months of conscientiously attending networking functions, upgrading her office's appearance, and engaging in advertising seminars. Frustrated and defeated, she considered closing her practice. Consider Bill: after spending a great deal of money to achieve certification in a specialty area and subsequently investing in such items as new business cards and stationery, he met the same devastating end—a small number of referrals not worth the investment of time and money.

Converging Processes

What causes failures when therapists do everything correctly? There can be many factors, ranging from poor clinical services, to an inefficient and costly business infrastructure (even solo practitioners have an infrastructure), to using outdated methods of referral development. Simply put, the business paradigm for practice building is quickly and radically changing. Close examination identifies four converging processes: technology, a flattening field, best practice standards/customer service, and the subsequent result of creating lifelong customers.

Technology

Google, blogging, Yahoo, HTML (hypertext markup language), podcasting, online scheduling, e-news, Adwords, PDAs (personal digital assistants), and secure socket layer e-mail are essential tools for surviving and thriving in today's private practice marketplace. A foreign language to many, these tools are quickly replacing antiquated practice-building techniques of yellow page advertisements, attending networking functions, having snappy graphics and logos, and blanketing the public with business cards or brochures. Outdated practice-building techniques are expensive, labor intensive, and ineffective. For example, a therapist choosing to send a newsletter to current and former clients realizes the following costs:

> $0.44 postage (current postage which will increase) per mailing
> $0.06 per envelope
> $0.14 per newsletter copy (black and white, self-serve, $0.07 per side)
> $0.03 per label
> ————
> $0.67 total per piece
> x 300 mail outs
> ————
> $201.00
> + $240.00 lost income ($80 per session x 3 hours of labor)
> ————
> $441.00 total project cost

Conducting a $441.00 mailing quickly becomes cost prohibitive on a monthly basis. However, with an e-mail merge program integrated with an electronic contact management system, the cost can be a few minutes of time and a simple point-and-click action. There are no costs for postage, envelopes, copies, or labels. In addition, the newsletter can be multiple pages, created in color, and include links and audio files. Clients receive fresh information rather than an infrequent and expensive newsletter typically sent when referrals are lacking. Technology eliminates cost and time barriers while enhancing the final product.

Clients can continue to receive the newsletter long after therapy ends because the cost remains the same whether sending 1 or 1,000 newsletters.

Therapists who use technology quickly become more credible. The e-mailed newsletter will include links to the therapist's Web site. The Web site will then provide additional services and resources. Blogging, for example, creates a situation by which clients, potential clients, and other professionals feel connected to the therapist, even if the therapist is a solo practitioner. Just a few years ago, this type of connection and credibility were not possible. Although some clients will demonstrate reluctance and resistance to technology and psychotherapy, eventual adaptation similar to technology in other service delivery areas will occur. Furthermore, as young adults become independent utilizers of mental health services, technology will be a natural part of their lives.

Technology increases cost efficiency, reduces administrative demands, enhances access to care, and maximizes focus on treatment. The resulting business climate characterized by fewer barriers and hierarchies (flattening) is a second significant change.

Flattening

Thomas Friedman (2006) presented a description of current globalization and economic trends he labeled as *flattening*. Flattening involves removing or diminishing technological, economic, or political barriers primarily for conducting commerce, thereby allowing small companies to compete with multibillion-dollar corporations. Economies implementing technology are becoming more interconnected, offering advantages and opportunities to many countries, cultures, and people. Advantages once afforded to the economic privileged are disappearing, affording people and countries the opportunity to succeed in professions once dominated by other cultures.

Flattening involves leveling the playing field, placing customers in a position to interact more directly with the provider of services. In psychotherapy, there have been numerous flattening events. One example of flattening is the elimination of psychiatric supervision. Legislation and licensing changes began eliminating the need for a psychiatrist's signature or supervision of services (hierarchy), allowing psychotherapists to eliminate one cost of conducting therapy, thereby removing a barrier to providing services—flattening.

Quite possibly the most significant, practice-altering flattening process involves technology and referrals. Until recently, clients telephonically accessed an "intake and referral coordinator." Clients provided some basic clinical information, and the coordinator (hierarchy) would typically provide a few names for the client to contact. The referral process, usually based on positive relationships between the coordinator and specific network therapists, created a situation in which in a network of many, only a few therapists were chosen and utilized by the coordinator. Today, the situation is completely different. A potential client accesses the online directory of his or her insurance company, conducts a zip code search, and then chooses from numerous therapists within a specified radius of that zip code. After reading varying therapist biographies, clients begin calling, e-mailing, or visiting Web sites in rank order of personal preference, *not* the coordinator's preference. Now, all therapists on a panel have an equal opportunity to gain referrals (the playing field is leveled). Therapists once truly the "preferred, preferred providers" are now in a sea of therapist names and with no qualities to distinguish them from others. An added complication is that some online directory search results are listed in alphabetical order. Therapists with last names beginning with B or elsewhere in the high alphabet have a poor likelihood of review by the potential client.

Contributing to additional practice implosion self-infliction is the lack of responsiveness of therapists to these directories. Despite being free, provided by the insurance company, and an important pipeline for referrals, many therapists do not complete their profiles. Furthermore, when a free or inexpensive therapist directory is offered to therapists, only a small percentage of therapists will actually take advantage of the offer. Other inexpensive practice-building tools (e.g., online scheduling, e-mail merge programs) are frequently shunned by therapists because they fear technology or lack technological literacy.

Traditional practice-building strategies are increasingly difficult to execute successfully in a flattening business climate. New paradigms are becoming necessary to survive and thrive in a flattening field. As early as 2000, more than half (53%) of Internet users were using the Internet to take better care of themselves or loved ones (Fox & Rainie, 2000). Astoundingly, from March 2000 to December 2002 Internet users seeking health information increased from 46 million to 73 million users, a 59% increase (Madden, 2003).

The challenge, of course, is that therapists view technology as "not for me." In the 21st century, technology is necessary and expected. Potential clients expect fewer barriers between services, and in a point-and-click world they expect immediate assistance. In a flattening society, practice-building therapists must implement strategies that meet consumer demands. For example, a current client can understandably expect the ability to schedule an *immediate* appointment. The emphasis is on immediate. Why should clients need to call and leave a voice mail or wait for a receptionist to arrive? Consider a cross-country truck driver who realizes he will arrive home earlier than expected and, at say 2:00 A.M., schedules an appointment via the Internet, using a wireless Internet connection.

Speed, access, and connectivity are fundamentally changing the client–therapist relationship. Technology and flattening now create practice situations in which therapists must pay attention to practice standards and treatment services extending beyond the psychotherapy room.

Best Practice Standards/Treatment Services

Placing emphasis on effective and efficient treatment models and therapy styles was commonplace during the 1980s and 1990s. Currently, growing in momentum is the rapidly expanding emphasis on best practice standards or, in business language, customer service. These standards focus on the whole of psychotherapy, not just the face-to-face interaction in the therapy room (Todd, 2006). They are the underbelly of psychotherapy. For example, variables such as access to care, coordination of care, and postdischarge follow-up are becoming vitally important treatment expectations, best practice standards, and customer service necessities.

Three significant publications—*Achieving the Promise: Transforming Mental Health Care in America. Final Report* (New Freedom Commission on Mental Health, 2003), *Crossing the Quality Chasm: A New Health System for the 21st Century* (Institute of Medicine, 2001), and *Mental Health: A Report of the Surgeon General* (U.S. Department of Health and Human Services, 1999)—outline and challenge health care professionals to deliver services considered "ceilings," not "floors." Many conclusions can be drawn from these reports, and here I synthesize the salient variables for outpatient mental health care.

1. Non-face-to-face services, services outside the therapy room, are as important as the actual psychotherapy services.
2. Consumers must have easy and fast access to providers and care.
3. Consumers must be able to "comparison shop." Consumers must have the opportunity to compare many variables, ranging from office location to therapist gender, to psychotherapy style.
4. Providers need to create profiles and benchmarks that allow easy comparison. Providers will also be profiled and benchmarked by third-party entities.
5. Providers will engage in evidence-based practice patterns. Both the style of psychotherapy and the effectiveness of the practice must have some sense of scientific or research backing.
6. Providers will engage in emphasizing prevention and anticipation of consumer needs.
7. Providers must engage in aggressive coordination of care.
8. Technology needs to be implemented in all practice settings, allowing for multiple forms of interaction with consumers as well as a more streamlined practice pattern.
9. Excellence at all levels of service delivery, not just "in-the-room" care, is

expected from all providers. The expectation is service delivery at the ceiling, not floor, level.

These initiatives clearly demonstrate that a service delivery system capitalizing on technology to provide outstanding customer service is becoming a reality. The New Freedom Commission on Mental Health made the following recommendation: "Use health technology and telehealth to improve access and coordination of mental health care, especially for Americans in remote areas or in underserved populations" (2003, p. 79). *Telehealth* refers to use of all forms of information dissemination involving telephony, Internet, and such. The New Freedom Commission suggested telehealth is underused for the distribution of mental health information in rural, underserved, and severe disability populations. The report cited video cameras and e-mail reminders as two examples that can easily enhance mental health service delivery.

The Institute of Medicine (2001) made a strong argument for continuous care—albeit not necessarily face-to-face care. Consumers should have access to care when they need it and in a method that allows easy access, whether by telephone, Internet, or any other means *not involving face-to-face visits*. This tenet clearly indicates the emphasis on outside-the-room services and the ever-increasing use of technology.

Mental Health: A Report of the Surgeon General (by the U.S. Department of Health and Human Services) asserted: "There is no 'one size fits all' treatment; rather, people can choose the type of treatment that best suits them from the diverse forms of treatment that exist" (1999, p. 453). Importantly, the phrase "people can choose" is a fundamental shift in service expectation exemplifying customer service. Choice is moving beyond a simple list of providers given via a telephone directory list. Choice is becoming sophisticated. Potential clients are starting to compare therapist Web site and associated features. Now, they can make choices involving variables such as appearance (if a picture is included), presentation (if a video introduction is given), all credentials, self-help tools available, experience, psychotherapy style, scheduling, and availability. Review of these variables, without actually speaking to the therapist (flattening), provides potential clients a healthy choice. Psychotherapists have fundamentally held to offering choices for clients, but until recently, it was more of a value than actuality. Clients, whether needing a preauthorization from their insurance company or a referral from their primary care physician, had limited choices for therapy services. Choice was typically a short list of providers.

A choice of therapists provides consumers a heterogeneous pool of psychotherapy styles. None of the reports mandated that mental health professionals choose a particular psychotherapy model. Rather, these publications emphasize developing treatment services focusing on high-quality standards for a particular health care sector. Importantly, intolerance of mediocre services is evolving, while reinforcement exists for professionals and agencies engaging in high-performance services. Third-party payers, governmental funding sources, and consumers are increasingly demanding higher-quality health care.

Most psychotherapists focus entirely on the therapeutic conversation. Lacking is the distinction between psychotherapy service and customer service. It is critically important that therapists begin to view administrative skills as the other side of the treatment coin.

Available technologies now afford owners of private practices the opportunity to provide exceptional customer service outside the therapy room. These services, combined with customers' ability to stay connected via Web site updates, e-newsletters, podcasts, and more are creating the explosive new practice-building category of lifelong customers.

Lifelong Customers

In virtually every profession other than psychotherapy, securing lifelong customers is a dream come true. Primary care physicians to plumbers, restaurant owners to attorneys, strive to deliver services that secure a client or customer for as long as possible. Customers who trust a professional return for services.

Psychotherapy clients are no different. In behavioral health care, during the evolution of managed care, a frequent plea from clients was the desire to remain with their "not-in-network" therapist. It is a frequent consideration when clients change insurance plans. Clients prefer staying with providers after experiencing high-quality services.

One practice standard is the offering of services and resources without face-to-face contact (Institute of Medicine, 2001; New Freedom Commission on Mental Health, 2003). On the surface, this standard seems impossible to meet and, if met, could lead to ethical violations related to dependency on the therapy process. However, as is well-known, clients do not like "starting over." Keeping in touch with them is an ethical practice and falls within the idea of best practice standards. Finding methods to provide non-face-to-face services decreases the client costs and increases assistance. Furthermore, maintenance of a trusting relationship provides opportunity for your former clients when they need another treatment episode. Today, technology allows us easily and inexpensively to create a relationship with our clients that can cross the lifespan.

Historically, following therapy, the only means to access the therapist was through voice mail, a telephone call, or by scheduling an appointment. Today, however, post-treatment clients can continue to access therapy information from their therapist via Web sites, e-news, blogs, and podcasts. In essence, they can stay connected to the therapist without therapist knowledge. Technology allows multiple forms of non-face-to-face service delivery before, during, and after psychotherapy.

As a family therapist, for example, you provide services to a family with a child diagnosed as having attention deficit disorder. The outcome of therapy is successful, and typically you may not hear from this family again. But perhaps 2 years later when this child is a teenager, the parents review your Web site information and listen to podcasts about raising teenagers. After implementing strategies discussed in the podcast, they continue to feel they need additional services. They visit your Web site and immediately schedule an appointment because they trust you and you offer online scheduling. Was the relationship ever severed between yourself and these clients? On one level, treatment was terminated. On another level, your clients stayed connected via your Web site—most likely without your knowledge. Provided your clients remain satisfied and feel their needs are being met, they may stay connected throughout their lifetime. Technology creates the opportunity for former clients to become outstanding advertising representatives of your practice.

When giving seminars, I ask therapists, "What do you give your clients and former clients—advertising representatives—for marketing and advertising your practice?" The typical answer is an appointment or business card. Challenging the audience, I ask, "When did you give the business card?" The usual answer is the first or last session. My next question is, "What will they get 6 to 12 months after they have completed treatment?" Typically, no one answers this question. Keeping former clients aware of your services is vitally important for practice building. Other professionals (e.g., realtors, attorneys, plumbers) continuously inform their current and former customers of activities through newsletters, postcards, and other means. They want to prevent the cliché: "Out of sight, out of mind."

Technological advances are making old paradigms and practice-building strategies just that—old. In a technological world where significant changes occur seemingly every month, small business owners need to keep pace with trends and services that complement their face-to-face psychotherapy. These changes are quickly turning firmly held practice-building beliefs and methods into myths and antiquated strategies.

Myths and Antiquated Practice-Building Strategies

Traditional practice-building strategies are antiquated, or simply myths, receiving little critical examination. It is important to identify and understand common myths and steer clear of these ineffective strategies. Although some of these strategies can generate business, it is essential to consider the return on the investment, your time, financial resources, and energy.

Today's business environment and technology require radically new ways to think of building your business based on technology, flattening, lifelong customers, and best practice standards. Web sites are replacing brochures. Click-through Web advertising is replacing yellow page advertising. Online scheduling is replacing voice mail and live operators. These changes have a drastic impact on practice-building strategies, and it is high time some myths and antiquated practice-building techniques are debunked.

Myth 1: I Must Attend Networking Functions

Let me summarize the general experience of attending a networking function:

Make sure I have excellent business cards—*expense*

Do I have quality brochures?—*expense*

Become a member of the networking organization—*expense*

Devote 2 or 3 hours of time at the meeting—*expense*

While at the meeting, feel anxious about "gripping and grinning" with people generally leery of my profession—*emotional expense*

Exchange business cards with those who are professionals at network marketing—*expense*

Following the event, go back to my office and send thank you notes to my new contacts—*expense*

Wait for the cornucopia of referrals. Now, there are three possibilities:

1. No referrals are made—high probability.
2. Someone refers a relative who has been in and out of counseling so many times that there is little chance of success. You see the client, yet despite your exceptional skills, the client and referral source (fellow networking member) are unhappy. Now, you are a failure to your *new* referral source, who will not understand why you failed— just that you failed—*big expense*.
3. You are successful with the new referral.

Does this process sound about right? Notice the number of expenses. Again, calculate these expenses in both time and money, and later you will see where you can more effectively invest both. The problem with networking functions is that fellow networkers will never witness your great clinical care, and there is little understanding of the clinical situation if there is a poor clinical outcome.

Another problem with networking functions is that professional networkers have the primary thought of sharing business with other business professionals. They are not thinking, "How do I get business?" In the networking field, it is of paramount importance to refer business so that eventually you receive business. Business professionals quickly recognize that mental health professionals rarely make referrals. For example, will you put up a cell phone exhibit from a specific company in your waiting room? Or, will you have a business card display in your waiting room filled with cards from plumbers, accountants, and financial planners? There are many issues surrounding such practices in behavioral health care, and it is a rare therapist who engages in such aggressive referral-sharing systems. Therapists expect referrals but have difficulty making referrals. Fellow networkers, quickly recognizing this dynamic, steer clear of spending time with you.

Traditionally presented networking strategies force me to question, "Are they in the real world? Do they know that I'm a therapist, not a networking hound?" I am not saying the presented information is bad. However, practice-building consultants touting the power of networking fail to recognize the specialization of the skills and the extroverted personality needed to accomplish those skills successfully. Marketing, advertising, and networking are skilled professions requiring training and experience. Would you expect a sales representative to have your skill to navigate a therapy session? Certainly, some may do quite well, but most will not. Similarly, some therapists can successfully manage a networking function, but most will not.

Myth 2: I Need an Elaborate Business Plan

No, you do not need an elaborate business plan. Gone are the days of elaborate spreadsheets, vision statements, strategic plans, and trying to anticipate events that make or break a practice. Although these traditional components of business planning can be useful in large corporations, today's practice building is about nimbly and quickly capitalizing on technology to enhance your services. For example, after developing a tight clinical and administrative system, our agency began noticing that we were no longer business planning. Rather, we were adapting to changes and requests from clients and setting goals and benchmarks. Since our clinical services, both in and outside the therapy room, were gaining a great deal of attention, we nearly eliminated the need to develop new referral development strategies.

Instead of business planning, start identifying practice-building strategies and tasks that lead to a few specific goals. Some of these goals, discussed later, may include:

- Increasing the direct referral rate (Chapters 1, 3).
- Decreasing the number of days a client waits before the first appointment (Chapters 1, 4).
- Increasing the percentage of cases involving collaboration (Chapters 1, 3).

- Improving infrastructure technologies to increase profit margins (Chapter 5).
- Increasing the number of loyalty building points (Chapter 2, 6).

From these goals, strategies evolve. Rather than a static business plan involving pages of ignored narrative, you have a living document involving benchmarks with monthly monitoring.

Myth 3: I Need a Substantial Marketing and Advertising Budget to Succeed

Merriam-Webster defined marketing as an ongoing process of planning and executing the marketing mix of products (product, price, place, promotion), services, or ideas to create exchange between individuals and organizations. Marketing tends to be seen as a creative industry, including advertising, distribution, and selling. It is also concerned with anticipating the customers' future needs and wants, often discovered through market research. *Advertising* is a form of communication whose purpose is to call the attention of potential customers to products and services and how to obtain and use those services.

Therapists tend to use these terms interchangeably. Important differences are that marketing stresses meeting and anticipating needs, whereas advertising emphasizes communication of services. Anticipating client needs in psychotherapy is an easy and free process. Without asking, clients often suggest needs beyond psychotherapy assistance. This type of research is invaluable. One psychotherapist, identifying that her clients were increasingly frustrated with delays to reschedule appointments, sought my consult. When I suggested using an online scheduling system, she responded, "My clients will not use the Internet." Knowing she was collecting e-mail addresses for an e-newsletter, I pushed her, "Why then collect their e-mails?" The "aha" phenomenon hit. Realizing that e-mail addresses indicate Internet use, she took the leap of faith and began offering online scheduling services via her new Web site.

Advertising, or *calling attention to your services*, involves many materials you already have: letterhead, envelopes, fax machine, e-mail, Web page. Every day, you communicate your services to clients and referral sources. A simple thank you letter to a referral source is advertising. A clinical report form sent to a primary care physician serves both as a high-quality care process and advertising. An e-mail to a client identifying self-help resources is excellent clinical service and advertising.

Consider this: If you see 200 new clients per year and with each client you coordinate care with one ancillary professional (200 new clients plus 200 ancillary professionals), you are "advertising" to 400 people per year. Virtually every corporation would covet the intimacy psychotherapists have with clients and referral sources. This type of marketing and advertising is *not* equivalent to the distressing activities most psychotherapists associate with marketing: cold calling, schmoozing, slick advertising media. Your advertising and marketing should focus on those witnessing your exceptional care. *There is no need to develop advertising that will "catch someone's eye." Your clinical services should accomplish that objective.*

Advertising (communicating) to clients and former clients, and referral sources can take many forms. Report writing, podcasting, and Web site information are all advertising mechanisms. These cost-effective methods eliminate traditional and expensive tools for advertising.

Myth 4: Business Cards Are Important

Truth be told, my business partner and I have not had business cards for over 5 years. At this point, we cannot even consider why we would have business cards. Yes, every now and then we find ourselves wishing we had some cards, but we use these opportunities to promote the practice more purposefully—beyond exchanging business cards. For example, a primary care physician who was making numerous referrals to our practice requested a live demonstration of our online scheduling system for his referral coordinator. After giving the orientation, the physician asked for business cards and handouts. I explained that we did not have any business cards, but I would get him brochures. When I returned to my office, I promptly sent 50 brochures. Two weeks later, he asked for 100 brochures. Always work in a manner requiring you to send information shortly after your interaction. Yet, do not send too much information. Creation of strategies that increase the frequency of contacts demonstrates reliability, creates confidence, and helps establish a lifelong referral source. "Getting back" to someone can be very advantageous. It increases the contacts, and when you get back to them, you can be more effective. I would rather have a primary care physician giving out brochures (with Web site information, clinician directory, office locations, and the like) than giving out a simple business card.

For some, business cards are a security blanket. I would challenge you to think of the last time a business card garnished a referral. You hope a 2 x 3 inch piece of card stock develops enough trust for someone unfamiliar with your services to refer a loved one for psychotherapy. I read an article about a private practitioner whose goal was handing out one box of business cards per 6 months. She believed this practice resulted in a solid return on the investment. The article did not elaborate on the results of this investment, but it did suggest that she maintain this practice. Stop and critically examine this strategy. Where and why might you engage in distributing almost 100 business cards per month? I cannot imagine attending that many networking functions, not even if I were just starting a practice.

Myth 5: I Should Develop a New Clinical Service to Keep My Practice Going

There are two possibilities if your practice lacks referrals. First, your current clinical skills are not good enough to generate word-of-mouth advertising. Second, your current infrastructure does not capitalize on advertising your clinical skills and outcomes.

The solution to either problem is not a new clinical service. Developing a new clinical service because you lack referrals is an act of desperation. I have witnessed many therapists trying to develop careers in such areas as corporate consulting and coaching. Some were successful; most were not. After spending a great deal of time and money, the result was a poor return on the investment. Many of these therapists return to providing psychotherapy services as their full-time work. Be careful to avoid developing a new clinical service out of financial desperation. It simply lacks the probability of success. The answer is not in developing a new service but rather drawing attention to your existing high-quality services. Do what you are good at doing.

It is appropriate to expand your clinical services. For example, say you work with many couples, and your emphasis is communication skills. You might add a communication skills class once per month. This class is not a new clinical service; rather, it is an expansion on a clinical service you are already offering—and a good practice-building strategy.

An entirely new clinical service requires marketing and advertising. If your marketing and advertising are ineffective for your current clinical practice, what makes you think your marketing and advertising will be effective with a new endeavor? Before starting down the path of a new venture startup, ensure you are doing so for the right reasons. Sticking with your current practice requires you to answer the important question: "How do I provide others the opportunity to recognize my high-quality work?"

Myth 6: Graphics and Logo Matter

Do graphics and logos really matter? Yes, for companies such as Nike, Chevrolet, and Subway. These companies sell *products,* and they must protect from the dynamic of "out of sight, out of mind." What do you sell? You sell a personal and private service. It is highly unlikely that your clients, during or after treatment, will walk around with your nifty logo on a T-shirt.

Therapists, particularly those experiencing referral development trouble or just starting a practice, are often eager to have a personal logo with some catchy graphic. They spend time and money developing something elegant for their business card. Then, a few years later, they ask, "What was I thinking?" They either do not like the logo, or they discover it really never made any difference except with their colleagues, who admired their creativity.

Psychotherapy Finances stated, "Unless you're famous, your own name has no intrinsic value" ("Marketing," 2008a, p. 1). I respectfully differ on this position. Honestly, following a successful treatment episode, what do you want the client and referral source to remember? I hope you answered "my name." As the author, I do not know you as the reader. Yet, I can tell you with 100% confidence that your logo should be your name.

Forget about catchy graphics and logos; keep your focus on brand recognition, which is clearly your name. You want everyone to know your name (business agency or personal). Your name is the equivalent of the Nike swoosh. Your name is your logo. Your name is the brand that needs an outstanding clinical reputation.

Graphics and logos do not build trust and reliability. Your task is to make sure that your name is associated with high-quality care. You do not need international fame, only local.

Myth 7: Yellow Page Advertising Is Important

I know there are many people who will dispute the myth that you need yellow page advertising. If a yellow page advertising system is working for you, maintain the campaign. Increasingly, customers search for providers within their insurance-approved panel, a specific online therapist directory, or through a Web search.

The need for an individual to use a telephone directory after being referred by a former client or health care provider indicates you need to focus on supplying referral sources with more tools to refer. Your referral sources need brochures, fact sheets, and your Web address for distributing to potential clients. Remember, you want clients to find you easily.

Therapists who list their services in a telephone directory are attempting randomly to generate clients unfamiliar with their therapy services. Therapists have no influence when a potential client will use the telephone directory and only a small influence—based on your advertisement—on whether they will call you.

Myth 8: I Need Newspaper Advertising to Build My Practice

Rarely do I give a seminar without someone asking, "Tracy, what about newspaper advertising?" First, pick up that local neighborhood paper—you know, the one you get delivered to your specific suburb or community—to see how many therapists are advertising. Estimate the number of therapists in the area. What is the percentage of them advertising? I bet it is less than 1%. Why? This is because it does not work! Many years ago, I was employed by a large corporation operating counseling centers. This company had an enormous advertising budget. They would run a large advertisement for many weeks in the major local paper, offering a free seminar on topics such as stress relief. The cost was $10,000 in print advertising. Approximately 200 people attended the free seminar (a cost of $50 per person attending) and, of those attending, maybe 25 people registered for counseling services (a cost of $400 per person registering). Maybe half of those registering kept their first appointment (a cost of $833 per person going to the first appointment). Although this corporation found this an acceptable outcome (i.e. they also had a secondary goal of keeping their name in public at all times), it demonstrates the risk of this type of campaign. By the way, they went out of business in just 2 years.

I know you are thinking, "But Tracy, I have seen so and so advertising every week for the last number of years." Yes, there are successful exceptions to every rule. So and so has found a niche and has a system that works. Again, however, this is one therapist out of how many in your area?

Selecting a therapist is not like buying a piece of furniture. Our value to potential clients relates to trust. How effective is newspaper advertising for communicating trust? Potential clients desire a psychotherapist with a positive reputation. I emphasize the word reputation; it is a cornerstone of practice building.

Newspaper advertising is the epitome of cold calling—attempting to secure business without any relationship with the potential client. Keep in mind the rule of six. A consumer must see an advertisement six times before he or she recalls the product or service. Therefore, you would need to run the advertisement six times before it becomes memorable.

Myth 9: Cold Calling Is Important for Practice Building

Imagine the time and money you will save by giving yourself permission *not* to attend networking functions, drop off brochures at random offices, run advertisements, or engage in awkward and stressful activities. *Cold calling* is the attempt to access referrals without an established reputation. The first logical question is, "Why would any therapist attempt this endeavor when the therapist already has dozens of established relations within the treatment community?"

There is no need to become a marketing machine, a networking guru, a Google search expert, or a business analyst. The strategic use of technology to increase communication and collaboration with health care professionals is advertising. Collaboration is not only expected, but also viewed as providing high-quality care!

Far more important than spending time and money advertising to those unfamiliar with your services is creating an automated treatment system naturally incorporating advertising into your clinical care. This process is founded on two assumptions. First, you are delivering high-quality care. We all know therapists with bad reputations. How do you know you are *not* one of them? This question may seem harsh or insensitive, but how do you know you are delivering quality service? Do you have 3 years of satisfaction surveys? Do your treatment summaries indicate something like "mutually agreed closing, goals met"? Are you receiving at least two thirds of your referrals directly from other treatment professionals and former clients? I hear therapists comment, "My practice is built on word of mouth, and I don't advertise." My follow-up question is what percentage of your practice is word of mouth? Is it 100%, 75%, 50%? How do you know the referrals are word of mouth? Without specific data collection systems, psychotherapists are like everybody else—they remember the positive exceptions and ignore the general rule.

The second assumption is that your practice has an automated system for advertising delivery of high-quality clinical care. When does a referral source see your name? How is your name communicated to the referral source? When and how does another treatment provider involved in the case see your name?

A business infrastructure capitalizing on advertising opportunities through normative treatment operations is far more trustworthy than increasing referrals through cold calling. Cold calling practice-building strategies perpetuate ignoring the development of an infrastructure capitalizing on high quality services. Cold calling is not cost efficient nor is it practical from a clinical perspective. All practices have naturally occurring practice building points. These natural interventions need refinement thereby providing you easy and cost effective means of practice building.

Myth 10: Cash Pay Clients Solve All Financial Problems

The myth that cash pay clients solve all financial problems is my favorite because psychotherapists buy the premise hook, line, and sinker. There is no such thing as an ideal private practice, just like there is no ideal small business. A cash-based practice exposes you to economic downturns. An insurance-based practice may limit your ability to capitalize on a booming economy. Even the best practices will experience cash flow problems. Every practice has its challenges. A private practice is susceptible to all the adverse conditions of a small business because it *is* a small business.

A common belief is to focus exclusively on a cash pay practice. Generally, keeping your revenue streams diversified helps create financial stability. During economically prosperous times, clients are more likely to pay by cash. Your practice management strategies can focus on cash pay clients. During economic downturns, when potential clients will pay a $40 copayment rather than a $120 full-fee session, you can work the insurance angle and recession proof your practice. Insurance panels provide economic protection. Yes, unbelievably, I said "protection."

I want to make a clear distinction between (a) belonging to an insurance panel and (b) implementing strategies to gain referrals from that panel. Being on a panel does not equate getting referrals. Your infrastructure of nimble and adaptable business patterns allows you to turn on or off referrals from insurance companies. This ability places a practice in a significantly more secure position than a practice based solely on insurance or cash pay. As your practice grows, you can begin terminating those insurance contracts with low reimbursements while retaining those that may have a modest reimbursement but low administrative labor.

There are unanticipated events that can compromise or enhance a private practice. Many years ago, our practice had an outstanding relationship with an employee assistance program with an interesting assessment model (prior to online directories). The expectation was that the first session was an assessment, and the second session was to make a referral, give resources, and go over questions with the clients. The employer wanted to ensure that employees, in times of distress, were referred to appropriate treatment providers with resources to help them. This was a noble goal of the corporation. The reimbursement rate was a flat fee of $180 per referral. Although by today's standards this rate may not seem great, it was a lucrative situation when considering it was a two-session model of assess and refer. Then one day, the employer changed the employee assistance program to an "assess-and-treat" model, reimbursing approximately $45 per session. Virtually overnight, this referral source became a riches-to-rags revenue stream for our business.

On the upside, a primary care physician group relocated to a new office complex two blocks from our office. They became a gold mine of referrals in a matter of months. They were also the ideal referral source. Despite some clients having limited financial resources (which we worked hard to accommodate), the majority of referred clients had a diverse range of reimbursement structures. This diversity continues to provide the practice with solid revenue streams.

Lower rates of reimbursement from insurance companies are partially to blame for the challenges associated with financially managing a practice. However, virtually all practices have serious infrastructure inefficiencies that *lose* money, sometimes significant amounts of money (Chapter 5 addresses this further). *Developing a diversified revenue stream, while eliminating inefficiencies, provides the foundation for a solidly built business in outpatient mental health.*

An important distinction is necessary between reimbursement rates and profit margins. *Profit margin* is basically the income or sales minus all costs for the production and distribution of the product or service. Psychotherapists focus almost exclusively on reimbursement rates rather than the more important profit margin of their practice. Profit margins provide a more accurate picture of your practice than reimbursement rates. Using a simple example, an inefficient business in psychotherapy earning $100 per one 50-minute session, $2.00 per minute, may have the following costs:

Answering service scheduling the client = $8.00 per call
Billing service charging 6% of collections = $6.00 ($100 x 6%)
Overhead (varies greatly per practice) = $7.50 per session
Documentation of session (15 minutes x $2.00 your labor cost) = $30.00
Care coordination (15 minutes x $2.00 your labor cost) = $30.00
Total cost = $81.50
Net profit = $18.50
Profit margin = 18.50%

Compare this to a business with a technologically sophisticated infrastructure earning $80 per one 50-minute session, $1.60 per minute, which may have the following costs:

Online scheduling service ($10 per month or $0.33 per day) = $0.33
Online payment with 3% collection rate = $2.40
Overhead (varies greatly per practice) = $7.50 per session (held constant with the inefficient system)
Documentation of session using electronic forms or templates
    (5 minutes x $1.60 your labor costs) = $8.00
Care coordination using technology (8 minutes x $1.60 your labor costs)
    = $12.80
Total cost = $31.03
Net profit margin = $48.97
Profit margin = 61.2%

The profit margin of $80 per session reimbursement is over three times better than the $100 per session. Psychotherapists constantly complain about the low reimbursement rates (with which I completely agree), but they do little to increase the profit margin of their practice by improving infrastructure inefficiencies. Although this example is simplistic, the point is that as you build your practice, *know* your profit margin calculations and use technology to improve these margins.

Final Note

Purposefully building a practice requires an administrative system and infrastructure that focuses on current clients, former clients, and collaborating treatment professionals. As you begin this journey of implementing technology and business-building strategies, it is imperative that you have a clear understanding of your strengths, limitations, and the necessary qualities for success. The business paradigm is quickly changing, and therapists need to assess their preparedness, skills, and attitudes to manage outpatient mental health businesses.

My presentation may seem a bit one sided, favoring technology. Admittedly, I am erring on the side of technology for two reasons. First, I have been successful by staying abreast of and incorporating technology. Furthermore, I observe other successful practices that are incorporating technology to increase efficiencies. Second, the times are quickly and radically changing. The last major business change, which was much slower, involved managed mental health care services. Many therapists were not prepared for the drastic changes that ensued and suffered the consequences. The impact of technology is far more reaching and happening much quicker than managed mental health care. Although you may not embrace all the technological strategies, incorporating a few "musts" may prevent your business from unnecessarily closing its doors.

You will find a number of sample forms throughout this book. Please feel free to use them, modified as needed, in your own practice. However, please note that I cannot guarantee the legality of the forms.

CHAPTER ONE

Self-Assessment

Why did you purchase this book? Is your practice failing? Are you starting a practice? Are you trying to upgrade to a more current and healthy practice? Be honest with yourself. When therapists build a practice, they need an honest appraisal of the causes and conditions contributing to current challenges. Therapists who ignore trends in the mental health industry find themselves rationalizing and denying circumstances. Statements reflecting missed trends include:

> "I didn't want to participate in managed health care." (not a participating provider)
> "My clients will not use a Web site." (not creating a Web site)
> "My clients won't use an online scheduling function." (not offering this option)
> "I only want self-pay clients. That is more money and less paperwork." (reflects focusing on reimbursement instead of profit margins and administrative infrastructure)

Working from a base of desperation or reactivity, as we know with our clients, is challenging. We lose patience, cut corners, and skip steps altogether. If your practice is desperately suffering, I encourage you to engage in whatever means you can to begin building your practice through methodical diligence and a long-term perspective. The strategies I present are not quick fixes. However, an aggressive approach should warrant a return on your investment within 6 months, and over the course of 18 months, you should be reaping the benefits of a practice meeting today's consumer demands.

As a private practitioner, you own and operate a small business requiring care and nurturing. All small business owners, ranging from accountants to attorneys to restaurant owners to plumbers, need competent management of their production, services, and internal processes (even when they are solo business owners). That means long hours, skill, and knowledge beyond service delivery while keeping current with the trends in the business. Too often, therapists conceptualize private practice without considering business infrastructure. If you do not want to participate in these endeavors and simply do therapy, you have choices. You can work for an agency, subcontract for a private practice, or hire someone to manage your practice. These are not bad options. They are simply options that remove you from the role of administrator or owner. It is critically important for you to look at your motivation to embrace business development and management honestly and fully if you choose to be a small business owner.

I hope your practice is doing well and you simply want to continue your track record. This healthy motivation will serve you well. A thriving practice may offer many differing services, such as consultation, training, education, writing, and forensic work. These options typically have significantly greater reimbursements and help diversify your business. However, such services typically result from high-quality psychotherapy services that gain reputation and notoriety.

Barriers to Practice Building

There are some general barriers to building a practice. I encourage you to consider if these barriers apply to you. If they do, as part of your practice-building plan include strategies to eliminate them. One of the more challenging aspects of this chapter is overcoming your discomfort with technology. Do not be afraid to seek consultation or some training to implement strategies. Although virtually every therapist pays for additional clinical training, training keeping your business solvent also seems like a good idea. Do not let your fears and anxiety stop you from adapting to the flattening world. Remaining in practice, thriving, and enjoying your profession require proceeding as a business owner managing a business. Being in charge of a business does not guarantee success, but it does increase the chance of success.

Money

In "Ice Cream vs. Therapy" (2008, October) *Psychotherapy Finances* interviewed Susan Haber, who stated that one reason therapists are not earning more money is that they are unwilling to charge more money. Owning a business is all about making money. Making money is dependent on collections, setting fees, and offering outstanding services. Therapists all want to earn more money, but few feel positive about collecting money. One example of therapist discomfort with money involves collections for no-shows or late cancellations. I have heard many rationalizations and excuses for not collecting on these debts. Without exception, every reason reflects not placing value on time and skill.

Attitude

"I didn't get into psychotherapy to run a business" is an absolutely defeated attitude. Get over it. There is a significant difference between those acquiring specialty skills and *choosing* to work for an agency, hence being an employee and having a sense of security, and the risk takers who leverage time and money to become a business owner. It is impossible to own a business without facing business challenges and dealing with the plethora of issues you "never went to school to learn." Analogous is a restaurant owner focusing solely on food, paying little attention to reservation scheduling, waitstaff demeanor, or cleanliness. A spectacular chef opening a new restaurant and stating, "I did not attend culinary school to worry about how the bathrooms are cleaned" will soon close the doors.

Private practice therapists who desire to stay in full-time private practice must drop their resentments that they did not get into the field to do paper-work, billing, or the numerous administrative tasks associated with owning and operating a small business. Successful owners of any business fully recognize and embrace that there is more to operating a business than simply providing the service.

Owning a small business has some powerful intrinsic rewards, such as control over your schedule, sole decision-making, determining when to take vacations, and pride and fulfillment because of a successful business built on your shoulders. Experiencing these rewards requires guts, risk, and hard work beyond providing psychotherapy services. If you want to experience these rewards, then it is critically important to embrace that owning a successful, full-time, small business is really an accomplishment of the few.

Adaptation

While attending a meeting of psychotherapists, I heard the statement, "My clients will never use online scheduling or therapy services." The therapist made the statement with such conviction that others immediately validated the position. It is possible that the therapist treats a specific demographic, resulting in such a confident claim. However, does that necessarily mean other therapists serve the same demographic? Or, possibly, sometime in the future the demographic changes but the therapist does not? No profession is immune to extraordinary changes brought about by technology and flattening. Believing you can own and operate a full-time business under the guise of some romantic notion of private practice is unrealistic. In business, there are two potential outcomes: adapt or fail. Psychotherapists, like all other business owners, need to make quick and regular adaptations to market conditions.

Current known technologies, and technologies not yet invented, will have enormous impact on the delivery of clinical services. Although the actual therapeutic conversation will remain important, technologies that add to customer service and interaction will increasingly complement in-the-room therapeutic conversations.

Therapists can certainly expect the day when out of necessity a client demands, not requests, therapy interaction via webcams (e.g., www.Mytherapynet.com). Consider the possibility of providing services to rural clients and those with disabilities and other severe situations that limit the privilege of getting into a car and driving to a nice office to sit and chat with a therapist. Technology will certainly create the opportunity to provide services to treatment populations unable to enter a therapist's office and engage in face-to-face conversations. Furthermore, via technology, those who continue to assign a negative stigma to psychotherapy services may begin to participate from a safe, unembarasssing distance until they become comfortable enough for the face-to-face services.

Certainly, some clients will not embrace your technological advances, but they can still be clients. They may not use online scheduling or e-mail, for example, but they can still call your voice mail and receive traditional paper mail. Over time, this population will reduce in size, while the population embracing technology will increase.

On a parallel process, as a therapist you may be fighting the ideas and tools of high technology. Yes, there are real time commitments. However, over time, as the consumer population expects more technology, can you afford *not* to invest the time to meet their demands?

Because technology will be increasingly embraced, used, and expected by consumers as they age (teens becoming adults), it will shape the psychotherapy field like never before. Consumer expectations will gravitate to increased interactions with psychotherapists. Of course, these will not necessarily be in the room or face to face. Consumers will expect webinars and teleconferences, streamed video training, podcasting, and blogging. Some already do. Many clients are expecting such simplistic customer services as e-mail reminders, online scheduling, and the occasional interactive e-newsletter. These expectations require quick and efficient adaptations by owners of outpatient mental health practices.

Gender Differences

A frequent comment made by women during seminars is that strategies involving technology and business favor men. Their argument is that men are more business and technologically oriented than women. My impression is that over the age of 40, men seem to have an advantage of implementing high-technology and business strategies. However, younger female practice-building therapists do not seem to encounter such challenges. I have met some incredibly outstanding and creative female practice-building therapists implementing business-planning strategies, including technology. These women grew up in a technological era, which is most likely contributing to their enhanced technology skills.

Competition

Competition is *the* area that universally seems to repulse therapists. Stories from therapists about their disdain of competing with fellow colleagues reflect a belief that all business competition is unhealthy. Lying, cheating, lacking ethics, and immoral business practices too often make news. It is your business, and choosing to take such a path would be unfortunate. However, there are many more businesses engaging in positive and healthy competition.

Practice building is fundamentally competitive. Securing a cash pay client, full fee, is a result of that client choosing you over another therapist—competition. Rather than denying that you compete, embrace it. Your ethics and morals will guide business practices. While on a trip to wine country, the sense of healthy competition was apparent. Wineries trying to sell wines would also recommend a specific wine of a local competitor. Competition is what you make it, healthy or unhealthy. Clearly, however, you cannot avoid it. The demand for customer services outside the therapy room will increase the profiling or rating of psychotherapy practices. Highly imaginable is a therapist directory with a five-star rating system of therapists. Imagine the name

Tracy Todd, PhD, LMFT ★ ★ ★

Why only three stars? What is the system of rating?

Profiling and rating can lack the obnoxious star rating and still provide challenges to your business. Potential customers searching for a therapist will certainly expect, rightfully so, variables to evaluate and compare service providers. Gone are the days that your degree and license held importance. Today, they only allow you eligibility for referrals. Potential customers and treatment stakeholders will increasingly look beyond those once-hallowed credentials and demand knowledge about such service variables as satisfaction rates, access standards, collaboration rates, and customer service variables that heighten the overall therapy experience.

Potential customers will expect to comparison shop like I compare electronic purchases. Does this sound cold? Maybe, but I feel it is a great step forward to empowering for meeting specific needs and expecting a totality of service, not simply a therapeutic conversation.

Organization

Quickly look around your office at the tools you are using to manage your business. Do you have an appointment book bursting with loose paper and sticky notes? Do your clinical files have papers and notes falling out? Practice building in the information age requires good organization to help minimize labor and increase efficiency. If you are highly organized, great. If not, consider what tools are necessary to help you become more organized. I am aware of a number of therapists who acknowledge their lack of organizational skills and hire someone to keep them organized.

Automation

It will be important as you work through this book to consider how you can automate every effort and task within your practice infrastructure. Can you enter e-mails easily into a contact management system that is privacy protected and easily utilized when needed for newsletters? Automation reduces labor, thereby increasing profit. Most psychotherapy business owners lack realization about the numerous possibilities existing to build their business through automation. One example of automation is sending correspondence to a client by simply "pointing-and-clicking" a prepopulated form letter using a contact management system.

Paradigm and Integration

Integrating technology into your practice is not complicated, but it does take some strategizing. It is important to ensure that efforts are not duplicated, and that each effort gets the biggest bang for the buck. For example, if your Web site allows printable self-help sheets but the printed material does not have your name, telephone number, and address on the printout, the effort is wasted. Someone holding your information cannot contact or refer to you. Each effort and strategy should serve multiple purposes with the goal of maximizing profit, reducing labor, and increasing advertising.

Math and Spreadsheets

Seriously, practice building does require the ability to do some math. Whether it is through the use of a calculator or a spreadsheet, mathematical skills are required. Calculus is not required, but I am amazed at how often I get the "deer-caught-in-the-headlight" looks when I suggest using spreadsheets with calculations for monitoring a practice. Learning basic spreadsheet functions is necessary for building and monitoring your business successes and failures.

Data Collection

For the most part, psychotherapists went to graduate school and took a class in basic research methods. It is probably the first class forgotten after graduation. The problem is that research is necessary for a small business owner. At a restaurant, is a new food selling more than another? At a local coffee shop, does introducing soy milk increase sales more than offering low-fat milk? You are a small business owner, and conducting research is a necessary business component for adapting and attempting new business development strategies.

Technological Tools

Although it should go without saying, a computer is a necessary tool for *Practice Building 2.0*. Most computers come preinstalled with the necessary components to run a highly efficient and technologically sophisticated practice. Although I more thoroughly address some of the technical components later elsewhere in this book, the following list consists of the minimal hardware and software needed in *Practice-Building 2.0*.

- Computer: virtually any computer purchased in the last 2 years will work. Some minimum specifics include Intel® Core™ 2 Duo T5670 (1.8 GHz, 2-MB L2 cache, 800-MHz FSB), 2-GB shared dual channel DDR2 SDRAM, 250-GB, video card, sound card, wireless connection (if you are choosing a laptop, which I strongly suggest).
- Office suite software: Spreadsheet, word processing, slide show development (e.g., MSWord, Excel, PowerPoint).
- Sound recording software to record and convert audio files to MP3 format. If you do not have this software, do not worry: I suggest an easy and affordable (free) solution to assist you.
- Video editing software, usually included in any newer computer purchase.

Should you use a Mac or PC? This debate is eternal, but from a business perspective, the functionality of the computer is most important. Your computer needs the above-mentioned capabilities; the rest is personal preference. One word of caution: although the interfacing platform differences are gradually being eliminated, there are still many technological tools more suited for PC users. However, the hearty Mac user can usually find ways around such obstructions.

Data Preparation

Before I go any further, there are a few important data points to discuss for practice-building strategies. It is important that you get the most accurate data possible. Do not engage in guessing as this will make all of your computations and projections speculative. Spend some time calculating the most accurate data.

Your first step is creating two spreadsheets that allow simple but comprehensive data collection and calculation. The first spreadsheet will assist you with best practice standards and performance of your practice. The second spreadsheet assists in creating a picture of your practice patterns regarding referral and revenue distribution. At this time, simply create the spreadsheets with the suggested categories and as you work through this book, I make suggestions for you to enter data to gradually build and complete a picture of your practice (Table 1.1 and Table 1.2). I have included multiple therapist names in Table 1.2 for those in a group practice. If you are a solo practitioner, then simply create a spreadsheet with one column.

Data Point 1: Average Number of Sessions.

Calculate your average number of sessions based on the last 100 clients. Lacking these data, calculating the return on your investments, establishing financial projections, and making decisions about general practice-building ventures is impossible. Do not eliminate any clients because they were "atypical." Remember, you need an accurate representation of your practice. The mean will help you in your calculations throughout your business-building efforts.

After you have completed your measurement of mean number of sessions for past clients, it is important that you create your business profile spreadsheet. From this point, as you close each case, simply enter the number of sessions in the business profile spreadsheet. Importantly, let the spreadsheet do your work for you. The mean is calculated by placing a formula in the spreadsheet. I have witnessed therapists with elaborate spreadsheets in which they enter all data but still use a calculator for computations. Such a system defeats the purpose of the spreadsheet and costs you a great deal of time. Using the spreadsheet formula function allows the data to calculate instantly each time a new data point is entered (Table 1.3).

Data Point 2: Reimbursement Rate

Using the last 6 months of treatment, calculate reimbursement per session. This data point is critical for budgeting and calculating return on investment (ROI). There are multiple methods of calculating reimbursement rates, salary, or earnings.

The first method (working hours) is based on all appointment times avail-

TABLE 1.1: BUSINESS PROFILE SPREADSHEET

Client ID	Closing status	Care Coor. 1= yes 2 = no	Offered appt. days	Accepted appt. days	Method of appt. set (SS1)	Ease of setting (SS1)	Level of progress at closing	Number Sessions	Refer to therapist (SS2) 1= yes 2 = no	Refer to agency (SS2) 1= yes 2 = no

SS1, Satisfaction Survey 1 is the administrative satisfaction survey distributed to clients following the first session. Further discussion of the survey is found in Chapter 2.

Satisfaction Survey 2 is the clinical satisfaction survey distributed to clients following treatment. Further discussion of this survey is found in Chapter 2.

TABLE 1.2. REFERRAL AND REVENUE DISTRIBUTION

Referrals per Revenue source	Therapist	Therapist	Therapist	Total
Insurance A				
Insurance B				
Insurance C				
Insurance D				
Insurance E				
Insurance F				
Other Insurance				
EAP A				
EAP B				
Other EAP				
Self-pay full-fee				
Self-pay 75–99%				
Total				
REFERRAL SOURCE				
Web site				
Online directories				
Providers (please indicate who below)				
HR/employer				
Providers (please indicate who below)				
Previous clients				
Other				
Total				
% direct referral				

EAP, employer assistance program
PCP, primary care physician
HR, human relations

TABLE 1.3: BUSINESS PROFILE MEAN NUMBER OF SESSIONS

Client ID	Closing status	Care Coor. 1= yes 2 = no	Offered appt. days	Accepted appt. days	Method of appt. set (SS1)	Ease of setting (SS1)	Level of progress at closing	Number Sessions	Refer to therapist (SS2), 1= yes 2 = no	Refer to agency (SS2) 1= yes 2 = no
								9		
								10		
								3		
								3		
								24		
								1		
								2		
								3		
								6.9[a]		

aThe last row of the spreadsheet will, of course, be your formulas. In this example, **6.9** is a result of a formula averaging the rows, thereby keeping the data live and eliminating labor to calculate a new mean when closing each client file

SS1, Satisfaction Survey 1 is the administrative satisfaction survey distributed to clients following the first session. Further discussion of the survey is found in Chapter 2.

SS2, Satisfaction Survey 2 is the clinical satisfaction survey distributed to clients following treatment. Further discussion of this survey is found in Chapter 2.

able for scheduling clients. This calculation is aggressive and results in lower rates but gives an indication of your true hourly rate. Assuming a standard 40-hour work week (160 hours per month) and collecting $6,000 per month, the average "reimbursement" rate equals $37.50 ($6,000/160). Using collections rather than generations is more accurate as it represents money in hand, whereas generating represents outstanding dollars, which are actually liabilities.

The second method (availability) assumes 30 sessions per week are available for appointments (120 per month) and a practice that collects $6,000; the average availability reimbursement rate is $50.00 per hour ($6,000/120). This method, although less aggressive, provides you with a reimbursement rate for your time available to see clients. Despite not filling each appointment, earning $50.00 per hour indicates your availability reimbursement.

Another less-aggressive method (scheduled) provides information about the reimbursement rate per session scheduled. If 120 appointments are available for the month, with 100 appointments scheduled, and the total revenue collection is $6,000, then the average reimbursement rate equals $60.00 ($6,000/100). Assuming collections for no shows and late cancellations, this data point indicates the reimbursement rate for scheduled clients.

All three methods provide a different financial picture. Using the working hours example, the therapist is being paid $37.50 per hour regardless of providing psychotherapy services, filling out paperwork, or reading the newspaper. This therapist may set a practice-building goal to get a "raise" of 20% ($7.50) to attain $45.00 per hour (most employees would love a 20% raise annually). The availability method provides information specific to the therapy hour, while the least-aggressive method, scheduled, provides a more generous result and is the method many therapists use to calculate reimbursement rates. Depending on your objectives, any of the methods is appropriate.

A common mistake therapists make when calculating reimbursement rates involves inflation of reimbursement. For example, if 140 appointments are available for the month, 100 sessions are scheduled, but only 80 clients keep their appointments, and total revenue collected is $6,000, this results in a reimbursement rate equal to $75.00 ($6,000/80 appointments). The problem with this calculation is that 20 appointments that should have generated income are not being calculated. Ignoring this lost revenue inflates the average reimbursement rate. Knowing your lost income is important because decreasing lost revenues is a goal of practice building (Worksheet 1.1).

Data Point 3: Referral and Revenue Diversity

Diversity in revenue streams and referral sources provides excellent protection

Collections per month	Hours worked per month	Hourly rate	Appointments available per month	Hourly rate	Appointments scheduled per month	Hourly rate
$6,000	160	$37.50	120	$50.00	100	$60.00
Month 2						
Month 3						
Month 4						
Month 5						
Month 6						
Month 7						
Month 8						
Month 9						
Month 10						
Month 11						
Month 12						
Means						

Note: Use your data to complete this worksheet.

TABLE 1.4

ASSESSING REFERRAL, REVENUE PATTERNS, AND DIRECT REFERRAL RATE

Referrals per revenue source	Therapist	Therapist	Therapist	Total
Insurance A	22			
Insurance B	0			
Insurance C	8			
Insurance D	9			
Insurance E	8			
Insurance F	5			
Other Insurance	0			
EAP A	10			
EAP B	5			
Other EAP	6			
Self-pay full-fee	15			
Self-pay 75–99%	12			
Total	100			
Referral source				
Web site	37			
Online directories	28			
PCP	15			
HR/employer	2			
Providers	7			
Clients/ former clients	11			
Other	0			
Total	100			
% direct referral	35			

Note. After this initial assessment of your practice, keep these data calculated on a monthly basis. Monthly calculations help you to spot trends more quickly and adapt to changing market conditions.

EAP, employer assistance program
PCP, primary care physician
HR, human relations

Conceptual Shifts in *Practice-Building 2.0*

against changes in the marketplace. A simple exercise is to pull 100 charts to calculate your referral distribution, direct referral percentage, and revenue stream distribution. Create a spreadsheet and begin entering the data for your last 100 clients (Table 1.4).

In this example, 35 of the clients were referred by another professional in the community or a current/former client, resulting in a 35% direct referral rate. Keep this data point "live" (as current as your most recent client). Was the data easy to collect given your current charts?

A *direct referral* is any referral that is made to you through "word of mouth." *Psychotherapy Finances* ("Mini-Survey," 2008) reported that

- 20% of therapists get 76–100% clients through word of mouth.
- 33% of therapists get 51–75% clients through word of mouth.
- 24% of therapists get 25–50% clients through word of mouth.
- 22% of therapists get 0–25% clients through word of mouth.

Some examples of word of mouth include former clients, a current client, or a treatment stakeholder directly referring to your practice. *Psychotherapy Finances* ("Mini-Survey," 2008) also reported that only 47% of private practitioners track the source of new clients. If you cannot easily calculate this data point because your administrative system does not collect this information, this is a high-priority task that needs immediate change in your intake process. *Every* new client should be asked the simple question, "Who referred you to me?"

Data Point 4: Access to Care

Access to care is an important service variable. Start implementing a measurement plan to monitor the time between a new client's initial phone call and the scheduled appointment. Best practice standards typically monitor three categories:

1. Scheduling routine appointments within 5 business days of initial contact.
2. Scheduling urgent appointments within 3 business days of initial contact.
3. Scheduling emergent appointments within 24 hours of initial contact.

Increasingly, insurance panels and grant-funding sources assess this variable. Clients feel reassured and confident when they see such statistics on your Web site:

- Routine appointments for new clients are typically *offered* within 3 business days of initial contact.
- Routine appointments for new clients are typically *accepted* within 4 business days of initial contact.

Keep in mind to create a data collection system for measuring this information. This data collection system should be part of your normative routine, not something you try to piece together every month. One method is to make a note of days offered and accepted per client when they schedule an appointment. For example, if you use an online scheduling system that provides a written notification of an appointment, simply make a note of these data points (Figure 1.1). It is important that these data get into your business profile spreadsheet (Table 1.5). In this example, the therapist is offering appointments, on average, 2.2 days from the initial contact made by the client. The therapist is scheduling appointments 4.4 days from the initial contact made by the client. You may not be able to create these data from your records but immediately start tabulating these data on all new appointments.

Formula: Return on Investment
The return on investment (ROI) is typically referred to as the amount of income generated from a project compared to the level of expenses for that project. We will use a simple ROI formula to evaluate potential practice-building projects.

Projected Return on Investment Formula
This formula for projected ROI "ballparks" some numbers and estimates to help you determine if a project is worth attempting. Estimate the number of referrals your projection will gain through the chosen endeavor.

$$\frac{\text{(Average number sessions x Estimated number referral) x Average reimbursement rate}}{\text{Average reimbursement rate x Number of sessions lost for project + Cost of supplies}}$$

Actual Return on Investment Formula
The calculation for actual return on investment will be used after a predetermined length of time following a project. If you implement a 30-day "call all referral sources" campaign, then the calculation will occur 30 days after the completion of the campaign.

$$\frac{\text{Total sessions generated x Average reimbursement rate}}{\text{Average reimbursement rate x Number of sessions lost for project + Cost of supplies}}$$

Tracy Todd, PhD, LMFT
7800 S. Elati Drive, #230
Littleton, CO 80120

BRIEF **THERAPY**
INSTITUTE
OF DENVER
www.btid.com

An e-mail has been sent to the counselor. They'll call you to confirm.

Receipt

Therapist Name:	Tracy Todd, PhD, LMFT
Voice mail for Therapist:	xxx.xxx.xxxx
Date of Appt:	Friday, 11/7/08
Time of Appt:	10:00–10:45 A.M.
Location of Appointment:	7800 S. Elati Drive, #230
	Littleton, CO 80120
Paperwork Download Password:	9999

Reminders:

1. Please print or save this receipt. This information is NOT stored and CANNOT be retrieved under any circumstances.

2. Download and complete your paperwork.

3. Contact your insurance company and get an authorization/approval.

4. A no show/late cancellation (less than 24 hours) fee of $100.00 applies.

Today's Date: 11/3/08

First available appointment: 11/4/08 (1 day appointment offered from initial contact)

Appointment scheduled: 11/7/08 (4 days from initial contact)

TABLE 1.5: BUSINESS PROFILE WITH DAYS OFFERED AND ACCEPTED DATA

Client ID	Closing status	Care Coor. 1= yes 2 = no	Offered appt. days	Accepted appt. days	Method of appt. set (SS1)	Ease of setting (SS1)	Level of progress at closing	Number Sessions	Refer to therapist (SS2) 1= yes 2 = no	Refer to agency (SS2) 1= yes 2 = no
			3	6				9		
			1	5				10		
			0	1				3		
			2	7				3		
			4	4				24		
			3	3				1		
			2	3				2		
			5	6				3		
			2.2ᵃ	4.4ᵃ				6.9		

aMeans of data represented and would be in the final row of the spreadsheet

SS1, Satisfaction Survey 1 is the administrative satisfaction survey distributed to clients following the first session. Further discussion of the survey is found in Chapter 2.

Satisfaction Survey 2 is the clinical satisfaction survey distributed to clients following treatment. Further discussion of this survey is found in Chapter 2.

Conceptual Shifts in *Practice-Building 2.0*

Projected Return on Investment Example[1]

Your goal for presenting a brown bag lunch seminar to a local organization is 5 referrals and therefore 35 sessions (5 x 7 which is your average number of sessions = 35 sessions). The seminar is 45 minutes with 15 minutes travel time each way and 3.5 hours of preparation in writing and producing the material (total of about 5 hours) and the cost of supplies is $100.00.

(5 referrals x 7 sessions each = 35 sessions) x $80.00 average reimbursement rate = $2,800.00

($80.00 average reimbursement rate x 5 hours prep/attendance time) + $100 Cost of supplies = $500.00

= 5.6 projected return on the investment

Actual Return on Investment Example

You choose to define success as those referrals directly resulting from the seminar up to 30 days post-event. You subsequently received 2 referrals with a total of 5 sessions (one referral attended two sessions; the other attended three sessions). You can identify the actual ROI after both cases are terminated.[1]

5 sessions x $80.00 average reimbursement rate = $400.00

($80.00 average reimbursement rate x 5 hours prep/attendance time) + $100 cost of supplies = $500.00

= .80 return on the investment

Is a .80 return on the investment acceptable? The answer is simply, no. This endeavor lost money. What is an acceptable ROI rate for your practice building efforts? That depends on your goals prior to the project. Certainly, an ROI less than 1.0 indicates the project lost money and is considered unacceptable. A ROI above 1.0 can be considered successful (not losing money is always a success). However, my general advice is as follows:

ROI 1.0–2.0 = Poor
ROI 2.0–3.0 = Good
ROI 3.0+ = Great

These data points and spreadsheets are simply the basics to get your new

[1]Frequently, regarding calculation assumptions, I use financial projections. Since there is a significant variance of reimbursement patterns, you should replace my example numbers with your specific calculations. You may also choose to modify the calculations based on your level of sophistication. I simply provide some sound methods that allow any practice-building therapist the opportunity to easily understand the complexities and challenges of various business endeavors. My assumptions include working 11 months or 48 weeks, a reimbursement rate of $80 per hour, and an average of 7 sessions per treatment episode.

practice-building projects under way, thereby allowing you to begin taking a picture of your current practice patterns.

Setting Goals

Depending on whether you are building a brand new business, enhancing your current practice, or your practice is in perilous straits, keep your goals simple, focusing on high-priority actions. As you work through this book, begin to list your priorities and goals and consider data-tracking mechanisms.

Fitness Checklist

Are you fit to be a small business owner? A quick Google search of "qualities of small business owner" results in many articles and assessment inventories about characteristics of entrepreneurs and small business owners. I have put the salient qualities into a simple checklist for your assessment:

___ Do I have the ability to think creatively *and* analytically?
___ Can I consistently come up with good ideas and consistently discard those that would be bad business decisions?
___ Am I competent in social interactions? Can I immediately make positive first impressions?
___ Do I have the drive to work long hours?
___ Can I work hard and stay focused on the areas of my business that I find boring, tedious, "not me"?
___ Do I have trust and faith in my abilities to succeed?
___ Will I seek help in the areas that I need help?
___ Am I highly organized and efficient?
___ Can I adapt to new technologies or strategies that increase my efficiency?
___ Am I in good physical health?
___ Can I tolerate risk?
___ Do I have positive stress relief activities?
___ Do I have a solid and extensive support system?

Of course, the more you answer "yes," the better your positioning for owning and operating a small business. More important, those questions receiving "no" answers or creating feelings of uncertainty should be areas that you begin incorporating into your practice-building plan.

Get Training, Support, and Consultation

Recognizing the potential barriers allows you to create strategies for support. It is important to acknowledge your limitations as well as strengths. Consultation allows you to build your practice more quickly while learning from someone with the necessary experience.

I strongly encourage you to examine how much money you spent on clinical training last year. These dollars include not only your registration fees but also how many clinical hours were lost. For example if a 1-day seminar cost $200 and you average six sessions per day at $80 per session, that equals $680 per day of training (6 x $80 per session = $480 + $200 training cost). Four trainings per year equals $2,720 of training cost. This next year, try budgeting at least $2,720 for practice building. Remember, a new clinical skill might result in a few referrals. However, developing a podcast has a high likelihood of generating many referrals.

Typically, therapists will spend hundreds of dollars and many hours per year on clinical training only to use some of the information some of the time. Yet, therapists rarely spend a dime receiving training on such issues as building a database, managing a Web site, or developing a template-based paperwork and charting system—skills used every day, with every client. My recommendation is that, after creating an efficient business infrastructure, a minimum of 25% of all training should focus on research and development of your business. Trainings on how to use spreadsheets and word documents more effectively, and how to create podcasts are just a few examples of business research and development.

A common and understandable question asked by small business owners of mental health practices is, "How long should it take for me to build my practice successfully?" The answer depends on the status of your practice.

Starting a Practice

Patience and infrastructure are the key components when starting a practice. Therapists starting their businesses as part time often begin with inefficient accounting, data-tracking, and documentation systems in place. Logistically, it is easy to have and maintain an inefficient system when documenting and accounting for five clients per week. As the practice grows, the excuse is, "I don't have the time to change my systems." If the practice does not grow, frustration sets in, and the attitude becomes, "Why bother?"

A startup practice needs about 6 months of development before opening the doors for new clients. Beyond the normative office location, accounting/financial management system, telephone and office supplies necessary for a startup, during those 6 months the following goals and tasks need completion:

- Develop and launch of your Web site with paperwork download, online scheduling, and online payment functions.

- Create a data-tracking system.
- Create your electronic file management system.
- Conduct a risk analysis for all privacy protection concerns.
- Develop satisfaction- and loyalty-building strategies for clients, former clients, and referral sources.

Two months before opening, it is time to develop all advertising targets and advertising materials. If you are starting a practice, you may lack a reputation for quality services. However, lacking a clinical reputation in the treatment community should not deter your efforts. Rather, it is important to highlight those services you have confidence will create loyalty and satisfaction. On your Web site and possibly in a brochure, it is critically important to advertise your customer services. Most therapists advertise standard and ineffective information: name, degrees, licenses, treatment style (e.g., solution-focused family therapy), and clinical populations they feel qualified to serve. This information does not separate you from the others. Advertise service variables such as your online scheduling, podcast, your video introduction, and paperwork download capabilities.

Provided you have numerous service variables that heighten convenience and potential satisfaction with your treatment, start advertising to your network (friends, family, ex-coworkers). Critically important is having an attention-grabbing service, typically on your Web site. This service distinguishes your practice from that of your competitors and can offset any negativity that may accompany questions of private practice experience. Demonstrating you are current and up to date with services adds credibility to your clinical service component (see Appendix A for more information).

Expanding a Practice

Those expanding a practice and integrating *Practice-Building 2.0* strategies have an easier path to integration. Understandably so, practices wanting to expand are often the most challenging to adapt. These practices have enough referrals to avoid financial panic and deservedly consider the practice successful.

Because referral source development is not a problem, these practices should focus 6–12 months on replacing inefficient infrastructure processes with processes that save time, reduce labor, and increase indirect income. For example, converting all charting to electronic forms with prepopulated drop-down menus will save time and reduce labor.

Working through this book, you will find numerous examples of unrealized revenue by reducing costs or labor. Using these examples, business owners wishing to expand their practices need to begin identifying, and prioritizing, these indirect income building strategies. More challenging, however, is the temptation to avoid or remain status quo because of success. If you are committing to expansion, begin creating your list of priorities and schedule due dates. Most important, do not let current success create a false sense of security.

Rescuing a Practice

Business owners in the unfortunate position of having a struggling practice are often the easiest to comprehensively engage in *Practice-Building 2.0* strategies. These businesses need aggressive strategies and interventions that yield fast, positive results. The general order of priority is as follows:

1. Building a Web site with nearly all the functions discussed in Chapter 4. A failing business is in the position of needing all Web site enhancements to quickly and decisively differentiate itself from competitors.
2. An aggressive strategy emphasizing satisfaction, loyalty (Chapter 2) and treatment stakeholders, clients, and former clients (Chapter 3).
3. Most important, avoid the temptation to spend money and time on antiquated practice-building strategies or strategies focusing on Ring 3 referral development (Chapter 3).

Summary

Barriers to building your business exist only if you let them. Honestly assess your fitness for owning a business and seek feedback from others. Understand your limitations and create strategies to enhance your skills and knowledge where you are vulnerable. Training in business, computer skills, and administration are as important as your clinical skills. Such skills are the foundation of your business, and you need to avoid allowing lack of skill to compromise your pursuit of small business ownership.

Like any other small business, data are necessary to capitalize on market trends, understand adverse trends, set goals for your business, and assess if business strategies are effective. You only need some basic data points and a method to collect and analyze the data easily. Knowing your business profile, not guessing, is critical for success in a highly competitive marketplace.

Key Points
1. You are an owner of a *small business* and conceptualizing your practice as such is more useful when attempting to start, expand, or rescue your business. The notion of "private practice" creates outdated concepts and paradigms.
2. Barriers exist to building your business. Understand these barriers,

account for them, and avoid letting them deter you from your goals.

3. All businesses need data to make informed decisions. Make informed decisions regarding your business.
4. Always set goals based on return on the investment (ROI).
5. There are differences between starting, expanding, and rescuing a practice.

Action List

1. Assess your technology. Do you have the basics needed in a computer, office suite, and sound and video recording and editing?
2. Create a spreadsheet that captures business profile data points.
3. Create a spreadsheet that captures your referral and revenue streams. Enter data from your last 100 customers.
4. Calculate your average number of sessions and access-to-care data points.
5. Choose a reimbursement calculation to benchmark your practice-building strategies.
6. Complete the fitness checklist and create a plan for those areas in which you may experience challenges.
7. Identify those who can train, consult, and support your business endeavors. Remember, they *do not* need to be fellow therapists.
8. Earmark a specific amount of money that you will use to invest in your training and education regarding infrastructure skills and tools over the next year.

Master Goal List

As we begin your practice-building efforts, there are master goals to begin considering. Some of these goals may not make sense quite yet, but they are important to keep in mind as you work through the practice-building strategies. These fundamental goals should result in your practice growing, thriving, and being built on a solid foundation to allow for protection against adverse market conditions:

1. Direct referral percentage greater than 80%.
2. Care coordination rate of 66%.
3. Web site with basic functions: paperwork download and online scheduling.
4. Automation of data collection and computation.
5. Use of technology to enhance infrastructure efficiencies, thereby increasing unrealized revenue.
6. Documented client satisfaction rate greater than 90%.

CHAPTER TWO

Satisfaction, Loyalty, and Lifelong Customers

"There are no such things as synonyms."
Tom Robbins, *Jitterbug Perfume*, 1984, p. 208

A great deal of psychotherapy is word manipulation. Different words conjure different emotions and cognitive states. The group typically labeled "referral source" often includes professionals in the community. Substituting the phrase "treatment stakeholders" significantly changes the context of the relationship. A referral source receives a thank you call or note. A treatment stakeholder is someone involved at any level of service delivery (e.g., referral source to provide additional services, such as a psychiatrist to prescribe medication) receiving more attention. Are those we provide service to clients or customers? Depending on the relationship context, both nouns apply. Changing *client* to *customer* fundamentally changes the relationship. The client–therapist, or patient–doctor, relationship is hierarchical with the client or patient in the subordinate role. Changing client or patient to customer creates a role reversal. As customers, expectations change between the provider or seller and purchaser of services. The customer creates demand with the provider or seller held in the accountable or subordinate position.

Psychotherapists often place clinical interpretation on uncooperative clients or poorly motivated clients. Examination of how customer service contributes to these clinical situations rarely occurs. I shudder to think how many clients labeled as resistant, noncompliant, or difficult simply did not engage in therapy because of poor customer service. For example, a potential client (financial planner) interviewing therapists contacted our practice to inquire about our administrative services. He was dissatisfied with the administrative services, not the clinical service, of a previous therapist. After making numerous requests to obtain financial statements his previous therapist reported that she only sent statements when necessary. Because he paid his bills each session, the therapist did not find this an important administrative task. When he did receive his statements, he typically found errors. He also reported that it was difficult to reschedule appointments with her. When trying to address these matters, he was told to stop being so difficult and that his complaints reflected his general clinical issue of "controlling." Although the interpretive leap was easy to make, it was simply wrong. How many of us would find it discerning to receive infrequent and inaccurate statements or to take days to reschedule?

Clients who experience hassles or challenges with your practice become aggravated. Although they may understand the situation, they are upset when starting a therapy session. These aggravations can range from a therapist starting a session late, to a client receiving an erroneous bill prior to the session, to having to make multiple telephone calls to schedule the appointment. Clients are customers and need attention to customer service variables. Relying solely on the therapeutic conversation as both treatment and customer service is not only poor clinical work but also terrible customer service.

Technology is changing the face of customer service. Customers can order a gizmo from a favorite electronic store and simply walk into the store, show their e-mail receipt, and walk out in less than a few minutes. If they are willing to wait, they can have it shipped directly to their door. Through technology, big business is becoming more intimate with customers.

Clinical Service Is Not Equal to Customer Service

Therapists in a quest to deliver the newest or most evidence-based clinical service mistakenly presume that they are delivering high-quality customer service. Credentialing associations and licensing boards, through continuing education, further perpetuate the notion that quality clinical services are synonymous with quality customer service delivery. Graduate schools train students to focus exclusively on what occurs in the therapy room, erroneously assuming, and perpetuating the notion, that experiences outside the therapy room experiences have little to no impact on clinical services. From credentialing services, to graduate school training, to continuing education, psychotherapists lack exposure to customer service variables and strategies. The erroneous assumption that "in-the-room" therapy conversations define customer service perpetuates ignorance and avoidance of the connection between administrative service variables and quality of treatment.

Therapist–Client Hierarchy

Psychotherapy services, steeped in the medical model of service delivery, are predicated on the hierarchy of professional–patient relationship. Although emphasizing clinical concepts such as joining and collaborating with the client, when examining service delivery variables the field of psychotherapy continues to place the therapist in a hierarchical position. Do you disagree? The simple act of asking clients to leave messages, eventually to receive a return call at the convenience of the *therapist,* places the therapist in a hierarchical position. Therapists who lack Web sites create situations in which clients cannot shop or compare services. Forcing potential clients to call and inquire about qualifications, rather than examining the qualifications on a Web site, is an example of relying on the therapist for information. These examples may seem insignificant, but they subtly demonstrate the hierarchical position of the therapist–client relationship. This position is quickly, and thankfully, changing with the new emphasis on best practice standards, technology, and the flattening of psychotherapy. Best practice variables that mandate that treatment establish ceilings, not floors, address the need for non-face-to-face service provisions (outside the room) as well as anticipate and prevent needed services. The therapist–customer business relationship is evolving to equal status as the clinical relationship.

Difference Between Product and Service

There is a significant difference between the quality of the product (psychotherapy service) and the quality of delivering that product (customer service). For example, Starbucks serves coffee and tea (product), with a system to deliver that product most patrons find so satisfactory they become staunchly loyal to Starbucks. Little thought is given to waiting in a line of three or four. Customers have come to expect and accept this situation. Why? They find the value of the coffee-drinking experience, friendly service, and coffee made exactly to their liking worth the short wait.

Customer service is significantly different than clinical service. Rarely, however, does the psychotherapy field consider *quality customer service.* Candidly, it is a bit worrisome when bureaucracies such as the National Committee for Quality Assurance and Joint Commission on Accreditation of Healthcare Organizations must give mandates to providers outlining customer service variables and benchmarks. Surprising are the typically harsh sentiments of many therapists toward customer service improvements. Following a meeting held by a third-party payer, I overheard many network providers complaining about the nonclinical expectations:

"Why do I need an office within one block of public transportation?"

"Expecting us to set a nonemergency appointment within 7 business days is absurd."

"How can they expect me to notify my clients' primary care physician in two-thirds of the referrals?"

These variables reflect an emphasis on customer service outside the therapy room. Yet, it is easy to ascertain how these variables may contribute or detract from the therapy experience in the room. Predictably, it would seem, waiting longer than 7 days for an appointment decreases motivation for change. The result is a likely cancellation or no-show. The problem is not solved, and the next crisis situation is simply looming. Another example involves not notifying a primary care physician or psychiatrist about lifestyle issues that compromise medication effectiveness, thereby placing both the therapist and the primary care physician in enabling treatment roles.

Customer Service Is a Business

Customer service is big business. To stay competitive, psychotherapists facing a flattening business model need to implement high-quality customer service processes. The business world is filled with books on how to deliver high-quality customer service. Corporations spend billions of dollars training employees to deliver high-quality customer service. I challenge you to find a single book, or identify a single conference, with the primary theme of the delivery of customer service while providing psychotherapy. More challenging would be offering such a conference and having therapists actually attend. Certainly more metaphorical than scientific, I did a quick comparison search on both Amazon and Google of the key words "mental health customer service" and "small business customer service." The Google search of mental health customer service yielded articles about counties needing to improve services for community health care centers, and the Amazon search resulted in a kaleidoscope of topics addressing treatment options but not service variables. More telling was conducting the same search using the key words "small business customer service." The Google results listed specific sites addressing how to improve your customer interactions regardless of service, and the Amazon search resulted in such titles as *May I Help You?: Great Customer Service for Small Business* (Mercer, 2003) and *Customer Service Made Easy* (Levesque, 2006). Although nonscientific, these results do suggest the field of psychotherapy, from a business development perspective, lacks maturity. It is important to start examining all aspects of service delivery outside the therapy room from pretreatment engagement to posttreatment follow-up, from interactions with clients, former clients, and referral sources to our own administrative procedures.

Psychotherapists are a dime a dozen. The challenge I pose is, "What makes psychotherapy with you extraordinary?" I am not referring to the quality of your clinical service. What is so outstanding that a former client, or customer, wants to brag about your services? A few years ago, a colleague and I were finishing a session at the same time. Her next scheduled clients were in the waiting room. Having previously made small talk with them, walking through the waiting room and, knowing my colleague was exiting her session, I jokingly said to them, "Watch out, she is crabby today." They chuckled, and I went to get the mail. On returning to the office, I discovered they had locked me out. They told me that they would not let me into the office until I said something nice about their therapist. Of course, I did some groveling, and they unlocked the door. Following the session, my colleague commented on her clients' appreciation of our services and sense of community. The clients felt connected with our agency, which was different from previous counseling experiences. They highlighted everything from online scheduling, to having self-help resources readily available in the waiting room, to a serious but not morbid environment, to the sense of community. This example demonstrates the principle of surprise and delight espoused by Starbucks (Michelli, 2006). My colleague's customers were both surprised and delighted at the entire therapy experience and continue to make numerous referrals to our agency.

Surprise and delight builds satisfaction and loyalty. There is an important distinction, however, between these qualities (Gitomer, 1998). Gitomer argued that satisfaction is important but is not the same as a loyal customer. He challenged corporations to consider strategies that develop loyalty. In behavioral health care, the idea of loyalty becomes imperative when considering practice-building efforts.

Customer Satisfaction

Customer satisfaction (Gitomer, 1998) is certainly ambiguous and varies across customers and products or services. Such ambiguity clearly exists with psychotherapy. Who do you want satisfied with your services? Some clients may be upset with interventions that break enabling patterns. What if confronting a client results in a treatment dropout? Maybe it was an appropriate clinical intervention. Alternatively, how do you ensure referral source satisfaction? How does the referral source define satisfaction? A referral source might define *satisfaction* as saving money, coordinated care, keeping the client out of crisis, or comprehensive and communicated treatment plans.

Satisfaction is multifaceted and complicated. A prescription-abusing, personality disordered professional you confront may end therapy thinking you are a terrible therapist (not satisfied). The referral source (e.g., primary care physician) may not understand the frequency of this occurrence (not satisfied). A more understanding referral source might find your intervention appropriate (satisfied). The spouse may be thinking, "Finally, someone said it" (satisfied). Relying entirely on the outcome of service delivery is a compromising position because of the various clinical dynamics associated with psychotherapy. In the corporate world, there are many service components examined for customer satisfaction. It is important to assess every step a client goes through from pre therapy appointment scheduling to posttherapy follow-up, asking the questions, "Are my customers satisfied with this step, process, or procedure?" "Are there any barriers to treatment?" One method of discovery is to administer a client satisfaction survey at the beginning of treatment (Form 2.1).

Consider sending a satisfaction survey following the first session. This administrative survey evaluates the perception of new clients regarding your access to care, online scheduling system, the office, and paperwork download system. You can learn a great deal with this satisfaction survey, thereby effectively and efficiently meeting the needs of clients. It is interesting to note that this survey can reflect changes in your treatment population. For example, ten years ago we only inquired about scheduling through a voice mail system. As we added a live operator and online scheduling, we needed to know the satisfaction level of each scheduling possibility. These data points created more confidence to emphasize online scheduling when advertising our practice.

After collecting enough data that you are confident in a specific administrative component such as scheduling, you can change the survey to assess another area. The survey can easily assess the functionality of a Web site, the office location, or any other processes you feel are important in developing immediate satisfaction with your clientele.

Administering another satisfaction survey following therapy is vitally important to assess clinical services (Form 2.2) This clinical satisfaction combines outcome measurements with satisfaction questions. Although each question examines a different aspect of satisfaction regarding the therapy experience, there are two questions I would find most important: "Would you refer family and friends to the Brief Therapy Institute?" "Would you refer family and friends to your therapist?"

These two questions suggest more than satisfaction. They represent a strong possibility that your former clients are satisfied enough with services that they have reached the state of loyalty. This loyalty is demonstrated by positive answers to the survey questions and strongly suggests developing lifelong

Tracy Todd, PhD, LMFT
7800 South Elati Drive, #230
Littleton, CO 80120
www.btid.com

SATISFACTION SURVEY 1

At the Brief Therapy Institute of Denver, we value your opinion about our services. This satisfaction survey is to evaluate your opinion about our Initial Services with you. Please take a moment to complete this survey (circle the most accurate response) and return it via the self-addressed stamped envelope we have provided. Thank you.

	Online 1	Live Operator 2	Voice mail 3	
How did you set your appointment?				
How easy was it to set the appointment with this clinic?	1 not	2	3	4 very
How convenient is the location of this clinic?	1 not	2	3	4 very
How comfortable is the office?	1 not	2	3	4 very
So far, how professionally has your therapist handled your situation?	1 not	2	3	4 very
If you used our Web site for information, how helpful was it? [http://www.address]	1 not	2	3	4 very
If you set an appointment *online*, how confident were you about the process?	1 not	2	3	4 very
If you set an appointment with the *live operator*, how confident were you about the process?	1 not	2	3	4 very
If you set an appointment through your *therapist's* voice mail, how confident were you about the process?	1 not	2	3	4 very
Although you are at the beginning of treatment, how confident are you about the potential success of treatment?	1 not	2	3	4 very
What suggestions do you have about our intake and appointment-setting process?	1 not	2	3	4 very

What suggestions do you have about our intake and appointment-setting process?

Office: West	Clinician: TT	Contract: Insurance A	Intake no.: 200803173

Tracy Todd, PhD, LMFT
7800 South Elati Drive, #230
Littleton, CO 80120
www.btid.com

SATISFACTION SURVEY 2

At the Brief Therapy Institute of Denver, we value your opinion about our services. This satisfaction survey is to evaluate your opinion about our treatment services. Please take a moment to complete this survey (circle the most accurate response) and return it via the self-addressed stamped envelope we have provided. Thank you.

How satisfied are you with the therapy you received?	1 not	2	3	4 very
How effective were the services you received?	1 not	2	3	4 very
How helpful have the services been for dealing with your problems?	1 haven't	2	3	4 extremely
Comparing your situation to before treatment, how would you describe your current situation?	1 worse	2	3	4 better
How confidential do you feel your services are?	1 not	2	3	4 very
Would you refer family and friends to the Brief Therapy Institute of Denver?	1 Yes	2	3	4 NO
Would you refer family and friends to your therapist?	1 Yes	2	3	4 No

What level of improvement have you noticed in the following areas since starting therapy?

Medical problems	1 not	2	3	4 great
Work/school problems	1 not	2	3	4 great
Alcohol or drug use	1 not	2	3	4 great
Out-of-control behaviors	1 not	2	3	4 great
Personal relationships	1 not	2	3	4 great
Personal relationships	1 not	2	3	4 great
Stress	1 not	2	3	4 great
Overall functioning	1 not	2	3	4 great

Office:	Clinician:	Contract:	Intake no.:
West	TT	Insurance A	200803173

clients. It is your choice what variables, whether administrative or clinical, you believe accurately assess your practice patterns. Importantly, regularly enter these data in your business profile spreadsheet (Table 2.1).

Let us take a moment to examine some data regarding administrative and clinical services.

Method and Ease of Scheduling

The data indicate that 63% of clients are using the online scheduling function compared to 17% using voice mail. It is important to note that those using the online scheduling system clearly indicated greater ease of scheduling their appointment and generally higher satisfaction than those using voice mail.

Refer to Therapist and Agency

The data indicate that 40% of clients would not refer to their therapist and 20% would not refer to the agency. This is an alarming statistic. Examination of the data indicates that those *not* referring to the agency are also the same clients who scheduled appointments via voice mail. These data strongly suggest that a practice-building therapist needs to make some decisions about his or her scheduling services. The current voice mail scheduling process is reducing referrals, and aggressive corrective actions are necessary. Does the agency eliminate voice mail scheduling and move toward only online scheduling? Is there something about the voice mail process that can enhance customer satisfaction and loyalty? This example demonstrates the difference between strategies in *Practice Building 2.0* and more traditional practice building strategies. Simply increasing referrals is not the answer. *Rather than subjecting new clients to a problematic process, correcting the process so current and future clients experience satisfaction is the correct course of action.*

Customer Loyalty

Gitomer (1998) described customer loyalty as fighting to retain your product or service. Loyalty goes beyond satisfaction. Loyalty is about a client or referral source committing to repeat services and experiencing services impressive enough to refer family and friends (bond). Loyalty creates distress if a client cannot see you. Satisfying events occurring across time create loyalty. Today's technology provides many opportunities for psychotherapy practices to create satisfying services and loyalty. Continuous contact across time is no longer impossible or cost prohibitive. Web sites and podcasts easily eliminate barriers to loyalty building and provide practice-building therapists the perfect forum for creating a connection with clients, former clients, and ancillary health care professionals.

TABLE 2.1: BUSINESS PROFILE WITH SATISFACTION SURVEY DATA

Client ID	Closing status	Care Coor. 1= yes 2 = no	Offered appt. days	Accepted appt. days	Method of appt. set (SS1[a])	Ease of setting (SS1[a])	Level of progress at closing	Number Sessions	Refer to therapist (SS2) 1= yes 2 = no	Refer to agency (SS2) 1= yes 2 = no
			3	6	1	4		9	1	1
			1	5	1	4		10	1	1
			0	1	1	3		3		
			2	7	3	2		3	2	1
			4	4	1	4		24		
			3	3	3	2		1		
			2	3	1	3		2	1	1
			5	6	3	1		3	2	2
			2.2	4.4				6.9		

[a]Over the years we have averaged an approximately 20% response rate for Satisfaction Survey 1 (SS1). This high percentage is most likely because the clients are just starting therapy, and we encourage them to return the survey. For Satisfaction Survey 2 (SS2), we average a 5% response rate. For both surveys, we provide a self-addressed, stamped envelope. I have increased the percentages in the example to demonstrate the emergence of trends and the return rates are not representative of our data.

SS1, Satisfaction Survey 1 is the administrative satisfaction survey distributed to clients following the first session. SS2, Satisfaction Survey 2 is the clinical satisfaction survey distributed to clients following treatment.

Conceptual Shifts in *Practice-Building 2.0*

Point-and-click technology becomes more than a tool. Technology creates a bond between all those involved with treatment to your practice. Through technology, the client and therapist relationship may terminate, but the customer and seller relationship continues. On termination, a former client can continue to receive therapy information and assistance through the use of e-newsletters, podcasts, and self-help videos and instructional sheets. From a best practice perspective, a loyal and lifelong relationship provides non-face-to-face services, anticipates client needs, provides prevention services, and allows customers quick and easy access to future services (New Freedom Commission on Mental Health, 2003). From a practice-building perspective, lifelong customers create many business advantages. These customers become great advertising agents when provided with ample mechanisms to refer.

Never before has the ability to build loyalty been so easy, quick, and affordable. Today, with Web sites, podcasts and videocasts, paperwork download capability, and e-mail reminders, a solo practitioner can easily achieve and build loyalty. The important practice-building component is strategically implementing technology. As customers become more sophisticated, they expect more convenient services.

I constantly look for excellent service delivery regardless of the product or services. Table 2.2 is a comparison of some outstanding service variables of various businesses and a practice implementing *Practice-Building 2.0* strategies.

Many of these strategies, such as newsletters, help create a connection with customers long after therapy concludes. Those loyal to your services can use the newsletter for self-help information *and* to advertise your practice. Loyalty creates a lifelong customer–provider relationship. Practice-building therapists need strategies and business processes to develop and maintain lifelong customers.

Lifelong Customers

Lifelong customers return to your practice in the future when they experience hardship or need your assistance. For example, Mary and Joe seek your services for their 9-year-old son, Sam, who is experiencing severe adjustment disorder because of their recent relocation. They are receiving conflicting advice from teachers, their pediatrician, friends, and family members. They want credible consultation regarding treatment options. After a few sessions, they are satisfied and confident with a parenting plan. Is it reasonable to assume they may need your services again when Sam is 14 years old and presenting adolescent challenges? What about when Sam is 20 years old, and he would like your services for some normative life issues? When Sam is 24 years old and considering marriage, will he seek your guidance? How about when Sam is 34 years old and dealing with his own parenting struggles?

TABLE 2.2. SATISFACTION AND LOYALTY-BUILDING TOOLS

Business Service Variables	Practice Building 2.0
Dentist—e-mail and phone appointment reminders	E-mail reminder
Realtor—"Get to know me" video	Video introduction on Web site
Realtor—Assess your home or the home you want to buy	Links to websites offering assessment instruments
Restaurant—Online reservations	Online scheduling
Fitness center—Tips for staying in shape	Self-help handouts available online
Business consultant—Self-help pods and video	Self-help podcasts, audio and video
Heating service—Furnace season tips and strategies	Seasonal newsletter and Web site posting of predictive issues
Auto dealer—Service feedback, purchase and oil change	Satisfaction survey at the beginning and end of therapy
Attorney—New developments immediately notifying client	Care coordination
Financial planner—Referral thank you and newsletter	Referral source thank you cards, newsletters

Characteristics

What creates a lifelong customer? Multiple satisfying events throughout numerous interactions and experiences with your practice create lifelong customers. Of course, a positive therapy experience precludes loyalty. Most therapists believe they deliver outstanding therapy to the vast majority of clients. Then, why do these same therapists have difficulty building and maintaining a practice?

There are most likely a few contributing factors that inhibit growth among psychotherapy businesses. First, the potential exists that therapists are not delivering the quality of therapy they really believe they are delivering. There is a significant difference between adequate therapy services that solve the problems presented by clients and services so outstanding that clients are converted to lifelong customers. A second reason that quality services do not convert clients to loyal, lifelong customers is the nearly complete absence of services outside the therapy room. The in-the-room services might be outstanding, but in a flattening world that increasingly emphasizes best practice standards, psychotherapeutic services must become more encompassing.

It is imperative that practice-building therapists begin assessing their business from a customer's perspective. Although I delve into these matters in greater depth throughout *Practice-Building 2.0*, it is important to recognize the intentionality necessary to accomplish this critical practice-building variable. Creation of a lifelong customer is no accident; it is an intentional process. As a business owner, the process starts long before a client becomes a customer and ends well after treatment concludes.

Becoming the therapist across the life span positively reflects the trusting bond created with your clients. Historically, the difficulty with maintaining a lifelong relationship involved pragmatics and cost. Doing so meant paper-storing addresses and sending snail mail. After a few years of practice, thousands of names are on a mailing list, and frequent mailings become cost prohibitive. Today, however, the situation is greatly different. E-mail and Web sites provide affordable and easy methods for staying connected. Technology creates a significant paradigm shift in conceptualizing every new referral. Rather than providing services that are adequate and moving on to securing another referral, therapists need to consider providing outstanding services that create a lifelong customer.

Ethics

Many therapists struggle with the concept of ethics, so it is important that we deal with the ethics and pragmatics behind the idea of a lifelong customer. A client across the life span is not the same as creating and exploiting client trust through dependency. These are two different circumstances. Building a lifelong customer–seller relationship is creating a business bond similar to a primary care physician, dentist, attorney, or accountant. These professionals are often with us throughout our life span. Consider your own primary care physician. Do you change primary care physician every time you have an ailment? No. We all want continuity.

In reviewing the code of ethics for the major mental health associations (American Association for Marriage and Family Therapy, 2001; American Counseling Association, 2005; American Psychiatric Association, 2001; American Psychological Association, 2003; National Association of Social Workers, 1999), it becomes evident that therapists must avoid exploiting a client by furthering their own interests or harming or compromising a client via the therapy relationship. Understandably, many therapists express ethical concern about clients becoming dependent on the therapy relationship.

Let us examine two different situations. First, a newlywed couple seeks your guidance on improving communication and setting boundaries with extended family members. After services are completed, they access your Web site for any pertinent additional information. For the next few months, it is quite possible you are posting articles, sending e-newsletters, and creating podcasts on depression. Since neither is experiencing depression, they find the information educational but not relevant. After addressing depression, your next topic is conflict management. Your former newlywed couple now finds the distributed information useful, and it assists them in developing an improved relationship. Is this an unethical or unhealthy therapist–client or customer relationship? No. As a matter of fact, according to the Institute of Medicine (2001) and the New Freedom Commission (2003), this scenario is the ideal treatment process and relationship.

Now, consider a second situation using the same clinical scenario. Shortly after successfully terminating therapy, the husband begins to access your podcasts on a variety of subjects. He begins to call your office and request, maybe even demand, information on communication and conflict management via the Web site and podcasts. He begins suggesting that he needs more frequent contacts or sessions. As the couple's therapist, have you done anything unethical? No. However, do you have a clinical situation that needs addressing? Yes. To this point, there have been no ethical violations, but rather clinical issues that need intervention. How the therapist chooses to intervene, or not, can result in ethical violations.

Having a lifelong customer is not a violation of ethics. However, how a therapist manages the relationship can be either professional and appropriate or unethical and harmful. The fact that former clients are accessing or receiving clinical information from you is not the contentious issue. How the client responds to the issue and your subsequent management of the clinical challenge determine if any ethical violations exist.

Summary

In a flattening world where technology fundamentally changes our relationships with clients and former clients, practice-building therapists need multidimensional business strategies and systems. In-the-room psychotherapy services are no longer substantial enough to gain new referrals, maintain existing customer relations, or attract relationships with other health care professionals. Practice-building therapists need to move beyond the concept that in-the-room expertise is enough to build and maintain a thriving practice.

Satisfaction and loyalty are practice-building outcomes resulting from a business owner's attentiveness to the variables that create such positive emotions

Conceptual Shifts in *Practice-Building 2.0*

among customers. Lifelong customers result from intentional and specific strategies implemented by a business owner. *The future of your business should not rest solely on the in-the-room experience of clients.*

Key Points

1. Satisfaction is a necessary but not sufficient condition for practice building.
2. Developing loyalty among clients, former clients, and referral sources will sustain your practice through the toughest of times.
3. A practice-building goal is to achieve a lifelong customer base.
4. Clinical services are not the same as customer services. You must distinguish between your product (psychotherapy) and outside-the-room services.
5. Customer and clinical service build satisfaction, loyalty, and lifelong clients.

Action List

1. Create an administrative satisfaction survey to assess your clients' satisfaction with the intake process.
2. Create a clinical satisfaction survey to distribute following therapy to assess client satisfaction with clinical services.
3. Enter specific data points into your business profile spreadsheet.

CHAPTER THREE

Rings of Referrals

Referral sources generally fall into three different categories: treatment stakeholders, clients and former clients, and unknown or unanticipated referral sources. An excellent method for clarifying your practice-building priorities is conceptualizing referral pools (advertising targets) as concentric rings. Ring 1, the "bull's-eye," includes referrals from treatment professionals in the community—treatment stakeholders (Figure 3.1). Some examples of treatment stakeholders include psychiatrists, primary care physicians, financial planners, and attorneys.

Ring 2 includes referrals made by clients and former clients. Ring 3 includes unknown referral sources lacking experience or knowledge of your treatment—

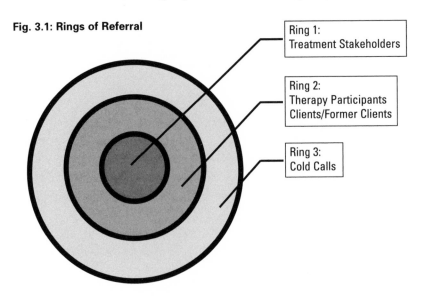

Fig. 3.1: Rings of Referral

Ring 1:
Treatment Stakeholders

Ring 2:
Therapy Participants
Clients/Former Clients

Ring 3:
Cold Calls

cold calling. Although creating strategies to enhance your chances of being on the first page of a Google search sounds exciting and profitable, consider these efforts only after successful implementation of Ring 1 and 2 strategies. *Practice-Building 2.0* strategies result in treatment stakeholders, clients, and former clients receiving virtually all of your marketing and advertising attention. Ring 3—unknowns and cold calling—may get no attention.

Logically, this prioritization makes sense. Yet, most practice-building efforts focus almost exclusively on Ring 3, unknown referral source development. The purpose of this chapter is to distinguish and identify differences between each referral target so that eventual practice-building strategies are prioritized and successfully implemented.

Ring 1: Treatment Stakeholders

Developing and maintaining an expansive network of treatment stakeholders is quite sufficient for a thriving private practice. Mackay (1997) gave numerous reasons why we should have a strong network, with job stability as one of his top 10 reasons. As self-employed business owners, our top priority is job stability. Treatment stakeholders are the highest level of priority when practice building. Every practice is unique and needs critical examination of treatment stakeholder potentialities. To start identifying treatment stakeholders, ask, "Who indirectly experiences or witnesses my clinical work, and who benefits from my high-quality services?"

Identifying Treatment Stakeholders

Treatment stakeholders include anyone associated with the care of a client. Treatment stakeholders become critically important to the success of your practice because they can elevate your credibility and reputation. Treatment stakeholders such as primary care physicians and psychiatrists, recognizing your high-quality care, become excellent advertising representatives. Some other examples of treatment stakeholders include:

- Nurse practitioners
- Intake coordinators for primary care offices
- Attorneys
- School counselors
- Human resource directors
- Employee assistance professionals
- Coaches
- Teachers
- Members of the ministry

Therapists who are not aggressively involving treatment stakeholders miss opportunities for developing a high-quality reputation and subsequent loyalty among this referral group. Not only do you enhance your reputation with treatment stakeholders but also you can help them deliver higher-quality services to the mutual client. Most treatment stakeholders recognize that psychological and relationship issues have an impact on the services they are trying to deliver. However, they either do not feel qualified to intervene or lack knowledge of who can assist them. Treatment stakeholders, in delivering services, risk providing poor services because of distressed clients. A team approach helps your mutual client, helps the treatment stakeholder become more effective in delivering whatever services they are offering, and establishes you as a credible treatment provider. Without collaboration, benefits to the mutual client may occur, but no one is aware of the services you are specifically providing.

Task. Review the file of your last three clients and list at least three potential or recognized treatment stakeholders for each client, regardless of whether you actually contacted the treatment stakeholder, and rate the level of clinical participation (Table 3.1). Were you able to accomplish this task? Did you, like many therapists, identify treatment stakeholders but not involve them in the treatment? With each identified treatment stakeholder who is not aware of your role in the entire treatment process, opportunities are lost for you to gain a reputation of a high-quality service provider.

TABLE 3.1. ASSESSING TREATMENT STAKEHOLDERS	
	Level of involvement
CLIENT 1	
Treatment stakeholder's name	
Treatment stakeholder's name	
Treatment stakeholder's name	
CLIENT 2	
Treatment stakeholder's name	
Treatment stakeholder's name	
Treatment stakeholder's name	
CLIENT 3	
Treatment stakeholder's name	
Treatment stakeholder's name	
Treatment stakeholder's name	

1= None; 2= I notified stakeholder of my care; 3= We have communicated, communicate regularly.

Conceptual Shifts in *Practice-Building 2.0*

Clinical Example. Jerry is a 42-year-old male referred by an employee assistance program (EAP) specialist for work performance problems related to recent episodes of high anxiety. During the assessment, you learn that Jerry has a history of anxiety, and the recent episode was precipitated by his employer asking Jerry to start giving presentations at work. His primary care physician has prescribed medications for 2 years to assist with Jerry's chronic anxiety. However, the primary care physician is now requesting that Jerry seek psychotherapy before changing or increasing medications. Concluding the session, Jerry and you agree on the importance of sending the Care Coordination Form to his physician, and Jerry signs the Authorization to Disclose form (Form 3.1 and Form 3.2, respectively).

Jerry also suggests contacting the employee assistance specialist as well as the director of human resources so they are aware he is taking the necessary steps to improve his work performance. Subsequently, Jerry and his physician mutually decide to hold off increasing the medication. You continue therapy, and Jerry begins improving his anxiety management skills and work performance. Jerry's primary care physician is pleased with the prompt services and coordinated care. The EAP specialist and director of human resources are pleased with the care coordination and progress. In this example, there are three treatment stakeholders in Ring 1 (primary care physician, human resource director, and the employee assistance specialist) and one Ring 2 customer (Jerry). As a high-quality provider meeting best practice standards, your care coordination efforts will also have the secondary effect of potent *advertising*.

Jerry and Primary Care. The relationship with Jerry is obvious in the importance of both care coordination and practice building. Clinically, it is vitally important that this relationship has open communication channels, thereby providing Jerry the best possible care. As a practice-building therapist, the more you can assist the primary care physician and the treatment of Jerry, the higher the quality of care and the more likely you will receive a referral from the primary care physician. *Your clinical care is your advertising.*

Jerry and the EAP Specialist. The EAP specialists are more than referral sources. They have inside knowledge about a work environment that can be vitally important to your practice-building efforts. Maybe Jerry works for an employer that is known to have a toxic or high-anxiety work environment. Possibly, his supervisor is known as verbally aggressive. On the other hand, the employer could be supportive and understanding toward mental health issues. Coordinating with the EAP specialist gives great insight about work dynamics, challenges, and logistics.

As with the primary care physician and human resource director, involving the EAP specialist also creates exceptional advertising. Typically, EAP professionals represent more than one employer and are aware of many organizational situations needing services. The EAP professional, having an extensive network needing more than simply psychotherapy services, provides an excellent source for practice building. Furthermore, the services requested are often more lucrative, enjoyable, and with the potential for creating lifelong organizational customers.

Jerry and the Human Resource Director. Many therapists are reluctant to coordinate through human resources, but care coordination is vital. Involving human relations allows you to assess Jerry's personnel and work performance issues. Is he exaggerating the impact of anxiety at work? What is his baseline performance, and how far away from that performance is he currently performing? Your coordination also signals to his workplace that he is receiving care. This collaboration is a best practice expectation and a potentially powerful practice-building alliance. The human resources director may have extremely relevant clinical information for you. With the human resources director, communication may be a one-way street. The human resources director may be giving you information, while you are minimally disclosing treatment information.

As with the primary care physician, the secondary benefit of care coordination is advertising. When the human resources director becomes confident that you are considering Jerry's employment welfare and hears that Jerry is taking positive steps to treat the anxiety, you begin developing a positive reputation. After treatment, the human resources director is in the treatment stakeholder referral ring, allowing your advertising efforts to focus on someone witnessing your high-quality services.

EAP Specialist and Human Resources Director. The relationship of particular interest is that of the human resources director and EAP specialist. Why? There is a very good chance they will discuss future problematic employee issues. It is hoped that the conversation will involve you. Furthermore, depending on your interests and qualifications, you can become their resource or referral source for other opportunities. There are lucrative opportunities in such activities as critical incident and stress debriefings, organizational training or consultation, and other organizational needs.

Close examination of Jerry's situation highlights that advertising is *only* related to treatment activities. The result of high-quality care eliminates the need for inefficient advertising and marketing. In this simplistic example, there are three natural practice building targets: primary care physician, human

FORM 3.1. CARE COORDINATION FORM

Tracy Todd, PhD, LMFT
7800 South Elati Drive, #230
Littleton, CO 80120
www.btid.com

Care Coordination Form[a]

Date:
To:
From: vm:
RE:

I am currently seeing this client for   Expected course of treatment
_____ Individual therapy   _____ Weekly
_____ Marital therapy   _____ 2x per month
_____ Family therapy   _____ Monthly
                                                _____ As needed

At this time, my working diagnosis is   Other concerns include
_____ Major Depression   _____ Suicidal tendencies
_____ Bipolar   _____ Homicidal ideations
_____ Anxiety Disorder   _____ Domestic violence
_____ Panic Disorder
_____ Adjustment Disorder
_____ Other _____

I have requested the client see you for
_____ Evaluation for pyschotropic meds
_____ Medication management
_____ Physical examination
_____ Other
_____ None of the above

Current medications client indicates taking:

Comments:

_____
Signature

[a]Signed Authorization to Disclose on File

Tracy Todd, PhD, LMFT
7800 South Elati Drive, #230
Littleton, CO 80120
www.btid.com

Authorization to Use or Disclose Protected Health Information

I, _____, authorize the use or disclosure
of my protected health information as described below:

1. My authorization applies to the specific information described:

   _____

2. I authorize the following person (or class of persons) to make the authorized use or disclosure of my protected health information:

   _____
   Therapist Name

3. I authorize the following persons (or class of persons) to receive and disclose my protected health information:
   Name(s):_____

4. I understand that, if my protected health information is disclosed to someone who is not required to comply with the federal privacy protection regulations, then such information may be redisclosed and would no longer be protected.

5. I understand that I have a right to revoke this authorization at any time. My revocation must be in writing (by a letter including name, address, telephone number, and reason why revocation is requested). I am aware that my revocation is not effective to the extent that the persons I have authorized to use or disclose my protected health information have acted in reliance on this authorization.

6. This authorization expires on   Date: _____ *or*

   Condition: _____.

7. I understand that I do not have to sign this authorization and that my refusal to sign will not affect my abilities to obtain treatment from my therapist or my eligibility for benefits.

8. I understand that I have a right to inspect and copy my own protected health information to be used or disclosed in accordance with the requirements of the federal privacy protection regulations found under 45 C.F.R. 164.524.

9. I can request a copy of this authorization at any time.

10. I agree that a photocopy or facsimile of this signed authorization form shall be considered as valid as an original signed copy.

I certify that I have had the opportunity to review this form.

_____   _____
Signature   Date

_____
Print name
Personal Representative: _____
_____ Parent _____ Court order _____ Power of attorney _____ Other

resources director, and EAP specialist. Using this example, if you have a case-load of 200 clients per year, there is the potential for 600 treatment stakeholders. After 4 years of practice, you have the potential of 2,400 treatment stakeholders experiencing your high-quality treatment. Despite some duplicates in this equation, you get the point.

There is absolutely no need to engage in network development with unknown people or agencies or to invest in expensive advertising campaigns. Treatment stakeholders not only will build your practice but also will sustain you through the toughest of times.

Conceptualizing treatment stakeholders as customers forces practice-building therapists to consider such ideas as convenience, ease of access, reputation building, and communication. A "stakeholder" requires more service than a referral source or another professional involved with a mutual client. Treatment stakeholders involved at any level of treatment should benefit from your building strategies by your anticipation of their needs and the unanticipated nuances of the mutual client.

Care Coordination

Practice-Building 2.0 emphasizes applying high technology to old-fashioned professional relationship building. Every clinician, on opening a chart, should examine how many potential treatment stakeholders exist. Industry standards, cases reviewed by third-party reimbursement systems, indicate that approximately two thirds of all cases should involve care coordination with those considered treatment stakeholders.[1]

Engaging in aggressive care coordination with treatment stakeholders not only satisfies the criteria of best practice standards, but is also exceptional advertising for your practice. Of course, it should go without saying that care coordination also requires discussing and obtaining authorization from your clients to coordinate care. Therapists often justify *not* coordinating care by stating that their clients do not want them discussing treatment with others. This dynamic requires careful examination. Therapists can erroneously assume that not coordinating care and protecting privacy is in the best interest of the client. For example, a client having an affair and experiencing depression may not want his or her therapist discussing the affair with the client's primary care physician, who prescribed an antidepressant, because the primary care physi-

[1]I have participated on numerous quality assurance boards for third-party payers at local and national levels. These payers have identified a goal for all clients of approximately 66% care coordination between the psychotherapist and treatment stakeholders (proprietary information). This means that, if you examine 100 client charts, at least 66 should have a signed authorization to disclose form and documentation of your communication with another service professional.

cian is the family physician. Yet, the therapist believes that the antidepressant is ineffective and needs adjusting. Does the primary care physician need to know about the affair? No. Does the primary care physician need to know the medication is ineffective? Yes. Informing your client that you have some obligation to ensure the entire treatment team is coordinated and that you will only discuss symptoms, not issues, is, simply put, great clinical care.

I have heard therapists state, "My clients don't want their issues discussed with others, so I don't coordinate care." Implicit in this message is the attitude of therapists to compromise care and continue enabling situations. Rarely do treatment issues need discussing, and coordination of care can occur without raising intensely private concerns. Trust and presentation are paramount when seeking authorization to coordinate care.

Ring 2: Clients and Former Clients

Practice-Building 2.0 places the next level of advertising priority on clients and former clients. These individuals, couples, and families become your second best practice-building force. After experiencing your exceptional treatment, those not shy about letting others know they attend therapy can begin making referrals. Many therapists consider clients and former clients the best source of referrals and advertising. However, there are barriers to clients and former clients referring others to you.

Referring Barriers

Introducing You. How can this referral pool effectively introduce you and your services? A business card might be enough, but do you want your practice-building efforts hanging on a simple business card? Your clients and former clients need tools to create an introduction. Web sites with video introductions are excellent tools for accomplishing this goal.

Embarrassment/Stigma. Although they are comfortable with therapy, your clients and former clients might be embarrassed to admit to others they sought counseling. Likewise, even if they are not, the person they are recommending your services might still associate a negative stigma to psychotherapy. How can you help both your clients and former clients overcome any referring stigma?

Referral Ambivalence/Anxiety. Even when your clients and former clients give outstanding testimonials to potentially new clients, those potential clients are likely to have anxiety about scheduling an appointment. A Web site with podcasts and video introductions may reduce anxiety experienced by potential new referrals.

Scheduling an Appointment. Scheduling the first appointment can be the most difficult step of the entire counseling process. Does your office offer multiple ways to schedule an appointment? Can you provide a method of scheduling that enables a potential new client to schedule immediately when motivated? Online scheduling is a great high-tech practice-building tool that allows clients, former clients, and new clients the opportunity to schedule an appointment all day, every day, even on holidays.

Needing Information: Insurance, Payment, Treatment Style. Even when a client or former client is comfortable referring others to you, can you help your former client by providing basic and practical information to potential new clients? Former clients will need assistance in addressing simple issues such as payment structure, insurance coverage, and office hours.

> BETTY (CURRENT CLIENT): You really should see my therapist.
> SALLY: Okay, but do you know if she takes my insurance?
> BETTY: I'm not sure, but I know she has an insurance list on her Web site.
> SALLY: Great. I will look it up.

This simple conversation is easy to imagine. Betty's therapist does provide a method to help Betty make the referral. Do not underestimate the power of this example. Without a Web site listing insurance coverage, what are the odds that Sally would call Betty's therapist and ask for insurance information?

With technology, Betty is able to make a referral and stay connected with her therapist. This significant shift assists in creating a lifelong customer and advertising representative, resulting in potent practice building.

Logistical Considerations

Understandably, questions exist about how aggressively and when is it appropriate to interact with treatment stakeholders, clients, and former clients. Clinical need should always be the first consideration for interactions. There are two types of interaction: active and passive. Active interactions are therapist initiated. For example, sending a psychiatrist a brochure is therapist initiated. Passive interactions are those that you may not know exist. For example, a former client who subscribes to a podcast from your Web site is doing so without your knowledge or initiation.

TABLE 3.2: INSURANCE MATRIX

Tracy Todd, PhD, LMFT
7800 South Elati Drive, #230
Littleton, CO 80120
www.btid.com

Accepted Insurance by Provider

Referral Source	Therapist	Therapist	Therapist	Therapist
Insurance A	X	X	X	X
Insurance B[a]	X		X	X
	X	X	X	X
	X			
	X	X	X	X
	X			
	X		X	X
	X	X	X	X
		X		
	X			X

[a]In subsequent rows, list third-party payers accepted.

Treatment Stakeholders

Active interactions with treatment stakeholders are limited to a few strategies. However, these strategies, when repeated, build your credibility and trust. The most important practice-building intervention is sending the Care Coordination Form via fax, mail, or e-mail. Besides meeting a best practice standard, your name is repeatedly associated with quality care. Some therapists comment that they "never hear back" from the primary care physician. That will happen, but does not mean that you should compromise quality care services. We consistently made coordinated care with a local primary care physician and never received a referral or response. After some investigation, we discovered his wife was also a psychotherapist. Did we discontinue sending Care Coordination Forms when appropriate? No. Did we stop expecting something in return? Yes.

The second active strategy is annually distributing a hardcopy of the Insurance Matrix and Treatment Population Matrix (Table 3.2 and Table 3.3, respectively). A good strategy is creating a one-page, two-sided laminated handout that includes this information plus your practice information. We visited treat-

TABLE 3.3: TREATMENT POPULATION MATRIX: CLINICAL SPECIALITIES

Tracy Todd, PhD, LMFT
7800 South Elati Drive, #230
Littleton, CO 80120
www.btid.com

	Therapist name	Therapist name	Therapist name	Therapist name
Abuse: physical, sexual		<18		
Adolescent problems	X	X	X	X
Affairs, infidelity	X	X		X
Alcohol abuse/addiction	X		X	
Anxiety, panic	X	<18	X	X
Attention deficit/hyperactivity disorder	Adult	X		X
Bipolar disorders	X	<18	X	X
Children <12 years		X		X
Chronic illness/HIV			X	
Communication skills	X	X	X	X
Depression	X	X	X	X
Dissociative disorders				
Divorce adjustment	X	X	X	X
Eating disorders				
Family problems	X	X		X
Financial	X		X	X
Gambling			X	
Gay/Lesbian/transgendered			X	
Grief	X	<18	X	X
Hepatitis C	X		X	X
Marital	X	X	X	X
Major mental illness	X		X	
Parenting in general	X	X		X
Parenting teens	X	X	X	X
Pelvic pain				
Premature ejaculation				X
Relationship with family	X	X	X	X
Relationship with people	X		X	X
Sexual arousal desire/disorders				X
Stepfamily issues	X	X		
Stress	X	<18	X	X
Work	X		X	X

ment stakeholders with whom we had coordinated care during the previous year and personally delivered the handout to the office staff. Frequently, the intake manager (for primary care physicians) would be delighted to meet us, and we would often see the last year's handout tacked up somewhere in the office.

Passive strategies with treatment stakeholders are those that you do not know are happening. Having some information available on your Web site for professionals creates the ability to visit your Web site when needing information. For example, having an online bookstore categorized by clinical issues may result in a treatment stakeholder visiting your website to find a book on a particular topic to recommend to a client and maybe soon to be one of your clients.

Clients and Former Clients

Active strategies for clients are few and simple: newsletters and emails. It is important to address communication issues during the first session. For example, our intake form asks the following question:

> I authorize the [agency name] to mail any correspondence regarding my treatment, satisfaction with treatment, updates about my treatment and educational programs during and after the completion of my treatment to my home mailing address or e-mail address.
>
> _____ Yes   _____ No

Those clients indicating "Yes" will receive information before, during, and after treatment. At any time, they can e-mail or call to "unsubscribe" to receiving information. This simple strategy helps protect the "out of sight, out of mind" phenomenon. Ask yourself, "What am I doing to prevent this situation?"

THERAPIST: Hi, I'm Samantha.

CLIENT: Nice to meet you.

THERAPIST: Nice to meet you too. I would like to take a few minutes to review your paperwork. Is that okay?

CLIENT: No problem.

THERAPIST: I noticed that you have seen a therapist in the last 2 years. Is that correct?

CLIENT: Yes, probably a year and half to 2 years ago.

THERAPIST: Did you find it helpful?

CLIENT: Absolutely. The counselor helped me with some job issues. I didn't lose my job!

THERAPIST: That's great. Do you recall the counselor's name?

CLIENT: Hmm . . . let me think. I remember she was located over at the Professional Office Complex. No, I don't remember her name.

THERAPIST: Is there any reason you did not try to go back to her?

CLIENT: No. She was good. I just thought it was easier to call the number on my insurance card, and they sent me to you.

This conversation reflects a history of a positive client–therapist relationship. However, over the course of nearly 2 years and *no* further contact from the prior therapist, the client lost investment in the client–therapist relationship. A good clinician lost business because the client no longer recalled her name. There are two major problems with this situation. First, the therapist lost a customer. Second, a satisfied customer, unable to recall the therapist's name, cannot refer family and friends.

As a practice-building therapist, strategize and implement methods that keep you in contact with clients and former clients. Fundamental groundwork includes

Informing clients how you plan to stay in contact with them
Seeking client permission to stay in contact
Implementing administrative procedures that allow easy and quick
    contact with clients
Routinely staying in contact.

Passive interaction strategies should be abundant. These strategies include such activities as podcasting and RSS (Really Simple Syndication) feeds, videocasts of self-help strategies, reading tips and strategies on your Web site, links to high-quality sources of information, online bookstores, and online scheduling. These customer service interventions build satisfaction and loyalty without any direct interactions with clients and former clients. Unlike the situation for previous generations of practice-building therapists, a Web site is a simple, affordable, and easy mechanism for providing clients and former clients a method to stay connected passively to your practice.

Ring 3: Unknowns and Cold Calling

The riskiest pool of potential referral sources for practice building involves people unfamiliar with who you are, what you do, or how good you are at doing it. These people may have a business card, brochure, and your Web site to review. However, they lack experience with your treatment. Ironically, it is amazing how many therapists consider Ring 3 the highest-priority referral development target. I consistently hear, "I dropped off my brochures," "I met so and so at the Chamber of Commerce meeting and gave her my business card," or "I had lunch at a networking function, and there were a lot of people interested in my services."

Strategies

Some examples of Ring 3 practice-building strategies include

- Attending networking functions
- Participating in health fairs
- Subscribing to yellow page advertising
- Using newspaper advertising
- Using AdWords campaigns
- Giving seminars to the public
- Dropping off brochures at offices

Ring 3 should only receive attention after successfully building your practice. Ring 3 allows you to experiment with strategies that yield a significant return on the investment. However, Ring 3 should never be the exclusive practice building strategy. Many therapists (including myself) have the desire, curiosity, and risk-taking mentality to answer the question, "What if?" If you do, then go for it. Just make sure you are pursuing Ring 3 after successfully developing practice-building strategies for treatment stakeholders, clients, and former clients—not because of desperation or panic. In Chapter 7, I suggest some strategies and marketing ideas for Ring 3.

Prior to embarking on risky practice-building strategies, creating a catego-rization of referral priorities based on the return on investment is necessary. I am surprised at how often therapists engage in practice-building events that lose money. Frequently, I hear, "Tracy, I did get a referral from attending the networking function." Great! That therapist still probably lost money. It is pos-sible that this one client will refer clients down the road, but was the event worth it, particularly when comparing this expenditure to other forms of advertising and practice-building efforts? Maybe you get infrequent referrals from such labor-intensive marketing, but when assessing this group for prac-tice-building strategies, it is critically important to calculate the return on the investment.

You project that attending a networking function will reap three referrals, therefore 21 sessions (3 x 7, the average number of sessions = 21 sessions). The event will take 3 session hours for attendance and preparation, and the cost of supplies is $75.

(3 referrals x 7 sessions each) x $80.00 average reimbursement rate = $1,680.00
($80.00 average reimbursement rate x 3 hours prep/attendance time) + $75 cost of supplies = $315.00

    = .33 projected return on the investment

Actual Return on Investment Example

You choose to assess your success 30 days post-event. You received 2 referrals with a total of 3 sessions (one referral attended two sessions, the other attended one session).

3 total sessions x $80.00= $240.00
($80.00 average reimbursement rate x 3 hours) + $75 cost of supplies = $315.00

    = .76 return on the investment

Everyone with a good idea believes it will generate more business than it actually does. Critically examining the success of a project requires more than yes-no thinking. Yes, a referral resulted from this laborious task. Yet, it was not worth the time and investment if the goal was a 2.0 return on investment (ROI). Prior to embarking on Ring 3 strategies, ask yourself the following questions:

Have I satisfied all possible practice-building strategies for Ring 1 treatment stakeholders?

Have I satisfied all practice-building strategies for Ring 2 clients and former clients?

Am I engaging in Ring 3 unknown practice-building strategies because of a planned strategy or out of desperation?

Have I achieved my direct referral rate percentage?

If you answered yes to all three questions, then give it a try. However, if you answered yes to all three questions, you probably will not even need to consider this option.

Summary

Unlike traditional practice-building strategies, *Practice-Building 2.0* avoids marketing and referral development strategies focusing on unknowns or cold calling referral targets. Rather, *Practice-Building 2.0* clearly differentiates treatment stakeholders, clients, and former clients as the lifeline of referral development. Care coordination, when engaged in frequently and consistently, establishes you as a high-quality provider. The net effect is reputation building, advertising, and a powerful practice-building process.

Avoid temptations to start mining referrals from low-probability, high-risk, and high-cost potentials (Ring 3 referral pool). Keep your focus on those familiar with your services and able to represent your practice positively to new potential referrals.

Key Points
1. Treatment stakeholders include anyone who is involved with your service delivery.
2. Aggressively incorporating treatment stakeholders into your service delivery meets best practice standards *and* simultaneously advertises your practice.
3. Treatment stakeholders should become your best advertising representatives.
4. Clients and former clients need to experience service delivery so outstanding that they are willing to disclose to others that they are attending psychotherapy and will refer to you.
5. Use care collaboration maps to ensure maximum therapy inclusion and advertising.
6. High-quality care coordination has a side effect as potent advertising.
7. Assess your practice-building strategies and whether they are focused on clients, former clients, treatment stakeholders, or the unknown referral pool.

Action List
1. Add the following question to your intake paperwork: "Who referred you to my practice?" Try to get an answer from every client.
2. Create a care coordination form if you do not have one.
3. Create an authorization to disclose form if you do not have a current form.
4. Specifically, identify those treatment stakeholders by names who have referred to you. Keep this list live.
5. Create an insurance accepted matrix.
6. Create a treatment population served matrix.
7. List some possible strategies to stay in contact with treatment stakeholders, clients and former clients.
8. Do *not* engage in Ring 3 referral development until you are completely satisfied with your direct percentage referral rate.
9. Calculate your goals for referral and revenue distribution. Using the data generated in Chapter 1, Table 1.4, indicate the goals you feel are necessary for your practice (Table 3.4).

TABLE 3.4: REFERRALS PER REVENUE GOAL SETTING

Referral Source	Therapist	Goal
Insurance A	22	
Insurance B	0	
Insurance C	8	
Insurance D	9	
Insurance E	8	
Insurance F	5	
Other insurance	0	
EAP A	10	
EAP B	5	
Other EAP	6	
Self=pay full fee	15	
Self-pay 75%–99%	12	
Total	100	
Referral Source		
Web site	37	
Online directories	28	
PCP	15	
HR/employer	2	
Providers	7	
Clients/former clients	11	
Other	0	
Total	100	
% direct referral	35	

Note. In this example, cash pay revenue accounts for 27% of revenue generated, and the direct referral rate is 35%. There are no correct answers but it is important that you set goals to evaluate your practice-building strategies. Try to evaluate your goals on a monthly basis and adjust your practice-building strategies for referral and revenue generation twice per year.

EAP, employee assistance program
PCP, primary care physician
HR, human relations

Rings of Referrals

PART TWO

New Technologies
for
Practice-Building 2.0

CHAPTER FOUR

Web Site Technology

This chapter discusses the Web site technology needed to build a practice.

Web Site Essentials

One practice consultant reported ("Still no Web site," 2006) that only about 35–40% of therapists had a Web site. Surprisingly, 2 years later and despite the overwhelming reasoning for Web presence, *Psychotherapy Finances* ("Mini-Survey," 2008) reported only about 38% of those in private practice had a Web site.

A Business Necessity

In a technology-driven world, a Web site becomes the equivalent of the front door of your business. Over 81% of Internet users expect to find health care information online (Horrigan & Rainie, 2002). It is simply a poor business decision to create a situation in which your clients go elsewhere for all their mental health questions. Although you cannot address every issue and your Web site will have links to resources, the starting point for treatment stakeholders, clients, and former clients seeking health care information should be *your* Web site.

Another consideration for owning a Web site is changing demographics. Teens and young adults—in fact, 91% of those under 29 years of age—use the Internet ("Latest Trends," 2008). These clients expect an Internet service delivery component. Although you may not work with this demographic, as they age they will become your clientele. Any previous resistance to technology from your clinical population will dissipate with this aging demographic.

Therapists who create Web sites tend to design and create content for the referral group that should get the least attention, Ring 3. A Web site meeting the needs of Rings 1 and 2 will undoubtedly meet the needs of Ring 3. Keep in mind that the goal of your Web site is to provide service that creates satisfaction and loyalty for your treatment stakeholders, clients, and former clients. The emphasis is not on generating random Ring 3 referrals.

I was hoping to facilitate a referral (I was the treatment stakeholder) to another psychotherapist and suggested that the potential client visit the Web sites of 10 possible referrals supplied on a referral list. Of the 10 referrals, only 2 had Web sites. After reviewing each Web site and finding one provider's Web site filled with resources, a professional biography, and a frequently asked question section, it was a no brainer which therapist the client chose. The other possible referral had a Web site that lacked any positive representation, credibility, or professionalism.

More important, because of lacking Web sites, eight potential referrals were immediately eliminated. One clinician averages 25 clients per month because of his Web site ("Still no Web site," 2006). For most practices, 25 new clients per month may be an ambitious goal to achieve, but not having a Web site clearly results in lost income (Box 4.1).

BOX 4.1
Unrealized Revenue: Web Site Appointment

Using a conservative estimate of just three new clients per month, scheduling appointments because you have a Web site equals $18,480 (3 clients x 11 months = 33 new clients per year x average of 7 sessions = 231 sessions at $80 per session = $18,480).

Any potential client using the Internet for psychotherapy information (e.g., online insurance directory, general research) expects to find a Web site. With apparently over half of psychotherapists lacking a technological front door, these therapists will find surviving in today's technological marketplace increasingly difficult.

While giving a seminar on practice-building, a participant made the statement, "We (referring to herself and two colleagues) just came from a workshop, and the presenter told us a good Web site would cost at least $1,500." Shocked, and in dismay, I clarified that was outrageous and erroneous. Yes, Web sites can cost thousands of dollars per month to build, maintain, or administer. However, a private practice does not have the technological demands of Amazon. A small business in mental health has very simple and basic Web site needs, resulting in affordable costs to build and maintain.

Web sites have many purposes. Some are purely informational (WebMD), others provide services (Expedia), yet others are retail outlets (Amazon). Your Web site will be primarily informational and, with the abundance of inexpensive technologies available, affordable. Depending on treatment population, your Web site features offering convenience can take many different forms, such as paperwork downloading, online scheduling, discussion forums, articles, and online payments. For example, a convenient feature for parents with challenging adolescents involves links to discussion forums, articles, and any other informational pieces you trust. These resources save parents time in the search for reliable information. Providing parents with these reliable resources creates satisfaction with and loyalty to your service. The beauty of this strategy is that you only need to implement the strategy once, and it benefits all parents wanting such information. Gone are the days of needing to provide such labor-intensive information repeatedly via copying handouts, or providing books and articles to each individual client.

Your Web site is also a great tool for connecting with clients and former clients. Your Web site can communicate your educational seminars, new service availability, or a news note. Providing these non-face-to-face services is a business necessity that allows former clients to stay connected, satisfies many best practice standard variables, and avoids the "out of sight, out of mind" dynamic. With RSS (Really Simple Syndication) feeds, many former clients might refer or return to therapy for a "tune-up" because of a timely informational podcast.

Competitive communication advantages include

- Podcasts of treatment strategies and tips.
- Book reviews and recommended readings.
- Scheduling information. Why lose a referral because you are on vacation? Post your time away from the office on your Web site and encourage visitors to use the online scheduling feature.
- Personal quotations. If you happen to be quoted in the local newspaper, prominently place this announcement on your Web site.
- Seasonal newsletters with RSS feeds that allow visitors to read and subscribe.
- Video role-plays.
- Timely "how to" responses to critical incidents.

The potential for communicating is endless. The beauty of a Web site is that communication is inexpensive and completed with just a few point and clicks.

Designing your Web site to include the technologies needed as discussed in *Practice-Building 2.0* gives you many significant competitive advantages over competing therapists. Helping a primary care physician's office to become reliant on your Web site's paperwork download system that allows patients to leave with "something in hand" is a serious advantage over other therapists in your area.

Therapists need strategies that integrate their Web site into the daily business patterns of treatment stakeholders, clients, and former clients. These direct referral sources often need answers to simple questions for those they are referring. For example, listing your office hours and telephone number and describing your method or style of doing psychotherapy are important pieces of information for treatment stakeholders to communicate to potential referrals. In a busy world, these simple pieces of information save a great deal of time and effort. If your office hours prohibit a client from choosing you, voice mail tag is eliminated. Although you lost a referral, the referring treatment stakeholder and client avoided a frustrating barrier to treatment.

Because treatment stakeholders are your primary referral pool, it is imperative to create the tools on your Web site to keep them satisfied and loyal. Generally, stakeholders benefit from the following on a Web site: name, address, telephone and fax numbers, picture, video introduction, bibliography, online scheduling, office hours, and paperwork download.

Depending on your treatment population your Web site can create other potent competitive advantages. For example, a sex therapist who knew her treatment stakeholders (i.e., gynecologists, primary care physicians) faced significant challenges when referring clients for sexuality issues created a Web page specifically for her treatment stakeholders; it focused on easing the transition of clients to psychotherapy. This strategy helped her eliminate a barrier facing other sex therapists, giving her the advantage.

Treatment stakeholders are significantly more sensitive to best practice standards. Although therapy style is important, they need confidence in your customer service. Advertise practice variables that enhance confidence, trust, and reliability. Provide practice information on such service variables as customer satisfaction, access data, collaboration percentage, and paperwork download.

Strategically implementing a Web site should accomplish three goals:

1. Make a sound first impression to the viewer about you and your practice patterns
2. Build satisfaction and loyalty among your treatment stakeholders, clients and former clients
3. Reduce your labor and costs of conducting business

The goal of this chapter is to provide you with necessary information about integrating Web sites and complimentary functions into the infrastructure of your small business. The technology described in this chapter allows you to make positive first impressions while reducing your labor and administrative costs, resulting in increased profit margins.

Web Site Functions

Web sites can have many functional components: education, advertising, sales, scheduling, downloads, and social networking, to name a few. Web sites, like most other business tools, evolve over time. Do not feel pressured to "have it all now." It is important to identify the high-priority items and gradually begin to implement them into your Web site functionality.

Design: Making a Good First Impression. Your Web site represents you and reflects your professional image. Web sites lacking a professional image will not turn potential customers into paying customers. When designing your Web site, look at your competitors' Web sites. Look for any deficiencies so your Website becomes the "state-of-the-art" site in your geographic area. A Web site should accurately communicate and reflect your personality and at the same time heighten your image. Consider the last time you researched a company before engaging in their services. You probably visited their Web site and in a few minutes made your purchasing decision. People view Web sites and make decisions quickly. In a technological world, your Web site needs to capture the attention of visitors and quickly turn these visitors into customers. Remember the cliché, "You never get a second chance to make a first impression."

When designing your Web site, focus on simplicity, organization, and clarity. Be mindful that you are not an advertising firm needing slick graphics and other impressive technologies on your home page. On the contrary, you should assume that your visitors are experiencing distress. There is a high likelihood that they are dealing with anxiety, depression, death of a loved one, a runaway adolescent, or the like. These are not people who want to be awestruck by your graphics, sounds, and unwelcome videos. These potential customers want to find information quickly and easily. Keep your home page well organized and easy to navigate. Even for those who might simply be browsing, there is a necessary balance of navigation with sophistication and organization. Compare Web pages 4.1–4.3.

Although *Therapy Center 1* (Web Page 4.1) is comprehensive in service description, the information is scattered. Most problematic on this home page is the uninvited music when you visit. Two quick modifications to this Web site would help significantly improve the home page. First, alphabetizing the problem areas would provide convenience so visitors can quickly locate whether

Home	**THERAPY CENTER 1**
About the Counseling Center	Individual, Family, Couples, and Group Therapy
About the Therapist	Seminars, Weekend Intensives, and Interventions
Clinical Philosophy	Sexual Abuse Survivors Addictions, Codependency, and Recovery
Scheduling Appointments	Challenging Adolescents Posttraumatic Stress Disorder (PTSD)
Specialty Areas	Adolescent Life Cycle Issues Family of Origin Issues Interventions
Additional Practice Areas	
Seminars and Workshops	Anxiety Depression Grief and Loss Eating Disorders
FAQs	Stress Management Couples Personal Growth and Coaching
Site Map	Weekend Intensive Workshops and Retreats
Contact Us	Daytime and Evening Seminars

THERAPY CENTER 2

HELPING PEOPLE ACHIEVE

Thank you for visiting our Web site!

Inspiring Therapy offers the following services:

- Success Coaching (personal and business)
- Individual Therapy
- Family Therapy
- Couples Therapy
- Group Therapy
- Seminars (for Organizations including Workplace, Religious Centers, Fitness Centers, and others)
- Supervision for professionals

Learn how to turn your challenges into opportunities!

Let's explore the possibilities for change that will allow you to achieve your goals!

- Enhance your relationships.
- Strengthen your family.
- Achieve your goals.
- Improve communication and other relational skills.
- Effectively manage stress.
- Deal effectively with life's events.
- Thrive in all you do!

It takes great bravery to seek assistance, no one has ever accomplished anything great without support.

| *Welcome* | *About Us* | *FAQS* | *Contact Us* |

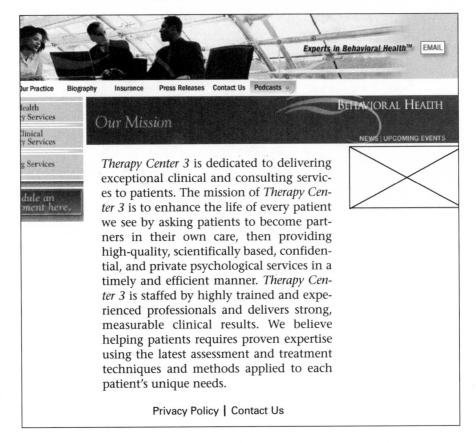

this practice meets their clinical needs. Second, giving visitors the option to listen to the provided music with a "play" button respects their privacy. Imagine a visitor to this Web site working in a cubicle and while the individual is searching for psychotherapy services, music suddenly starts playing, thereby inviting questions from office mates. Be sensitive to the possible locations of Web site viewing. Gone are the days of viewing sites at home or simply in the office. People can view sites on mobile devices, laptops, in coffee shops, and at library kiosks.

Does the *Therapy Center 2* Web site in 4.2 tell you anything about the services provided or the psychotherapist? No. The home page is motivating but not necessarily capturing. It has that "feel good" message but does not communicate any substance about the provider or services provided. This site is poorly organized and focuses on reflecting the style of the therapy center rather than clearly selling the services and meeting client need.

In contrast, *Therapy Center 3* is well organized, descriptive, and comprehensive. Furthermore, it allows a visitor the *option* of audio by indicating podcasts are available. This site also provides easy navigation. Through the use of tabs along the top and links on the left side, a visitor can quickly identify the needed information. The site looks much more professional than the other two, and it immediately offers the opportunity to schedule an appointment.

Task: Design Your Web Site. Designing a Web site is easy. Get seven sheets of blank paper and place the following titles, one title per page, on each page:

Home Page
Therapist Biography
Business Information
Scheduling
Client Resources
Treatment Populations Served
How I Work

Take a few minutes to visit a number of Web sites (e.g., Amazon.com, WebMD.com, BTID.com), and you find that most Web sites are designed in two-, three-, or four-column format. You might change your format but start by creating three columns on each page and identify what you feel are important functions of and informational pieces about your business (Figures 4.1–4.7). I provide some examples of sections per page, but you should modify to your preferences.

You now have the basic elements of a Web site. Keep in mind, that text is a turnoff and graphics sell. There are a number of Web sites from which you can purchase pictures for less than a few dollars, including: www.fotolia.com and www.istockphoto.com. Purchasing a few photographs rather than using stan-

FIG. 4.1: HOME PAGE

| Home Page

Therapist Biography

Business Information

Scheduling

Client Resources

Treatment Populations Served

How I Work | Welcome to my Web site . . .

Office Location

Phone number

General business hours | Picture goes here

Schedule appointment [link goes here] |

FIG. 4.2: THERAPIST BIOGRAPHY PAGE

Home Page Therapist Biography Business Information Scheduling Client Resources Treatment Populations Served How I Work	Credentials Education Experience [Keep this information short and concise: highlight experiences relevant to your practice]	Picture or video goes here Schedule appointment [link goes here] Self-help tip

FIG. 4.3: BUSINESS INFORMATION PAGE

Home Page Therapist Biography Business Information Scheduling Client Resources Treatment Populations Served How I Work	Insurance accepted [provide a link to my insurance matrix] Online payment function goes here Phone number to billing service (if you have one)	No show, late cancellation policies [link to a PDF document]

FIG. 4.4: SCHEDULING PAGE

Home Page Therapist Biography Business Information Scheduling Client Resources Treatment Populations Served How I Work	[Scheduling function goes here] Intake paperwork [link to PDF document of intake paperwork]	First Session Jitters [link to a document or possibly a podcast normalizing first-session anxiety]

Home Page Therapist Biography Business Information Scheduling Client Resources Treatment Populations Served How I Work	Books to read, by category [link to Amazon]	Self-help tips [Podcasts, videocasts, blogs, PowerPoint with voice narration can go here] Newsletter

FIG. 4.6: **TREATMENT POPULATIONS PAGE**

Home Page Therapist Biography Business Information Scheduling Client Resources Treatment Populations Served How I Work	[Provide a brief statement about the treatment populations served] [link to Treatment Populations matrix]	Possibly list community resources

FIG. 4.7: **HOW I WORK PAGE**

Home Page Therapist Biography Business Information Scheduling Client Resources Treatment Populations Served How I Work	[Provide a description of my style of therapy (cognitive behavioral, solution focused, other type)] [Describe what clients can expect from treatment]	[Outline customer services that differentiate your services from others, for example, online scheduling, satisfaction surveys, data I have compiled about satisfaction or appointment offered and accepted.]

dard graphics creates a more professional look and will communicate your personality and style more effectively.

Positive Representation. The Web site design does not need to be sterile. Reflect your personality in the design. Have some fun. However, keep in mind the balance among professionalism, navigation, speed, and your personality.

One important technical consideration when posting content is your writing style. Psychotherapists, who have a minimum of a master's degree, usually write in academic style. This style is not helpful for gaining referrals. When possible, have someone who writes advertisements critique your Web content. Such stylistic details as first or third person, and passive or active voice, make big differences when attempting to convert visitors to customers.

A Web site cannot be neglected. Your Web site should reflect changes and updates on a frequent basis. A terrible mistake is including information on your Web site that is outdated. For example, newsletters, whether e-mailed, are part of an RSS feed, or simply posted on your Web site, provide freshness. However, it is better *not* to have a newsletter on your Web site than to have a few newsletters dating back many years. A 2-year-old newsletter that continues to be the only newsletter on your Web site gives the impression of inattentiveness. Another common error is inviting e-mails for additional information, then not responding. I have accessed Web site "contact us" sections never to hear back from them. Lack of response reflects poorly on your business. Demonstrating attentiveness and speed impresses. Frequently review your site. Look for broken links, outdated items, or other mysteries of cyberspace that have crept into your site.

Content, design, and administration reflect your practice. Increasingly, potential clients are investigating backgrounds and treatment processes. Whether you have a Web site or not, you are being Googled. If you have a Web site, does it accurately represent you? I cannot stress the importance of positive representation.

Usability. In computer–human interaction, *usability* refers to the ease with which people can navigate and execute functions on your Web site to achieve their goals. There are companies that exclusively focus on usability of Web sites. These companies will engage focus groups, do interviews, and virtually tear apart a Web site to assess if it truly meets the goals of the business. You do not need to hire such a company, but you should conduct a usability study whenever you add new technology to your site and at a minimum once per year. Enlist the help of family and friends and seek feedback from clients to ensure that you have a usable Web site. For example, no one will use your paperwork download function if it is difficult to locate on your Web site. Potential customers, as well as current customers, may be accessing technology while under distress. Therefore, it is important to make all technology simple and easy to navigate.

Speed is one usability factor that involves two components. First, how fast does your Web site download for viewing? Although downloading speed is becoming less of a factor as users convert to high-speed access systems (e.g., cable, fiber optic), therapists will often have a high-resolution photograph on the home page, and because of the format and density (resolution and size) the page may download slowly. The slower the loading speed, the higher the potential of a visitor leaving your site. Keep in mind that graphics and video take time. When using video introductions locate them on a separate page, not on the home page. Keep your home page simple so that it can download quickly through any type of Internet connection.

When considering navigation, the second component of speed is clicking efficiency. The home page should allow different types of viewers the opportunity to get to information they seek quickly. For example, a current client seeking a book mentioned in a therapy session will want to find your resource section quickly.

Your goal is to help visitors quickly locate what they seek. For example, a client wanting to schedule an appointment could experience the following click path: Home page *click,* About Us *click,* Therapist biography *click,* Our Locations *click,* Contact Me *click,* call for an appointment. A potential customer realistically may point and click five different times before getting to a Web page with a telephone number to schedule an appointment. Comparatively, on our basic design the click path is Home page *click,* Scheduling *click,* Online Scheduling function. This path results in the visitor pointing and clicking twice before scheduling an appointment.

Keep the point-and-click number as minimal as possible. I have visited Web sites on which scheduling an appointment can take up to six clicks, if I can find how to schedule an appointment. Regardless of your goal, always count the number of clicks to meet your primary objective (usually scheduling an appointment). A general rule is that your most important function or goal should never be more than three clicks away from any Web page on your Web site.

Modifiable. The single most important variable when considering a Web site hosting company involves *your* ability to modify the content. If you need to submit changes to the company or person and those changes are dependent on their time constraints, you will quickly become frustrated with the services. As you become comfortable with your Web site and the design, you will want to start adding things such as links, video, audio, and podcasts. Does your Web hosting company give you this option? Although you might be thinking, "I will never do this stuff," it is quite likely you will eventually add content. Make sure that when purchasing services from a hosting company they give you a mechanism to make instant changes to that Web site.

Interactive. Interactive Web sites are the norm. Interactivity allows a visitor to explore, play, and access resources on your site. Interactive Web sites have functional purposefulness. Potential clients, current clients, former clients, and treatment stakeholders interact with your Web site, and hopefully will build satisfaction and loyalty. For example, accessing the online bookstore section of your Web site provides them the opportunity to review and possibly purchase a resource you suggest. Another example of interactivity involves paperwork download. New referrals can download and complete intake paperwork at their convenience.

Uploading Documents. To offer such features as paperwork downloads, podcasts, and videocasts, you Web hosting company must provide a mechanism to upload files and documents. Be specific about what they will allow you to upload to their system. Some companies have file size limitations. Such limitations are important to understand because video files can be large. Nothing is more annoying than to have time set aside to accomplish such projects and then find your hosting company blocking your work. Inquire about the ease and size limitations before purchasing your Web site or services from a hosting company.

Portable Document File Writer.[1] Using Google search, type "pdf writer."[1] You will have your choice of many programs. Most have free demonstrations that allow you to try their software with a few of your documents. Give each a try, and when you find one that works to your satisfaction, make the purchase. Most are inexpensive and easy to use. Converting a document to PDF (portable document format) protects your information because it can only be printed and completed in hardcopy format, whereas uploading, for example, a Word file would allow someone to download the entire file in electronic format and manipulate the content.

Paperwork Download. Providing the option of downloading paperwork creates an incredible sense of convenience, satisfaction, and cost savings to your customers. New clients, after scheduling an online appointment, simply

---

[1]Because many businesses and resources are unstable and may cease to exist overnight, I instruct you on how to conduct a Google search for locating technological tools. This method of resource identification will provide the most up-to-date resources available.

download paperwork to complete prior to the appointment. Clients often comment about the efficiency of our office, making statements such as, "I wish our [any service professional inserted here] was this efficient."

Think of the numerous situations for which you wanted the initial paperwork prior to a first appointment. Often, the office asked unanticipated questions, and you felt rushed, resulting in giving incomplete and inaccurate answers. Maybe you use your own set of assessment questions, and a paperwork download system will conveniently help potential clients effectively prepare for the first appointment. With seemingly new regulations and laws resulting in more paperwork, offering the opportunity to complete it prior to the intake session can provide a buffer against potential dissatisfaction with the paperwork process.

Another advantage of providing paperwork downloads is cost shift savings for your practice. Your time spent making copies is time not making money or developing income-generating processes (Box 4.2).

BOX 4.2
Unrealized Revenue: Intake Packet

A clinician seeing 200 new clients per year and having an intake packet consisting of six pages, has costs of approximately $0.42 per packet (7 cents per page), plus the time to go to the copying center (estimate 30 minutes = $40 for labor). This results in $124.00 per year of costs shifted to clients and away from the practice ($0.42 per packet x 200 new clients + $40 for labor = $124 per year).

Your paperwork downloads can include much more than administrative forms. You can also include any specific handouts you wish your clients to have prior to the first appointment. For example, one particular handout that our clients find very useful is our "First Appointment Orientation" (Form 4.1). Clients, unaware of our style of treatment, comment that this orientation is one reason for scheduling with our practice.

Technical Components

Analytics. Analytics is a free service from Google that allows you to understand how your Web site is used. With this information, you can learn which pages are most viewed, which pages are not viewed, the effectiveness of an advertising campaign, and many other statistics about your Web site ("Making Web Marketing," 2008). As you begin integrating Web site technology, this information becomes an enormously powerful tool for heightening the effectiveness of your Web presence. For example, what are the results after purchas-

First Appointment Orientation

Thank you for choosing the Brief Therapy Institute of Denver Inc. for your behavioral health care services. We recognize you have many choices and we appreciate your trust in us.

We appreciate your downloading and completion of the paperwork prior to your first session. Completing the paperwork allows your therapist the opportunity to spend more time on clinical than on administrative issues.

Some things to keep in mind:
- Remember that you can download and print, review, or ask for a complete set of Brief Therapy Institute of Denver Inc. privacy policies.
- Your therapist will review and answer any questions about this paperwork or other matters.
- Please bring your authorization number if given to you by your insurance company.
- Please bring your insurance card.
- We will need information about your copayment or deductible. If you do not know this information, please contact your insurance company and ask for an explanation of benefit coverage for mental/behavioral health issues.
- We will need your primary care physician's telephone number.
- If you have seen a counselor or psychiatrist within the last 2 years, we will need a telephone number for contact.
- It is helpful for the therapy process if you bring a list of goals for therapy. This will help you and your therapist make better use of the first session.

Goals for Therapy: Please List

ing an online directory listing that links to your biography page, not your home page? After 30 days, did your biography page experience increased traffic? If yes, did that traffic result in increased clientele? If you experienced increased traffic but no additional clients you might need to make changes to your biography page.

Data Storage. Data storage becomes an increasingly important issue as you build your Web site. Although storing text or paperwork requires minimal space, as you begin adding photos, graphics, audio, or video, you will quickly devour storage capacity. When purchasing and designing a Web site, inquire about expansion rates and lag time to increase your storage.

Although 250 megabytes (MB) of storage capacity sounds ample when you have two text pages consisting of less than 1 MB of space, when adding a video introduction and possibly two self-help videos, you will quickly exhaust 250 MB. Now, you need more space. How much will that expansion cost? How long will it take your hosting company to increase storage capacity? Maybe your self-help videos are income generating, and you consider adding a third self-help video but hesitate because the cost is prohibitive. Your hosting company may not allow you to increase beyond 1 GB without purchasing an entirely new service (possibly expensive), or they are incapable of increasing the capacity. Consider these potential barriers as you develop your Web site.

Unless you are storing a Tolstoy novel on your Web site, paperwork storage is insignificant. Hosting companies tend to have inexpensive introductory offers. Always ask about pricing and processes associated with upgrading your Web site. What was once a great introductory offer may become a financial nightmare. Shop around for a Web site hosting company that allows you to grow at an affordable rate.

Client Data Storage. A second area involving data storage that therapists tend to overlook but quickly migrate toward is client data storage: name, address, telephone number, e-mail address, and the like. Storing any form of client information falls under privacy regulations, even if you are only storing names and telephone numbers. Relatedly, is there storage and then transmission of the data? For example, I have met providers that ask clients to enter information into a Web form and that information is e-mailed (privacy and security concern) to the therapist's e-mail account (privacy and security concern). At this point in Web development, a simple Web site system is becoming complex. Protected health information is stored and transmitted, thereby opening up an entire area of Web site and privacy protection complexities.

Storing any client information requires firewall protection and encryption. It is critically important to differentiate between business data and clinical or personal health care information. Paperwork downloads, online scheduling features, your video introduction, audio recordings, and podcasts are business data storage variables. Other than someone stealing this information, there is no risk to others (customers or clients). Many therapists get ahead of themselves and start using their Web site for storing clinical and personal data. For example, it is easy to create a function that allows clients to complete a symptom inventory that is instantly available, via e-mail or Web access, to a therapist. It sounds efficient but has many complications regarding technology and privacy. Prior to storing client data, seek consult from your Web hosting company, and seek some privacy training.

Shared Server. Unless you purchase your own server your Web site is located on a shared server. This means that your Web site space is shared with numerous other businesses, thereby making your Web site and potential data storage vulnerable. The analogy I use is the difference between a gated home community and large apartment complex. In a large apartment complex, there is usually a central mailbox location. A single key is needed to gain access to the mailbox of anybody within that complex—you just need the correct key. The gated community requires you to access the security system for the gate to the community and then requires another key for the mailbox area and another key for your specific mailbox. In a shared server, you are with many other businesses. Choosing to store clinical data via your Web site requires that you address security issues with specific guarantees from your hosting company. Keep in mind that hosting companies host thousands of businesses that are *not* collecting health care information and therefore not necessarily subject to legal and ethical considerations. Do not be surprised if you find yourself educating the hosting company about privacy laws.

Security Indicators. Web page(s) collecting information of any kind should have a secure sockets layer (SSL) certificate. *Secure Sockets Layers* are tools that encrypt information a user is sending to you (TechTerms.com). Web sites that use SSLs are identified by Web addresses beginning with https rather than the normal http. You can obtain an *SSL certificate*, which is a file placed on your Web server that legitimizes your business (TechTerms.com). Third parties such as Verisign (www.verisign.com) or Thawte (www.thawte.com) confirm your Web site, thereby allowing the placement of the certificate on your Web site. These are easy technological tools to integrate, and they demonstrate the sensitivity needed when collecting and transferring any personal information.

Metatags. Metatags are great services for retail but not necessarily for professional psychotherapy services. *Metatags* are key words placed on a Web page but are not visible to the viewer (TechTerms.com). The idea of metatagging is that by placing key words within a Web site, the Web site moves up the list in searches. Instead of being listed number 87 in a search list, with effective metatagging you could move up to, say, 23 in the search result list. This strategy would be a primary consideration if your practice-building efforts were focusing on Ring 3 referrals. However, the focus of *Practice-Building 2.0* is providing services to Rings 1 and 2, thereby eliminating the need for metatagging.

Online Scheduling

Access to care is possibly the most important customer service variable. Is your access to care process providing convenience and satisfaction, or is the process a barrier to business growth? Treatment stakeholders are sensitive to the speed your office can "get someone in." When new clients are motivated, the longer the wait, the higher the likelihood they do not schedule, schedule with someone else, or cancel their appointment.

In a flattening world, potential clients are closer and more connected to therapists than ever before. Via online directories, Web sites, and online insurance profiles, they are able to learn about you without your knowledge. Potential clients are in a position to compare multiple therapists immediately. It only makes sense for your Web site to stand out when compared to other providers. One essential tactic is providing potential clients the opportunity to schedule an appointment immediately. A potential client reviewing your site, after examining your credentials, wants to schedule an appointment *now*. It may be 9:00 A.M. and the potential client is now motivated to schedule an appointment, following a distressing evening. Do you want that client calling multiple providers and choosing the provider who happens to be the first to call back?

Voice mail is great for leaving messages and for clients resistant to using technology or online scheduling services but is antiquated as an exclusive scheduling system. Clients can leave lengthy messages that an operator or receptionist cannot record. Most therapists indicate in their outgoing message that they return phone calls within 24 hours. Imagine feeling distressed and only knowing that your therapist will return your call sometime within 24 hours. Furthermore, this system places the therapist in the power position as clients are dependent on your schedule. Simply put, voice mail provides poor customer service for scheduling appointments.

Receptionists and live operators provide that "personal touch" that therapists believe is important. However, is the receptionist present 24 hours per day? You might have a live answering service, but can the service schedule appointments or only take messages? Our practice had a receptionist but over the course of 18 months after implementing online scheduling, virtually all appointments for new and returning clients were scheduled via the Internet. There was no longer a need for our receptionist. Receptionists and live operators add to overhead, involve personnel issues (attendance, performance) and have limited office hours.

Almost everyone prefers action over talking. One common example involves an elderly couple with the husband experiencing depression. Because the couple was also experiencing chronic medical problems, the couple's primary care physician (a frequently referring treatment stakeholder) suggested therapy. This couple expressed an unusual amount of appreciation at their first appointment about scheduling an online appointment. They reported that, after calling our office and getting voice mail instructions informing them they could either leave a message or go online to schedule an appointment, they immediately scheduled their appointment online. They reported online scheduling was so refreshing because their doctors have scheduling systems that require them to sit attentively by the telephone until someone calls them to schedule their appointment.

It is important that when using online scheduling, you prominently display this feature. Ensure that visitors can easily access this function. The deeper it is buried in your Web site, the less likely it will be used.

There are many treatment stakeholders who want instant access to your service and scheduling. Take a moment to consider your multiple referral sources and why they would like you to have online scheduling (Table 4.1).

Some treatment stakeholders are involved in care (i.e., primary care physicians, school counselors), while other stakeholders' role in the treatment process is simply making the referral. A financial planner, working with a couple, informed the couple that until they improved their communication she would not continue their financial planning. They heeded her suggestion and asked for a referral. The financial planner accessed our Web site and, using the online scheduling system, immediately scheduled their appointment. The couple was incredibly impressed with the financial planner and the seamless manner of accessing services. The beginning of building satisfaction and loyalty started taking hold.

As another example, psychiatric hospitals have discharge standards that hold them accountable for scheduling services at the discharge meeting. At the discharge planning meeting, the planner visits your Web site, views your schedule, and immediately schedules an appointment. After scheduling the appointment, the planner prints the appointment time, telephone number, address, and map to give to your new client. This process provides a great service

Treatment stakeholder	Possible need for online scheduling
Primary Care Physician	Possible immediate assistance to mutual patient
School counselors	Possible immediate relief to frustrated parents
Psychiatrist	Demonstrate collaboration with mutual clients
Attorney	Easy transition and coordination of services
Financial Planner	Improved reputation and services of the planner
Employee assistance program	Improved reputation and services of the planner
List some of your stakeholders and the reason they may appreciate online scheduling:	
Stakeholder	Reason
Stakeholder	Reason

because neither the discharge planner nor the new client needs to leave multiple voice mail messages to various therapists. The discharge meeting can conclude rather than lingering for a return phone call from a therapist. Convenience and loyalty are being forged with the treatment stakeholder (psychiatric hospital).

Clients and former clients will find the online scheduling a true convenience. Our primary intention when implementing online scheduling was capturing new clientele when individuals visited our site. This goal was quickly achieved, but the secondary benefits of online scheduling quickly became apparent (Box 4.3).

BOX 4.3
Unrealized Revenue: New Clients via Online Scheduling

Conservatively estimating two new clients per week results in $49,280.00 generated per year from online scheduling (2 new clients per week or 8 per month x 11 months = 88 new referrals x 7 sessions each = 616 sessions x $80 per session = $49,280).

Current clients, needing to reschedule appointments, began leaving voice mails to the effect of, "I need to reschedule, but don't worry about calling, I will jump online and reschedule." We happily realized our telephone time rescheduling appointments was significantly reduced. Another population benefitting from online scheduling is current unscheduled clients (e.g., those not immediately scheduling appointments during their last session). These returning clients simply capitalized on the opportunity to use online scheduling rather than calling and leaving messages (Box 4.4).

BOX 4.4
Unrealized Revenue: Time Saving

Approximately 90 minutes per week of time saving was realized with online scheduling, resulting in an additional $5,280.00 per year (90 minutes per week at $80 per hour = $120 of labor savings per week, $480 per month x 11 months = $5,280). Furthermore, 90 minutes per week x 4 weeks = 360 minutes per month x 11 months = 3,960 minutes per year or 66 hours per year in time savings.

Online scheduling for clients and former clients provides convenience, satisfaction, and loyalty. Appointments are scheduled 24 hours per day, 7 days per week, 365 days per year. As a business owner it is a great feeling to be involved in life, not work, and get a text message of a scheduled appointment. The process of scheduling did not take time away from my enjoyment, family, or friends. Furthermore, I know the person scheduling the appointment is extremely satisfied with the process (4-plus years of data collection), thereby creating a win-win situation.

Online scheduling is a potent instrument when engaging in Ring 3 advertising strategies. Increasing traffic of potential clients to your Web site is a good accomplishment but not good enough. A reasonably successful advertising campaign (Ring 3 strategy) results in potential customers viewing your Web site at all hours of the day. Why make them wait for a call back? Someone reviewing information at 2:00 A.M. or on a Sunday afternoon or a holiday will appreciate this opportunity to schedule an appointment, thereby laying the foundation of a loyal lifelong customer. If they are already online, why force them to change the medium of interaction from Web to telephone to schedule an appointment? Visitors to your Web site are online and quite possibly very motivated for an appointment. Forcing these potential clients to

     pick up a telephone
     dial your phone number

listen to a voice mail message

leave a voice mail message

wait for you to return their call at *your* convenience

get your call, possibly at an inconvenient time

simply places too many barriers for scheduling an appointment. New clients using an online scheduling system are scheduling when motivated and at their convenience. They can indicate a convenient time for a return call. When you do so, again it is at their convenience, not your convenience.

Before adding an online scheduling feature to your Web site, carefully consider security and privacy mechanisms of the system. There are many online scheduling companies providing very convenient functions without consideration to health care privacy policies.

Collecting Information. Online scheduling, although providing a significant convenience and service to both provider and consumer, is complicated by privacy regulations. When choosing an online scheduling system, keeping information sanitized is important.

Some online scheduling systems provide clients and potential clients the "convenience" of drop-down menus and prepopulated fields. For example, a typical question includes reasons for seeking services:

Why do you need an appointment?

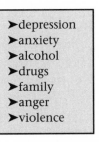

This convenient method, using drop-down menus, results in storing personal information. A client already feeling anxious may understandably choose to avoid using online scheduling. Ask yourself, do I want my personal health care information stored somewhere in cyberspace simply to make an appointment? Your answer is probably "No."

Sanitizing information protects client privacy by keeping the stored information minimal and noninvasive.

Why do you need an appointment? (optional)

Please describe. 75 character limit.

This format has several advantages. First, it is optional. New clients can *choose* not to indicate the purpose of scheduling an appointment. Second, clients have the option to disclose what they feel comfortable disclosing. A new client might indicate, "Challenges related to communicating with my teenage son." Another advantage gives new clients the opportunity to describe their unique situation rather than needing to pick an option they feel does not completely represent the clinical issue.

The point is to provide your clients as much control as possible when entering information, thereby reducing utilization barriers. As information becomes increasingly less sanitized, privacy regulations and risk analyses become more important. One good resource for online scheduling that is extremely simple and protects client privacy is Healthe-scheduler. (www.healthe-scheduler.com). This system keeps privacy concerns minimal while retaining the power of online scheduling services.

Storing Information. Because you are storing personal health care information in a different company's system, data storage is an important consideration with online scheduling. Online scheduling is probably the only area of a practice involving the storage of personal health information *away* from your business computer. This storage of personal health information *away* from your computer is subject to privacy rules and regulations. Although these regulations are highly variable, the question every business needs to answer is, "How complicated do we want our online scheduling system?" Each piece of collected and stored information adds complexity.

Having a "reservation" perspective that collects minimal personal information and focuses more on reserving the scheduled time provides an easier method of getting your new and current clients scheduled into your system and increasing privacy, safety, and security. Relying too much on another company to protect regulated privacy information may be too risky an endeavor for most practice-building therapists. Although there may be a few extra steps with a simpler system, consider these steps as insurance against privacy and security challenges.

Retrieving Information. What happens when a client schedules an appointment? Is your office immediately sent the information? Is a simple alert sent that someone has scheduled an appointment? What is the process to access and retrieve this information? What happens after you retrieve the information? These are questions that need answers prior to implementing an online scheduling system. Because most scheduling systems are designed for purposes other than health care, for which privacy regulations can be lax, many Web site design companies add an online scheduling system without giving any consideration to privacy policies.

Data Transfer. I have met a number of therapists with online scheduling systems that immediately transfer the personal health information into a contact management system or calendar. On the surface, this step has great appeal. A system by which a client name is stored and then transferred to your calendar system involves some important privacy protection considerations:

- Where is the data coming from?
- How is it stored at the originating location?
- What exactly is transferred?
- How will it get transferred to your calendar?
- Once in your calendar, is your schedule password protected?
- How do you back up the information?

These questions need specific answers, risk analyses, and privacy policies.

Data Retrieval. Unlike a system that stores information and then has a transfer mechanism, manually retrieving the information then deleting the information might be the safest method to protect privacy. Accessing information via a secured Web site with a unique provider password and user ID protects from client data transfer challenges. You simply retrieve and delete the information. Although this process may create a few extra steps, those steps can help keep your high-technology practice-building efforts less risky.

Privacy Policies. I am not aware of any specific privacy policies or expectations regarding online scheduling. However, there are some stringent expectations regarding the storage and transfer of personal health information. Once you have decided on an online scheduling system, you then need to conduct a risk analysis and write policies and procedures regarding the storage of personal health information. Finally, all clients and potential clients need notification of these policies.

Many online scheduling systems require customers to become a "member" and create a user ID and password to access and use the system. The fundamental idea behind a membership system is more security. However, there are some substantial problems with this type of system. First, do customers want another ID and password to remember? The online scheduling system is to help your clients, not to add another burden. Related is the distinct possibility that a new intake, not yet trusting the system, may turn away and schedule with another provider. When visiting a site and asked to "register," do you move to another site? A second challenge involves data storage over time. Each piece of data entered, including the creation of the ID and password, *is now stored on a server at a location you do not own or can influence*. A client scheduling a first appointment is creating a record with an ID, password, and the necessary information you require to schedule an appointment. It seems a bit risky to store this information on a shared server, probably in another part of the world, with a company that could be out of business tomorrow. Now what? How do you get that data back? More scary, where does the data reside, and who has access to it? If you only have one session, that record continues to exist in perpetuity. Are you willing to take the necessary time, monthly or annually, to delete such records? Are you provided the option of regularly deleting records, or are they stored and then used or sold to other vendors without your knowledge? If the company goes out of business or is purchased, will your contract remain valid? These are challenging and important issues to address before entering into an agreement with an online scheduling system that has access to personal health information of your customers.

Admittedly, when it comes to privacy, I am cautious and conservative. I tend to error on the side of how I would want *my* information handled. Also, I still believe that technology is a tool to enhance my relationship with clients and customers, not replace the relationship. Therefore, I am comfortable having a system that not only reserves a time for clients but also forces me to call, confirm, and start building a lifelong relationship with them.

Online Payment System

As we all know, collecting money is not only an important practice-building skill, it can be the most challenging. Eliminating barriers to collection is vital for the success of your practice. Online payment systems provide financial protection for your practice and convenience for your customers.

Typically, online payment systems offer you a "merchant terminal," which is simply the equivalent of a credit card terminal in your office. If your office has an Internet connection, you can accept a credit card payment and use the online system as a terminal. This feature also offers you financial insurance for no show or late cancellations. Creating financial disclosures and agreements, allowing you to automatically bill a customer's credit card for not giving 24 hours notification, is a sound business practice. You immediately get reimbursed for the no show or late cancellation rather than trying to collect this money. With an online collection system and financial agreements to bill for no shows, your practice will continue to earn money without the cost of bill collecting and nonpayment (Box 4.5).

Everything from clients with copayments or deductibles, to full-fee cash pay

BOX 4.5
Unrealized Revenue: No Shows

Two no shows or late cancellations per week can cost a practice $7,040.00 per year (2 no shows per week = 8 per month x 11 months = 88 no shows x $80 per no show = $7,040.00).

clientele can easily, and conveniently, benefit from this service. Clients simply use your Web site payment feature to pay for any outstanding bills. Before starting an online payment system, develop your financial agreements and disclosures and credit card payment policies for your business (Form 4.2 and Form 4.3, respectively, are examples).

If you accept insurance, often it is difficult to calculate a client's financial responsibility until an explanation of benefits arrives. At that point, the billing service, or you, can discuss with your client the amount due and have the client immediately make an online payment. Many times, our billing agent, while resolving outstanding billing issues, would either assist customers in immediately paying their balance via our online payment system or immediately charging their credit card. An online payment system provides multiple options for helping your practice reduce accounts receivable. It is time to compare how systems offered in *Practice-Building 2.0* are significantly different from more traditional methods for billing and collections (Table 4.2).

In this example, collecting for late cancellations and no shows 100% of the time increases your income and at the same time reduces labor. This reduction of labor is critically important for solo or small group practitioners. The time and frustration of collecting this revenue strips you of emotional energy and practice-building time. This example demonstrates how streamlining your infrastructure, rather than charging more per session, increases your income.

Online payment systems also assist treatment stakeholders with referrals who "don't have the money right now." Knowing these same people are likely to spend $25 per month on lattes, alcohol, dinner, or movies, stakeholders can persuade them to attend counseling and use a credit card for the copayments. Paying for mental health is a far better investment than paying for immediate gratification.

The elimination of barriers for payment is a significant financial benefit for potential clientele. Those desiring either to use insurance or to self-pay have an easy option for payment. Advertising this option via your Web site creates a practice-building situation that provides convenience and satisfaction to all three rings of referrals.

Tracy Todd, PhD, LMFT
7800 South Elati Drive, #230
Littleton, CO 80120
www.btid.com

The Brief Therapy Institute of Denver, in compliance with national standards of ethics, is required to disclose all billing and financial matters regarding psychotherapy services. We are further required to have financial matters reviewed on a regular basis. As a client of the Brief Therapy Institute of Denver Inc. you understand:

1. The usual and customary rate for providing direct face-to-face psychotherapy services is $120.00 per hour, $75 per 45 minutes.
2. You will be billed $75 for not giving a minimum of 24 hours notification of cancellation. This outstanding balance must be paid prior to additional psychotherapy services being delivered.
3. Your insurance company/HMO reimburses services at an approximate rate of $50 to $70 per session, depending on the insurance. Sessions are either 30 or 45 minutes in duration, and your copayment is the same regardless of duration.
4. Your copayment is due at the beginning of each session.
5. You will be billed for noncovered services such as telephone consultation, crisis intervention, report writing, care coordination with other providers (for example, primary care physicians and psychiatrists) at a rate of $2.00 per minute in excess of 5 minutes.
6. Any legal reporting, consultation, or coordination will be billed at a rate of $2.50 per minute.
7. We will periodically review the financial status of your account to address questions or concerns you may have regarding reimbursement issues involving third-party payers and balances due to the [your name or practice name].

Additional Comments/special conditions:

Please discuss any questions or concerns you may have regarding the financial arrangements concerning your psychotherapy services. We hope we have clarified some of the more common questions we receive about our financial arrangements with insurance companies and HMOs.

_____   _____
Signature   Date

_____   _____
Signature   Date reviewed

Please ask your therapist for a copy if you would like one.

Tracy Todd, PhD, LMFT
7800 South Elati Drive, #230
Littleton, CO 80120
www.btid.com

The Brief Therapy Institute of Denver uses PayPal, the highly secure online credit card payment system. We can accept MasterCard and Visa. By signing the line below, you agree to have your credit card information securely stored by [your name or practice name] until your file has been closed. *You also authorize your therapist, or billing representative to charge your credit card for any outstanding financial responsibilities. Charges are typically made for such items as copayments, no show/late cancellation fees, and deductible payments.*

_____
Signature

1. First and last name as it appears on your credit card:

_____   _____
First   Last

2. Card type (please circle):   **Visa**   **MasterCard**

Card Number: _____

Expiration Date: _____

Card Verification Code: _____
The verification number is a 3-digit number printed on the back of your card. It appears after and to the right of your card number.)

3. Payment schedule:

_____ Make a one-time payment of $_____

_____ Make a recurring payment of $_____ after each session or for

no show/late cancellation

_____ Other/Special instructions:_____

_____

4. Billing Address:

_____ My billing address is the same as it appears on the paperwork

submitted at intake.

_____ My billing address is different from that submitted on the intake

paperwork.

Street address: _____

City:_____ State:_____ Zip Code: _____

5. Contact Information

E-mail address: _____

Home phone number: _____

If you have any questions, please do not hesitate to contact your therapist or our insurance and billing specialist at (123) 456-7890.

TABLE 4.2: COMPARING *PRACTICE-BUILDING 2.0* AND TRADITIONAL SYSTEMS

	Traditional	*Practice Building 2.0*
No-show	Collect outstanding at next appointment or before scheduling. Low probability of collecting, say, $80	Signed agreement at intake allowing the immediate charging of a credit card for no-show or late cancellation
	Billing for the services incurs materials cost, labor, and postage; multiple billings may be needed to collect. Estimate labor at $5.00 Materials cost estimate $0.20 Postage = $0.44 Total cost = $5.64	Charge credit card Fee of 2.9% + $0.30 per transaction = $2.32 ($80 x 2.9%) + $0.30 = $2.62
Collection cost per 100 sessions billed	$564.00	$262
Revenue lost, including session fee, per 100 incidents	$80 x 100 sessions = $8,000	$80 x 100 sessions = $8,000
Hassle	High with poor collection ratio	Minimal, with virtually 100% collections
Difference	Assume a 50% collection rate: $80 x 100 sessions = $8,000 + $564.00 (billing) = $8,564 50% = $4,282	Assume 100% collection rate: $80 x 100 sessions = $8,000 + $262 (fee) = $8,262 minus traditional collections ($4,282) = $3,980 additional income per 100 lost sessions compared to the more traditional method

There are a few simple considerations when choosing an online payment system. The first is cost per transaction. Typically, a percentage of each transaction is collected by the online payment system. These fees are usually less than 5% per transaction. However, watch for hidden fees. For example, if you do less than a specified monthly transaction amount, you may be assessed an additional fee. A second factor involves ease of integration into your Web site. Some systems require you to have a technician add the feature; other systems, such as PayPal, have an easy method of integrating online payments. Finally, consider security. Although you may not choose PayPal for your online payment system, PayPal provides a good benchmark for comparing security systems.

Insurance Accepted and Treatment Population Matrix

It is essential that the hardcopy matrices you create and distribute to treatment stakeholders are posted on your Web site. These matrices help eliminate phone calls by saving time of those inquiring about your insurance acceptance policies and treatment populations. A nice Web-based strategy is linking each therapist's name to the therapist's biography page. Therefore, a visitor desiring family therapy simply needs to click "Therapist Name" and is then directly taken to the therapist's Web page. This strategy minimizes the point-and-click path. Linking the treatment issue to Web pages within your Web site provides additional convenience. For example, someone clicking "depression" might be taken to a Web page with some assessment questions, a podcast about depression, and a slide show of self-help skills (Figure 4.8).

Purchasing a Web Site

Before implementing any of the *Practice-Building 2.0* Web-based strategies, a practice needs a Web site. There are many companies offering affordable Web development and hosting services. A simple Google search of "Web hosting" will result not only in companies but also in "top ten" lists of the best, least expensive, highest customer rating, and more. This chapter outlined the technical and functional Web site components needed to flourish in a flattening and best practice standards private practice. Like anything else, know what you are purchasing. Outline the goals and priorities of your Web site and shop for the best service meeting your needs. From that point, you can begin identifying companies to provide you a Web site (Table 4.3).

Cautions

There are many Web site hosting companies that want your business. Some of these companies are no more than mom-and-pop shops that are "here today and gone tomorrow." Seek references about length of time in business, how many clients they have, and what are their emergency procedures if they lose data or have a catastrophe. Remember, as you grow and your Web site serves more functions, the more important your Web site becomes. For example, when our practice went to almost exclusively online scheduling, we had to ensure that the Web site and online scheduling function were functional 24/7. A simple lag in service is costly. We met with the company hosting our site, and they satisfactorily explained their emergency procedures.

FIG. 4.8: EXAMPLE LINKING WEBSITE

Clinical Specialties

	Therapist name	Therapist name	Therapist name	Therapist name
Abuse: physical, sexual		<18		
Adolescent problems	X	X	X	X
Affairs, infidelity	X	X		X
Alcohol abuse/addiction	X		X	
Anxiety, panic	X	<18	X	X
Attention deficit/hyperactivity disorder	**Adult**	X		X
Bipolar disorders	X	<18	X	X
Children <12 years		X		X
Chronic illness/HIV			X	
Communication skills	X	X	X	X
Depression	X	X	X	X
Dissociative disorders				
Divorce adjustment	X	X	**X**	X
Eating disorders				
Family problems	X	X		X
Financial	X		X	X
Gambling			X	
Gay/Lesbian/transgendered			X	
Grief	X	<18	X	X
Hepatitis C	X		X	X
Marital	X	X	X	X
Major mental illness	X		X	
Parenting in general	X	X		X
Parenting teens	X	X	**X**	X
Pelvic pain				
Premature ejaculation				X
Relationship with family	X	X	X	X
Relationship with people	X		X	X
Sexual arousal desire/disorders				X
Stepfamily issues	X	X		
Stress	X	<18	X	X
Work	X		X	X

(Fig. 4.8 continued on opposite page)

Home Page Therapist Biography Business Information Scheduling Client Resource Treatment Populations Served How I Work	Books to read, by category [link to Amazon] Depression [list books on depression]	Self-help strategies about depression and link to scheduling services Newsletter

Free Online Directory Presence

Do not forget to take advantage of online therapist directories provided by insurance companies, professional associations, and other organizations. These directories are free, and many therapists do not fully utilize all the functions and potentialities. Do not turn down free advertising! A place to start looking is your professional association. Does it have an online directory? For example, the American Association for Marriage and Family Therapy offers members a free listing at TherapistLocator.net (www.therapistlocator.net).

After identifying and registering with free directories, you need to maximize your presence in that environment. Do you have your picture posted, Web site listed, or as many features as possible integrated into your directory listing? Conservatively assuming two referrals per month results in approximately $12,320 of revenue per year (Box 4.6).

Web Site Options

Podcasting

Assuming you take the extra step to create podcasts rather than simply uploading audio files, podcasts become powerful practice-building tools. Podcasts serve many purposes and become an excellent vehicle for developing satisfaction, loyalty, and lifelong customers. I would recommend that you choose

---

BOX 4.6

Unrealized Revenue: Web Site Appointment

Two referrals per month x 11 working months = 22 referrals per year x average of 7 sessions = 154 sessions x $80 = $12,320.

TABLE 4.3: WEB SITE CONSIDERATIONS

	Basic	**Notes**
Disk space	2GB is a good start	Make sure you can easily and affordably increase
FTP access	You upload files	Inquire what software you may need
File Size Limitations	In the beginning not important because pages will be mostly text	Important as you consider adding video and other large files
Tech support	24/7 support; cost	Is support the same when you add advanced components (video, shopping cart, and the like)?
Bandwidth	Not an issue when starting	Important issue as you add sound and video
E-mail	Should offer personal mailboxes	Inquire about secure and encrypted mailboxes
Shopping cart	May not need when starting	May want to sell items such as online classes at a later date
Price	Compare; most will be the same (less $50 per month to host)	Learn hosting and administrations fees as your site develops and you customize additions
References	Minimally inquire about longevity of company, security of data	Ask if they have any other health care providers

some sort of icon representing sound files on your Web site. Such icons are signals for visitors that there is an audio file present. Be creative with your icon.

Introductions. Keeping your podcasts short, 3 to 5 minutes, eliminates time barriers from listening. Treatment stakeholders who gain an improved understanding of your treatment and service delivery style can effectively introduce your services. For example, a primary care physician listening to your self-help podcast about depression can offer simple cognitive-behavioral techniques to a potential new client and suggest that the client visit your Web site to gain further information. Whether in the primary care physician's office, at home, or at work, the client becomes positively introduced to you and your methods. This same client, listening to a few self-help podcasts, is benefiting from the information while your practice benefits from great advertisement.

Complement Treatment Stakeholders. Because podcasts can provide basic skills and information about any given topic, they can become resources for treatment stakeholders. Treatment stakeholders, learning a bit about clinical issues, can more effectively deal with clinical situations, thereby helping them appear knowledgeable. For example, a solution-focused therapist may have a podcast that highlights the importance of searching for exceptions to symptoms. Treatment stakeholders, knowing this is your treatment style, can continue the theme with mutual clients. Consider your own personal confidence when you perceive multiple professionals working together on your behalf.

Immediate Intervention, Immediate Advertising. Whether a current, former, or potentially new client, podcasts give people immediate information, and information is empowering. Everyone knows the effect of how a simple "to do" list benefits those experiencing distress. Imagine the advertising impact when a few simple steps benefit a visitor to your Web site. Beyond a doubt, this is a great form of advertisement. Unknowns, listening and possibly subscribing to podcasts, are in a position to become loyal customers. Virtually every major corporation would covet the opportunity to have a potential customer *voluntarily request* information on a subscription basis.

The unknown referral pool includes many clients ambivalent about counseling services. When listening to your podcasts, they can become comfortable with you and your style, thereby moving them into a more motivated state of mind for counseling.

Powerful Tool Needed at Critical Times. Since podcasts are extremely easy to produce and upload, they provide a vehicle to capitalize on immediate events or crises. If this sounds a bit like ambulance chasing, it is. A sports clothing store promotes the local team's jerseys if the team makes the playoffs. During the recent gas crisis, automakers promoted fuel efficient and hybrid automobiles. *Good business capitalizes on unfolding events.*

For the most part, high-stress events are predictable. For example, during tax season, posting a podcast for managing financial stress creates a win-win-win situation. The listener gains information (win). An accountant may benefit from a referral from your Web site (win). Your practice wins because it helped someone in need. Podcasts dealing with holiday stress, back-to-school issues, family vacation issues, or New Year's resolutions are all seasonal and fitting for the moment. Clients and former clients, learning you provide seasonal podcasts, will return to your Web site throughout the year to collect tips and strategies. This connection to your practice builds loyalty and lifelong customers.

Revisit Interventions: Clients and Former Clients. Podcasts are great for clients and former clients. Clients benefit from listening to therapy self-help techniques following sessions. Podcasts create a sense of reinforcement. For example, when working with a couple on communication skills, the couple can go home and revisit communication skill information. Podcasts are great for many different presented problems. List your common tips and suggestions and make some short podcasts to assist your clients.

Former clients are possibly the group benefitting most from podcasts. Following therapy, maybe many months, they can review information and skills discussed in therapy. Accessing reminders of clinical suggestions without needing face-to-face services (best practice standard) allows them to maintain positive skills and strategies. Former clients also use podcasts to refer clients. For example, a former client who knows a neighbor who struggles with some anxiety may refer the neighbor to a relaxation podcast. The neighbor, using the basic skills, realizes minor relief and appreciates your approach. Your podcast is helpful, is great advertising, and increases the potential for a new referral.

RSS Feeds. Most Web browsers allow automatic subscription to RSS feeds. Go to any well-known Web site (i.e., *USA Today*, *The Wall Street Journal*) and choose a story. Examine that Web page and you are likely to find something like

Subscribe with **RSS**

Tech Terms describes this universal symbol as indicating the opportunity to subscribe to similar stories, podcasts, videos, and the like. The podcast publisher, such as Poderator (www.poderator.com), creates this symbol and the code for Web sites. Someone visiting a Web site simply needs to click on the symbol, and the person automatically subscribes to the podcasts. Although simple audio files can accomplish many goals, they lack the power of RSS feeds that produce podcasts. Podcasts are subscriptions. If clients subscribe to your feeds, then whenever you post a new audio file, clients, former clients, and unknowns who subscribe will receive the podcast. This automation keeps your practice "in sight and in mind" rather than "out of sight, out of mind."

Do not avoid the simple step of converting audio files to podcasts because of the perceived complication. The ease of producing RSS feeds also creates some subtle and potentially powerful advantages. First, there are automatic programs that search for new podcasts to list in directories. If you take your time to tag your podcast, that directory will list your name and office and provide important background information about your practice (e.g., address, treatment populations served, and more). Now, you are engaging in *free* advertising.

Recording Considerations. There are many reasons and purposes for creating audio recordings to post on your Web site. These recordings can range from introducing yourself to providing self-help advice to creating the foundation for podcasting. Audio recordings have the advantage over video recordings as they take up significantly less space on your Web server, they are easy to create, and multiple formats can be created: Windows Media Audio (WMA), Moving Picture Expert Group Phase 1 Audio Layer 3 (MP3), or Advanced Audio Coding (AAC).

Creating audio recordings is easy. Virtually all computers have a recording device adequate for this purpose. The second needed piece of hardware is an independently powered microphone. This type of microphone has its own power source (i.e., battery or alternating current). Avoid those microphones that rely solely on the computer to generate the power for sound. Surprisingly, sometimes the most challenging piece of hardware to purchase is a microphone. Do not rely on microphones that are "built in" your computer or camcorder. These microphones simply do not have the ability to record quality sound for podcasting or your videos. Do not be afraid to take your computer to a store and to have a sales associate test various microphones to find the one that creates the best recordings. I would suggest looking into a wireless, lavaliere microphone as this type usually creates high-quality sound recordings, and you can use it with both your computer and your camcorder.

Before adding sound, consider the storage space of your Web site. Audio files quickly use storage space. For example, a .wav recording uses approximately 10 MB per minute of recording time. Recording, or converting, to an MP3 format uses 3 MB of storage per minute. For this reason, most audio files are MP3 files because they have great sound quality and require less space. Other advantages include cost savings (due to less used space) from your Web hosting company,

MP3 is a format that is easily listened to on any type of computer (PC or Mac), and MP3 is an easy format to convert for other uses.

Creating an MP3 recording is easy and requires little software or technical knowledge. The first step is to determine whether your computer already includes an MP3 converter. Within the recording sound tools, you may find a question asking what format you want your sound recording to be. If an MP3 option exists, choose it. If not, you will need to download some software, usually free or inexpensive. Do a Google search and type in the phrase "sound recording software." Your search results should return many recording software programs. The important consideration is the ability to record in MP3 format. A popular and easy-to-use program is Audacity (http://audacity.sourceforge.net). This program is free and converts your audio files into MP3 format. This program is exceptionally easy to learn and has great documentation. Audacity records audio files and with a few simple clicks converts the file to MP3. Another, more expensive, option is to purchase a handheld MP3 recorder. The top-end recorder is about $400 (Edirol recorders), but there are many less-expensive devices. After recording audio files in MP3 format, the sound files are ready for publication to your site. The advantage is that this method does not need a computer to make a recording. Also, it directly records into MP3 format.

One important consideration is the bit rate when recording. The *bit rate* represents the amount of data processed per second. The lower the bit rate, the lower the quality of sound. The higher the bit rate, the higher the quality of sound (TechTerms). Sound quality examples include

32 kbits sound like an AM radio station.
96 kbits sound like an FM radio station.
128–160 is the standard bit rate; some difference in sound might be heard.
192 bits sound like digital radio.
224–320 bits provide CD-quality sound.

Audio files for Web sites and podcasting are typically recorded at 128 kbits. The sound is quite good for practice-building purposes. Also, as the bit rate is increased, so is storage space on a hard drive. The bit rate is a setting on your recording software and is easily adjusted to meet your needs.

Another consideration is the actual sound recorded. Anything beyond your voice (e.g., music) may need some form of licensing agreement. There are many companies, such as Sounddogs.com (www.sounddogs.com), that sell sound effects. When choosing to use sound effects, ensure that you have the appropriate permissions and licenses to do so.

Many ask, "Why should I podcast when my clients can go to my Web site and listen to the audio file?" The difference between an audio recording available on your Web site and a podcast is whether the MP3 file is distributed to subscribers or whether individuals need to come to your Web site to get the information or file. An analogous example is whether you stop by a store to pick up a newspaper or have the newspaper delivered to your doorstep.

A podcast is automatically distributed to those subscribing to an RSS feed. After creating an MP3 file, there are numerous free and easy programs that create the RSS feed, thereby creating a podcast. The converter will create tags, labels, and the like, allowing a podcast to be searched on the Internet and listed in directories. Poderator (www.poderator.com) has a site that is very easy to use and navigate. Someone with an aggregator can listen to the MP3 file at his or her convenience as it is downloaded to the computer after you have uploaded it to your Web site. Podcasting provides more opportunities for listenership.

The technical considerations of podcasting are labeling and tagging. Depending upon the software it is important to remain consistent with a labeling and tagging system. For example

Artist = Your name
Album name = Your practice name
Song title = Title of podcast
Key words or tags = Your name, your practice name, key words describing the podcast
Album cover = Your picture

Following this format creates a consistent cataloging of podcasts. For directories (just like iTunes or Napster), your name becomes the artist, your album is the practice name, and the picture associated with the album cover is your picture or practice name or logo.

Videocasting

For any podcast or audio file, you could use a video file or videocast. However, video consumes space on a server. Since video files are large, judicious use is necessary. The two primary purposes for videos are introducing yourself and role-playing skills.

A video introduction provides potential clients a better introduction than a simple audio file or plain picture. A video introduction allows the joining process to occur prior to meeting your new client. Clients begin to have confidence and comfort with your style and presence. They see, hear, observe, and evaluate whether they can have a therapeutic relationship with you.

Treatment stakeholders who want to learn about your services can do so by visiting your Web site and viewing videos. This process helps to demystify who you are and establishes you as a credible referral source. Put yourself in the position of referring a client to someone for services. When referring to a psychiatrist, would you rather give the client the psychiatrist's business card or show the psychiatrist's video introduction? Which do you think the client would prefer? Video is powerful.

A client referred by a psychiatrist reported that in making the referral the psychiatrist showed my video introduction. The client appreciated my straightforwardness, liked my messages, and even noticed that I was not wearing "stuffy clothing," as he put it. After discussing my treatment style, while still in the psychiatrist's office, the client scheduled an appointment using the online scheduling function. The psychiatrist noted the appointment date and time and was able to forward relevant clinical information. This client indicated that the psychiatrist had our Web site bookmarked on his computer and stated that he had my narration nearly memorized because he would watch my video introduction and review my credentials and therapy orientation with all referrals. It is time to pause and break down this process to assess the significant advantages of the presentation in *Practice-Building 2.0:*

- The referring psychiatrist personally attests to my skill.
- Bookmarking indicates to clients that psychiatrist makes frequent referrals, which suggests satisfaction with services.
- Together, the psychiatrist and client can address questions or concerns about my services or treatment style.
- The psychiatrist is more confident that the referral will take place because he or she helped schedule the appointment.
- Clinical information is forwarded prior to the first appointment.
- The client is more educated about me at many different levels: appearance, voice, style, skill.

Consider the power of advertising when a referral source attests and tunes in to your commercial with a potential client.

When creating your video, get feedback. Therapists often "overtherapize" their message, which can be a turnoff, or they are nervous and the message is cold. A simple 3- to 5-minute introduction not only should include good content but also should demonstrate your confidence and a positive demeanor.

The other purpose for a video recording is demonstration. You can demonstrate helpful techniques: deep breathing, communication skills, conflict resolution skills, role-plays. Remember, videos take up an enormous amount of storage space, so try to keep them short. Videos on YouTube are simple and only a few minutes long. Video demonstrations are also useful for demonstrating skills and coping techniques. A simple 3- to 5-minute video may be just enough of a reminder for clients and former clients of some more basic therapy information (e.g., communication skills).

Short videos can be highly effective. On a more humorous note, a friend and I decided to eat at a "crab pickin'" restaurant. Lacking experience or knowledge in crab pickin', we jumped on YouTube and found about 25 videos on how to pick crabs. None of these videos was longer than 4 minutes. We watched a few and headed out fully confident in our abilities. When they dumped that bushel basket of crabs on our table, we dug in like pros . . . confident and able.

Of course, psychotherapy techniques can be more complicated, but the same dynamic is in play. Watching a video and having some knowledge, combined with some session discussion, can be all that is needed to put your client and former clients in a zone of confidence. A potential client visiting your Web site will see you in action. Your video will help the potential client determine if he or she could have a positive working relationship with you. This non-face-to-face service is exactly what the Institute of Medicine was referring to when discussing the provision of health care education and prevention (2001). As a practice-building technique, you are both assisting without being present and advertising your skills and practice. Imagine your clients and former clients showing the video to friends, family, and others. There is no better advertising than watching *you* in action.

Many therapists believe a video demonstration is "giving away" revenue-generating information. On the contrary, videos help generate business, not lose income. Strategically created videos will serve to provide potential clients an orientation to your style, provide the basis of loyalty, and eventually develop a lifelong customer. In short, videos are *great* advertising.

Videos can be posted on your Web site similarly to an audio file. You can create an RSS feed, and the video is automatically sent to anyone who has subscribed to that feed. These RSS feeds create connection. Ring 3 potentials might be connecting to you by subscribing to the RSS feed. They know you and become comfortable with your style, thereby heightening the potential to schedule an appointment. It is certainly more clinically useful and cost-efficient for potential clients to determine that you are someone they could not work with than for them to come to your office, have one visit, and not return. However, many more clients who are shopping for a therapist will see your video, experience your Web site in its totality, and select you as a therapist. Why? There are many more therapists without Web sites, pods, and videos. Maybe sometime in the next 15 years or so, all therapists will be on par with technology, and then the potential client will base decisions on other variables. However, those therapists with technology have the advantage for a number of years.

Technical Considerations. A digital camcorder is handy for creating the video components of your Web site. However, unless you plan to create many videos, I would avoid purchasing a digital camcorder for practice-building purposes. Your video introduction and a few other videos do not justify the expense. Locate a family member or friend and ask to borrow or rent their camcorder. If you do need to purchase one, a digital camcorder that is "good enough" will cost about $400. An important feature of your digital camcorder is that it has firewire output. A firewire allows video to transmit to your computer at speeds that allow you to store and then edit your videos. As computers have evolved, there are some with built-in cameras that allow you to record "talking heads." However, these cameras cannot record role-play demonstrations. Also, these cameras are "just good enough" to share videos with family and friends. It is unlikely that the quality is good enough for a professional-looking Web site.

The video-editing software in computers is almost always satisfactory for you to create the necessary video files for your Web site. Usually preinstalled, these programs only take a few minutes, even for someone who knows little of video editing, to learn. Now, video-editing software is created to be extremely easy to use so that families, grandparents in particular, can make videos of children and grandchildren to send and save.

Recorded videos use an enormous amount of space on a hard drive. If you intend to add a great deal of video, then I would suggest looking into a video condenser. This software compresses your video to a smaller size but usually at a quality loss. The high-end condensers can be costly, so it is probably better to maintain your format, just limit the video on your Web site.

The difference between posting video and videocasting is the same as the difference between audio files and podcasting. Therefore, it is a positive strategy to add the RSS feed so that your videos are distributed to those subscribing to your information.

Blogs

Short for Web logs, blogs are running commentaries about specific topics. Blogging technology is easy to implement. There are many free sites that offer the technology for your Web site. Using Google, search "blogging." The results will have sites listed for setting up free blogs. On a cautionary note, it is important to monitor blogs because it is easy to post inappropriate responses and comments. Make sure you can delete such entries. The last thing you want is someone attacking another on your Web site blog. Also, some blogs may be time sensitive. For example, "This weekend I'm going to be meeting my stepkids for the first time; any thoughts about what *not* to do?" Writing a response on Monday is not helpful and demonstrates that you are not paying attention to your blog.

The odds are pretty good that you have read a blog or two but probably not posted to a blog. Blogs allow the creator or moderator to get feedback and understand what readers are questioning or thinking. Similar to you, many clients will read blogs but not necessarily post comments. Ensuring anonymous blog posting will help elicit contributions. However, do not expect great participation. First, successful blogs require many visitors (i.e., highly visited sites such as USAToday or ESPN). It is a numbers game. Second, unlike posting your comments about your favorite sports team or a controversial issue, discussing personal issues is more difficult. You may post a blog and never get a comment.

While reviewing some blogs of therapists, I found a blog of a therapist asking, "Where are my readers?" The therapist posted a blog begging clients, former clients, and visitors to write something. There is no need for such pleading. Even when no one responds to your posting, blogs can stimulate referrals. Consider it another page of advertising. Your blog post indicates you are capable of working with that clinical issue or population. Also, blogs are searchable, meaning that search engines such as Google often index your blog and practice name. Therefore, you have a greater potential of being listed in search results of Ring 3 members randomly seeking services. Our experience has resulted in few posts, but numerous clients arrive for first appointments stating that the blog topic is exactly what they would like to discuss.

Blogs provide a sense of community and provide you credibility. Clients, former clients, and treatment stakeholders can feel part of your practice's community, while unknowns become acquainted with your services. As blogging develops, you may want to consider experimenting with the blog.

Flash Converter

A flash converter changes the format of media (e.g., PowerPoint, video) to a smaller size, thereby helping to maximize storage space. Often, however, there is degradation of quality. Flash converters range in price from free to expensive. To get an overview of the types of products available for flash converting, do a Google search on "flash converters." You will only need a flash converter if you begin to deplete storage space due to media on your Web site. PowerPoint presentations, videos, and audios can all be converted to a flash format. Typically, a long PowerPoint presentation should be converted due to space issues. If you are ambitious and start publishing self-help videos, Webinars, and other multimedia presentations to your Web site, you will definitely need a flash converter to save you the cost of increased storage space on a server.

Amazon Associates Program

Although a Web site is not a get-rich scheme, every penny counts. Your Web site should have an extensive selection of self-help books that complement your style of psychotherapy. If you are taking the time to list each book, then spend the extra minute or two to link to Amazon. Becoming an "associate" for Amazon can result in additional income from book sales. Participating in such programs enhances convenience for your clients, improves your reputation as knowledgeable of resources, and makes you money (Box 4.7).

BOX 4.7
Unrealized Revenue:Amazon Associates Program

If you are receiving 15% from Amazon (Amazon Associates Program) and your Web site referrals directly result in $400 in book sales per year, you will earn $60. Selling $400 worth of books, each averaging about $25 per book, means you are selling 16 books per year, a very achievable goal.

Summary

Today's marketplace expects—soon will demand—that small businesses in mental health have basic Web sites and Web site functionality. Customer satisfaction is increasingly measured by non-face-to-face services available. Your Web site is the perfect tool for meeting demands. Including simple functions such as paperwork download and online scheduling capabilities positions your business for staying technologically competitive. It is time to compare traditional practice patterns with those presented in *Practice-Building 2.0* (Table 4.4).

Key Points
1. Web sites are inexpensive and easy to build and modify.
2. Storage space is easily expandable and affordable.
3. Online scheduling provides enormous power in building your practice.
4. Podcasting maximizes distribution and advertising of your practice.
5. Keep video minimal due to space and streaming challenges.
6. Paperwork download capabilities provide convenience and satisfaction.
7. Your bottom line should be to integrate technology to streamline your practice and heighten efficiencies.

TABLE 4.4: COMPARING ACCESS TO CARE

Traditional practice	*Practice Building 2.0*	Notes
Potential client chooses three names from an online directory or is provided names to call and interview	Potential client gets your name and Web address from treatment stakeholder, client, former client (direct referral)	Practice Building 2.0 goal of 80% direct referral rate
Potential client calls all three clinicians with a high probability of leaving a voice mail with all three	While on the Web site, learns your credentials and style of therapy and can schedule online	No competition because client is following recommendation of someone he or she trust. Web site achieves a best practice standard of providing information for potential client
Potential client awaits the return call of one of the providers, providers are in a race with the each other	Potential client immediately schedules an appointment, in the notes section enters a general statement of problem and convenient times to be called	Best practice standard of easy and fast access to care met; client has information about you and can inform you of any important messages; Satisfaction and communication potentially enhanced
One therapist calls the client and one of three options occurs: 1. Schedule appointment 2. Client already scheduled appointment with different provider. 3. Therapist and client determine there is a mismatch and client referred elsewhere or client chooses not to schedule	Your new client receives a receipt with appointment time, telephone number, address to your office, and reminder to download intake paperwork; client downloads and completes paperwork; you call client to confirm appointment and introduce yourself	Best practice standards of offering multiple forms of interaction and service delivery beyond in the room service are met; provides convenience to client, communication with client
Although client was asked to come early for appointment, client arrives 5 minutes late and needs to complete paperwork.	You receive an e-mail and text message that an appointment time has been filled; you log on to the Web site at your convenience to collect client's information; after information received, it is deleted from the server, thereby completely protecting client privacy	Best practice standard of privacy protection achieved; information gained at your leisure, no need to rush or take time out of your schedule

(Table continued on following page)

Traditional practice	Practice-Building 2.0	Notes
Start session late and either cut into next appointment time or have less time with client	Client downloads intake paperwork and completes when convenient	Clients experience convenience and satisfaction; access to care streamlined. If clients are late, they have completed the paperwork
End session by giving client a business or appointment card with next appointment; collect copayment and review cancellation policies	End session by giving client a business or appointment card with next appointment; explain that cancellations are via telephone but rescheduling can occur online	Gives client multiple forms of communication and interaction with practice
Client cancels and wants you to call and reschedule	Client cancels but reschedules online	Reduces time spent on rescheduling process by you and your client; saves on labor costs; enhances satisfaction and loyalty
Play voice mail tag until rescheduled	Already scheduled	Satisfied customer
Client chooses not to return to treatment; use billing system to try to collect the late cancellation fee	Bill client's credit card, which you have a signed agreement to do	Reduces labor and increase income

Action List

1. Research Web hosting companies that meet your needs and purchase a Web site.
2. Research and purchase a PDF converter.
3. Begin designing and building your Web site.
4. Assess your access to care.
   ___ My telephone number is easily located on my Web site.
   ___ The prompts on my voice mail are customer service oriented and provide information for leaving a message
   ___ When the caller can expect a call back
   ___ Emergency procedures
   ___ Another option for scheduling

___ Data indicate that I am offering appointments within 5 business days of initial contact.

___ Data indicate that I am accepting appointments within 7 business days of initial contact.

___ Clients can schedule an appointment 24 hours a day, 7 days a week, 365 days a year.

___ The online scheduling function is easily located on my Web site.

___ The online scheduling function is quick and easy to use.

___ The online scheduling function provides a receipt with opportunity for me to send a customized message.

___ It includes directions and phone number.

___ It provides an immediate response to me and my client.

___ My live operator can direct customers and treatment stakeholders to the online scheduling function.

5. Research online scheduling companies considering your level of privacy concern. Purchase a system and integrate it into your Web site.

6. Research and purchase an online payment system.

7. Post your Treatment Population and Insurance Accepted matrices on your Web site.

8. Learn how to make audio recordings in MP3 format.

9. Learn how to create RSS feeds and test your system.

10. Learn how to make videos and post to your Web site.

11. Create RSS feeds for videos.

12. Research whether you want to incorporate a blog.

13. Integrate your online library into the Amazon Associates Program.

CHAPTER FIVE

Technology Beyond Your Web Site

W eb Sites and associated functionalities are an excellent start for practice building. Integral to the strategies in *Practice-Building 2.0* are the technologies that few treatment stakeholders, clients, and former clients will see but almost all will experience. This chapter is about the behind-the-scenes strategies that emphasize labor reduction and income generation, thereby increasing unrealized income opportunities.

Efficient infrastructure technology results in streamlined office processes. For example, consider the irritation when calling a service center and repeating information such as your name, address, and the problem each time a transfer occurs. Do you ask clients for specific information more than once? If yes, how can technology eliminate the redundant steps? Similarly, when a client schedules an appointment, how will you note the days offered and accepted from the initial contact? Rather than creating a frustrating exercise at the end of the month of searching for the data and calculating this statistic (which heightens the probability of discontinuance), create an infrastructure system that automates how these data are tabulated when scheduling each new appointment.

I once had a seminar participant tell me, "Tracy, I know I need to take the time to learn how to use my word-processing and contact management program more effectively, but I just don't want to take the time." Rather than implementing a point-and-click contact management system utilizing template forms, thereby increasing efficiency, this therapist chose to engage in costly labor activities, thereby reducing profit margins.

There are many treatment processes (also known as paperwork and case management) that require a high degree of labor and, honestly, are so tedious everyone tends to avoid them. These tasks have associated labor costs and frequently direct revenue costs. Streamlining these tasks through technology reduces the amount of time engaging in nonclinical tasks with the added benefit of increasing unrealized revenues.

Essential Infrastructure Technologies

There are a few simple infrastructure technologies that will greatly reduce labor and costs while improving your abilities to coordinate quickly and securely with treatment stakeholders, clients, and former clients. Regardless of whether you are starting, rescuing, or expanding a practice, accomplish these essentials in the next 6 months.

Electronic Contact Management System

An electronic CMS is *critical* for implementing the strategies in *Practice-Building 2.0*. Examples of CMS include MSOutlook, Entourage, and ACT. These systems range from simple to extremely complex (and expensive). Any program that can store the following information will suffice: name, telephone number, fax number, address, e-mail address, Web address, and simple notes (not psychotherapy notes).

The program should allow sorting of files by differing categories. For example, one file may include clients, another former clients, and another treatment stakeholders. Functions of the software should include integration of word-processing and e-mail tools, allowing creation of letters directly from the program. For example, you want to send a letter to a former client, Jane Smith. From the CMS, you simply click her name and then click the "create letter" function, and the word-processing program immediately allows letter writing with Jane Smith's address prefilled. There are numerous advantages to this system. First, it is expeditious. Name and address are automatically inserted into the document, and the entire letter or form is also created. Second, this event (letter writing) is date stamped and stored, providing verification of the action. In the event your records are ever called into question, you will have an automatic date stamp that verifies your actions.

How will you collect the information for your CMS? Easily collecting and entering information and never needing to worry with this step is the goal. On a simplistic level, the client enters his or her information on the paperwork printed from your Web site. You then enter the information into a CMS. When will you enter the information? How can the information be entered quickly and easily? Do you have a form for collecting this information? (Form 5.1).

FORM 5.1: BASIC CLIENT INFORMATION

Client Information

Name:_____

Address:_____
          Street   City   State   Zip

Birth date:_____   Age:_____ Gender: ____ Male ____ Female

Relationship status: ____ Married   ____ Separated   ____ Single
                     ____ Divorced   ____ Cohab.   ____ Child

I agree to pay my co-pay of _____ at the end of each session.

If I am self-paying, I will pay _____ at the end of each session.

Whom should we thank for the referral? _____

Contact Information

Home phone:_____ Best time to call: _____

Can we leave a message?_____

Work phone:_____

May we call you in confidence at work:_____

Can we leave a message?_____

Parent to contact if client is a child: _____

Insurance Information

Name of insured (if different from patient):_____

Address of insured (if different from patient): _____

Gender: ____ Male ____ Female   Birth date:_____

Social Security No. _____

Insurance company:_____

Phone: _____

Address: _____

Member ID No. _____ Group Number:_____

Insured's employer:_____ Status: Employed

           Terminated ___   LOA Authorization No. _____

Insurance Type: ___ HMO ___ PPO ___ Other   Deductible: _____

Who would you like notified in case of emergency?

Name:_____

Relationship to you:_____

Address:_____

Home phone:_____ Work phone: _____

From Form 5.1, any or all information can be entered into a CMS. The critical pieces of information are name and address so you can easily send correspondence (Figure 5.1).

Storing basic information (i.e., client name, address, telephone number) in your CMS literally drives practice efficiency. A CMS creates a streamlined practice infrastructure, eliminating barriers and time-consuming efforts, thereby increasing opportunity to engage in other practice-building efforts.

With a CMS, care coordination becomes fast and easy to accomplish. Treatment stakeholders' names, addresses, and telephone and fax numbers are simply a point and click away. As a clinician, you are more inclined to send a quick notice to a school counselor if you have that person's contact information readily available. This communication provides opportunity for consistency in communication thereby building a reliable reputation. Some other useful functions of a CMS include:

- the ability to point and click to compose e-mail and letters
- envelope and label making
- date-stamping activities
- creation of "tickler" reminders

FIG. 5.1: EXAMPLE CMS ENTRY

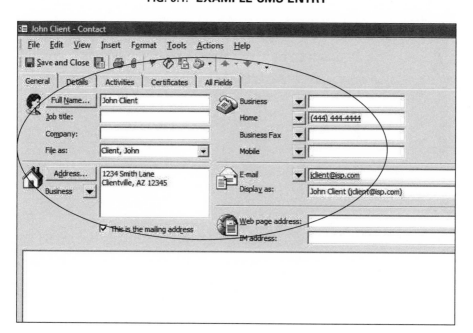

The CMS integrated with word-processing programs significantly enhance your productivity. For example, sending a care coordination notice to a primary care physician 3 weeks following a session involves some simple steps:

1. Enter a reminder on the date you will send the notice.
2. The reminder alarm will activate on that date.
3. You click the primary care physician's name.
4. Select "write a letter" in the action field.
5. Open a form or template for the clinical notice.
6. Enter client-specific information.
7. Save and print the letter.
8. Print the address on the envelope.
9. Mail or fax the notice.

The total time for this process is less than 8 minutes (I have timed myself when sending such reports) (Figure 5.2).

The bottom line with treatment stakeholders is that they are receiving frequent, consistent, and trustworthy information from *you*. The more streamlined your mechanism for delivering this information, the more likely you will engage in consistent communication. Many therapists start out by sending information via handwritten envelopes and typing new letters for each piece of correspondence; then, lacking a streamlined and inexpensive system, they discontinue the efforts after a few months. Technology reduces barriers, allowing efficient and effective practice-building strategies. After designing a

FIG.5.2: EXAMPLE OF FUNCTIONS AVAILABLE IN CMS

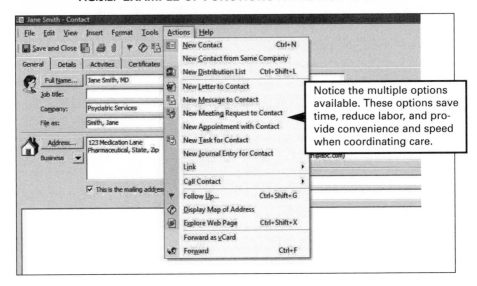

New Technologies for *Practice-Building 2.0*

newsletter, with a few simple point-and-click actions, it is distributed to specific individuals and agencies. This additional infrastructure component significantly increases communication and the potentiality to develop lifelong customers.

Remember, fewer than half of private practice therapists collect information on who referred clients to them. Using Form 5.1 on receiving the information about the referral source, the information should be directly entered into the CMS. When you determine that care coordination is necessary, you can then obtain and enter the referral source information (mail address, e-mail, and the like). After about 18 months, you will start to recognize the same names, and this entire step will be minimized to new referral sources and treatment stakeholders.

Dedicated E-mail Account

A dedicated e-mail account provides added security by separating private practice e-mails from personal e-mails. The best option is to have a business e-mail account. Virtually every Web site hosting company also includes basic mailboxes. For example, if you own ABC Mental Health, your Web site address could be www.ABCMentalHealth.com. You would then have a mailbox with the format, therapistname@ABCMentalHealth.com. Importantly, set your e-mail account to send a user name rather than your e-mail address. This way, when someone receives an e-mail from you, the item displayed in the "From" portion of your window is your name, for example, "Tracy Todd." Otherwise, upon receipt the "From" line will read "therapistname@ABCMentalHealth.com," which clearly compromises privacy as anyone quickly viewing the recipient's screen will notice that he or she is receiving e-mail from a psychotherapy center.

Another important function is to create a completely separate folder for receiving e-mails from your business account. Why is this so important? First, clinical e-mails should never be mixed with personal e-mails, which increases the risk of missing a critically important e-mail. Also, others may have access to your personal e-mails, thereby violating privacy regulations. Second, creating a communication policy for clients who wish to communicate via e-mail allows the possibility of creating an auto responder. Autoresponders are helpful tools for reminding clients of policies and procedures and vacations or indicating, "If this is an emergency, call 911." With personal e-mail accounts, your choice is to send all family and friends an autoresponse (which they may not appreciate) or never send your clients an autoresponse (not a particularly good idea).

Often, for an extra few dollars per month, you can have a *secure and encrypted* e-mail system. These e-mail accounts have added layers of security protecting your client communications. Since these accounts are usually affordable (less than $5.00 per month), they are a nice feature to include particularly if you intend to engage in any type of clinical communication via e-mail with your clients.

E-mail Merge Programs. There are two methods for merging. One is the traditional software that installs on a computer. The second is a license to a Web environment that stores the e-mail addresses and then with some software allows the user to generate a list for distribution. However, because the company is actually storing and sending e-mails, it prices the license based on how many and how often e-mails are sent. For a number of reasons, I tend to discourage using an online licensing e-mail distribution product. First, if you are using e-mail reminders, you will be storing your e-mail in two locations: your computer and in a Web environment for the mail merge. Second, what happens to your data (e-mail addresses) if the company goes out of business? Third, e-mail addresses can be considered personal health information; under privacy laws, does the hosting company have the necessary privacy guards to protect your clients' personal health care information (e.g., name plus e-mail address)? Fourth, what permissions and guarantees do you need to send personal health information to another company? There are simply too many complications and risks associated with these platforms compared to an easy-to-use add-in programs.

An add-in e-mail merge program works like a regular mail merge, only with e-mails. The critically important advantage of using an e-mail merge program is client confidentiality. Without such a program, you have two choices. One is to send your materials individually to each recipient, which defeats the purpose of technology. Second, you can send the material with many names in the distribution list, which is inadvisable as you are breeching confidentiality.

Depending on your CMS, using Google, search "e-mail merge add in" or "e-mail merge add in Mac" to get results for the numerous programs available. These programs save a great deal of time, provide extra confidentiality, and maximize practice-building efforts. One good program is Addins4Outlook (www.addins4outlook.com).

These types of programs allow you to retain your records and control. Privacy is based on your policies and procedures, not those of a company that may have little experience with privacy regulations and health care concerns.

Optimizing technology by integrating an e-mail merge program with your CMS provides speed, additional functionality, and significant reduction of costs. Because you have permission to e-mail clients and former clients and possibly treatment stakeholders, sending electronic notifications is far superior

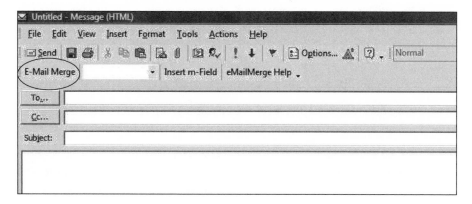

to paper notifications. Your e-mail merge program allows you to create one e-mail and send it to the entire group. Monthly notifications of any new information are an easily accomplished task that establishes you as the local expert, thereby heightening your reputation (Figure 5-3).

Distribution Cautions. Another e-mail use involves announcements. Referring to the example in the introduction, a snail mail distribution to 300 clients, former clients, and referral sources costs approximately $435.00. After a few years, a distribution list could easily surpass 1,000 contacts, which converts to thousands of dollars if you are using paper-and-postage mail. Whether e-mailing 300 or 3,000, the cost is design time as distribution costs remain the same. There are three important considerations when sending e-mail announcements and newsletters:

1. A CMS is necessary for storing and sorting information.
2. An e-mail merge program is required to save time and protect privacy.
3. Permission to receive announcements via e-mail is necessary.

Using e-mails to distribute information about your practice requires you to inform clients of risks associated with receiving your e-mails (e.g., someone else discovering they receive a mental health agency's newsletter) and to avoid accusation of spamming. The Federal Trade Commission CAN-SPAM Act (2003) outlined what is and is not considered spam. Assuming your practice is not involved in spamming activities, one of the more important rules involves allowing the reader or receiver to unsubscribe from the e-mail distribution system. As e-mail distribution lists expand, so does the risk of being flagged by an Internet Service Provider (ISP) as a spammer. If a recipient of your distributions flags your e-mail as spam, the ISP may take action. Although you have permission to send, your e-mail may start to be monitored as spam. Although not fail safe, including the following statement will help guard against being flagged as a spammer:

> You are receiving this e-mail because you have granted permission for my practice to send you e-mail correspondence. If at any time you wish to discontinue receiving e-mails, simply unsubscribe, and you will be taken off the distribution list.

The "unsubscribe" should be a hyperlink command that prompts an e-mail directly to your office. Legitimate businesses offer methods of unsubscribing that are monitored by ISPs. However, those involved in spamming do not provide this option.

Electronic File Management

Not to be confused with electronic medical records systems used in hospitals, physicians' offices, and large community health care centers, electronic file management is simply converting paper forms to a digital format. For example, frequent letters and charting forms converted to digital format provide you the opportunity to use prepopulated drop-down menus to save you an enormous amount of labor physically writing information by hand. Session charting must become the most streamlined process of the entire clinical system.

An electronic file management system has many advantages over handwritten and paper documentation. First, client files are easy to back up, helping your practice comply with privacy protection and security standards. Consistently copying files to a thumb drive provides protection against data loss. A second advantage is data retrieval. Simply point and click, and you have client information on your screen. A third advantage is that data within a file are easily searchable. This feature is particularly nice for those larger client files. Letters, sessions, and correspondence are easily located with a "find" command. A final advantage is a decreased need for storage space.

I am continuously surprised by the number of therapists who continue to use paper and pen to document each and every session. Regardless of the type of documentation—intake, session, letter to treatment stakeholder—with a little technology, documentation can easily become a point-and-click system. At the beginning of every session, client information is easy to locate on a computer. Many therapists report, "I can have the paper chart readily available." Yes, but there are increasingly major challenges with paper charting. I have not met a single therapist who creates a backup copy of paper charts, a necessary condition with current privacy protection regulations. Second, password protection on every file, regular backups, easy storage, and the ability to find and create documents quickly are far superior in efficiency to paper files and storage. Also, electronic files are searchable. If you are looking for a specific piece of information, you simply use a "find" command, thereby saving the labor and frustration of trying to read each page to locate the information. If a paper file exists because someone sent a letter, there can be a simple note in the electronic file regarding the existence of the paper document. Paper files are easily stored and significantly reduced in size. Anyone practicing a few years becomes shockingly aware of the challenges with storage and retrieval. With electronic filing, at a designated time, transferring all closed cases to a flash drive, then deleting the files from the computer, now reduces your storage to the size of a finger. The remaining paper files fit easily into one box, also easily stored. My recent move and subsequent storage of files was striking. Paper files contained in many boxes became painfully difficult to catalogue and store. Because I was leaving the state, my business partner needed access to the files and catalogue. Now, imagine looking into a secured storage area and seeing a wall of boxes and needing to find a single file. Yikes. She had this experience 3 months after my move. Contrast this situation to my last year of charting, which I provided to her on a flash drive. If she needs to find a file, she uses the security code to access the table of client names and then opens the appropriate file number. She prints the file and checks to see if there is a paper file. If there is a paper file, she can look into a small box of paper files to find the additional documentation. If you plan on being in a practice very long, electronic filing is a must.

Although it is not an everyday occurrence to find a chart that is 6 years old, it is an everyday occurrence to prepare charts for sessions. Most clinicians pull the paper charts of clients they are seeing that day or week. Spending time searching for files, examining files for a piece of information, or documenting takes time. With an electronic file, any information you need is a point and a click away. It takes seconds to locate a file number, and, using a search or find function, locate any needed information.

Efficient practice management builds a practice. Reducing labor increases the overall reimbursement of your sessions, and the removal of labor barriers increases the consistency of engaging in outside-the-room activities. Increased consistency establishes a high-quality reputation among treatment stakeholders, while reliability builds loyalty and lifelong customers confidently referring to your practice. Reduction of case management labor provides time for other activities that specifically address *Practice-Building 2.0* strategies. I think you get my point.

BOX 5.1
Unrealized Revenue: Documentation

Staying conservative and estimating a reduction of documentation time by 10 minutes per chart with an average of 25 clients per week, the saving is 250 minutes per week or $14,080 per year in labor (10 minutes per chart electronically x 25 charts = 250 minutes; 20 minutes per chart handwritten, hardcopy x 25 charts = 500 minutes. This is a saving of 250 minutes or just over 4 hours per week x $80 per hour = $320 per week x 4 weeks = $1,280 per month x 11 months = $14,080. In addition, 250 minutes per week x 4 weeks = 1,000 minutes per month x 11 months = 11,000 minutes or 183 hours saved per year.

So, you ask, "How does this build my practice?" Simply put, you have labor reduction. With a digital documentation system, using drop-down menus, the time to chart each session can be approximately 5 to 8 minutes (compared to 10–15 minutes when completed by hand) (Box 5.1).

With standard form letters, the entire letter simply requires only specific pieces of information. This important infrastructure mechanism reduces labor and improves consistency because labor is not a barrier to completion. For example, clients who do not reschedule canceled appointments often need some prompting (Form 5.2). In this standard "check in" letter, the only information needing completion is the client's name and the upcoming closing date. Creating the letter and addressing the envelope simply requires opening the CMS and choosing "New Letter to Contact" to complete the form letter, and then using a "create envelope" command to address the envelope. These small steps may not seem like huge time savers, but when collectively added over the course of months, many hours of time for advertising become available.

An electronic file system communicates at the metalevel the efficiency of a practice. During case collaboration with treatment stakeholders, clients will often report, "My primary care physician said she did not receive your faxed information." I simply look in the chart and inform them of the date faxed. The next comment usually is, "I suspected that it was his office that lost it; it is such a zoo over there." Technology communicates organization. This organization and continued consistency and reliability increase satisfaction and loyalty, and creates lifelong customers.

Although a paperless file system is a great goal, unless you invest in scanning systems that convert documents and take the time to engage in this laborious task, it is highly unlikely that any small outpatient practice can be completely paperless. Inevitably, some paper is generated that needs storing, but reducing the actual paper file by nearly 90% is possible.

FORM 5.2: CHECKING-IN LETTER

> Tracy Todd, PhD, LMFT
> 7800 South Elati Drive, #230
> Littleton, CO 80120
> www.btid.com

Date: [auto entry)]

From: Tracy Todd, PhD, LMFT

To: [type in client name]

Regarding: "Checking in"

I hope you are doing well.

It has been some time since I have heard from you, and I wanted to take a moment and follow up to see if you needed additional services. Please feel free to call me at _____ if you would like to schedule another appointment. You can also schedule an appointment at our Web site, www.btid.com, and then select my name. If I do not hear from you by [type in date], I will assume you no longer desire my services and your file will be closed. However, you may call at any time, and we will be happy to reopen your file.

Thank you for letting me serve you.

Setup. Virtually all word-processing programs have template or forms commands. The forms option allows you to convert any document to include drop-down menus and prepopulated fields. For example, if your session documentation requires indicating whether the client is suicidal, you might have a question such as

Is the client suicidal? Yes ___ No ___
In this example, your documentation requires marking yes or no.
Is the client suicidal? Yes ___ No _x_

However, when using forms, a prepopulated default answer is created:
Is the client suicidal? No

The "no" answer is automatically prefilled. Unless you specialize in crisis counseling, most of your answers will be no. Why spend time and effort every session marking no? Make this the default answer, but when needed, you can simply point, and click, and choose yes.

Suicidal or homicidal Ideation:

Consider the numerous default responses of any documentation. There is no reason to expend labor over default answers. Okay, so you are thinking, "Tracy, this is really such minor labor, why is this important?" One question seems insignificant, but what if your charting system has 20 questions with default answers? Now, the time saving becomes significant, especially when multiplied over more than 25 sessions per week.

Compare Form 5.3 and Form 5.4. Physically documenting the session by hand involves answering questions that have default answers, whereas, for example, up to 15 answers can be prepopulated with drop-down menus and default answers using templates and forms.

Task. First, compile all forms and letters used in your practice. Examine each form and for each question fill in the most common (default) answers, for example:

Does the client present that their situation is:

Better ___
Same ___
Worse ____

These might be the three answers that you have as options. Assume the most common answer is "better." The form would appear as

Client, Presenting Problem: Better

Yet, if a client tells you that his or her perception is that things are worse, you would simply click on the drop-down menu and choose "worse."

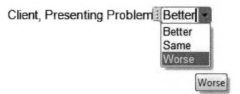

Client, Presenting Problem: Worse

Creating form fields is easy. Depending on your word-processing program, you can either take the tutorial or use the online help center for learning how to create form fields. Every practice form should be converted to forms or templates because of the enormous time savings.

Last Name: *Smith*   **Sess #:** *7*

Date: *6/19/09*   **Case #:** *2008003123*   **Length of Sess.:** *50*   **Time of Sess.:** *4 p.m.*

Members present: John, Sally, Brenda

Oriented X3:	Yes *x*	No
Suicidal or homicidal Ideation:	Yes	No *x*
If yes, high risk strategy implemented:	Yes	No
Alcohol abuse:	Yes	No *x*
Quantity:		
Frequency:		
Drug use:	Yes	No
Type/Quantity:		
Frequency:		
Assessed Substance Abuse:	Yes	No *x*
Assessed Addiction:	Yes	No
Physical/Sexual abuse:	Yes	No *x*
If yes, reported:	Yes	No
Domestic Violence:	Yes	No
If yes, plan set:	Yes	No
Has diagnosis changed?	Yes	No *x*
If yes, to what?		

Does treatment plan need updating (update every 3 months)?   Yes   No *x*

Homework attempted:	Yes *x*	No		
Homework completed:	Yes	No *x*		
Client, Presenting Problem:		Better *x*	Same	Worse
Therapist, Presenting Problem:		Better *x*	Same	Worse
Level of progress toward goals:		Great	Some *x*	Poor
Referred to MD:	Yes	No *x*		
Referred to PCP:	Yes	No *x*		

Data: *Family reports continued progress at all levels: improved communication, more effective parenting. Bill and Cindy are discussing issues in private rather than in front of children. They are creating unified messages prior to disciplining children. Joshua and Sue report that there is less fighting in the home and they are feeling that parents are not always angry but they don't like that they can't seem to get their way at times. Bill reports some additional stress due to layoffs at work.*

Assessment: *Parents are very motivated to make positive changes and appear to be taking positive steps. They are appearing to be more confident in their strategies. Bill's stress level appears normative for the work conditions and should be monitored if it has bearing on marital relations.*

Tasks assigned: *Maintain strategy.*

Plan: *Assess goals next session. If work stressors do not adversely impact family, will begin to space sessions to once per month.*

Date of next session: *8/1/09*   **Time**: *5 p.m.*

Therapist Signature: *Tracy Todd, PhD, LMFT.*   Date: *7/16/09*

FORM 5.4: SESSION DOCUMENTATION: Template Form

SESSION DOCUMENTATION

Last Name: **Sess #:**

Date: **Case #:**   **Length of sess.:**   **Time of Sess:**

Members present:

Oriented X3:   Yes x   No

Suicidal or homicidal Ideation: Yes   No x

If yes, high risk strategy implemented: Yes x   No

Alcohol abuse: Yes   No x

Quantity:

Frequency:

Drug use: Yes   No x

Type/Quantity:

Frequency:

Assessed Substance Abuse: Yes   No x

Assessed Addiction: Yes   No x

Physical/Sexual abuse: Yes   No x

If yes, reported: Yes   No

Domestic Violence: Yes   No x

If yes, plan set: Yes   No

Has diagnosis changed?   Yes   No

If yes, to what?

Does treatment plan need updating (update every 3 months)?   Yes   No x

Homework attempted: Yes x   No

Homework completed: Yes   No

Client, Presenting Problem: Better   Same   Worse

Therapist, Presenting Problem: Better   Same   Worse

Level of progress toward goals: Great   Some   Poor

Referred to MD: Yes   No

Referred to PCP: Yes   No

Data:

Assessment:

Tasks assigned:

Plan:

Date of next session: **Time:**

Therapist Signature: *Tracy Todd, Phd, LMFT*   **Date:** auto fill with current date

With the forms template, many responses can be prepopulated and other fields can include drop-down menus.

Client ID	Name
200803172	Client name
200803173	Client name
200803174	Client name
200803175	Client name
200803176	Client name
200803177	Client name
200803178	Client name
200803179	Client name

Your second task, after converting all paper documents to forms, is to create a blank electronic client chart. Place all electronic forms into a single file in the order you prefer to enter information, and save this file. This "new client" electronic file is opened for each new client, then stored using the system you created for storing client information.

Before you begin entering clinical information into your electronic file management system, you need a system to identify and password protect client files. Privacy regulations elevate this task to number one priority status. Despite the importance, implementation is easy. One simple system is to create file names based on year, therapist, and number. For example, file number 200803178 indicates the following information:

2008 = Year chart opened
  03 = Therapist number
 178 = Client number

If you are a solo practitioner, you can eliminate therapist number. With a group practice, each therapist is assigned a number. In this example, the therapist number is 03. Following the first session, assign a *case number* to the paper and electronic file. This method assists in minimizing the use of client names on materials to protect privacy (Table 5.1).

This simple spreadsheet in Table 5.1 with client ID and associated name is password protected and stored in an area of your computer only you know about. I would suggest *not* storing it with a file name such as "client names." This client ID can then be entered as the identifier in your Business Profile spreadsheet (Table 5.2). Although you could add the client name to this spreadsheet, someone accessing this spreadsheet would gain significant knowledge about your clients and their clinical issues. For this reason, you should consid-

TABLE 5.2: BUSINESS PROFILE WITH CLIENT ID

Client ID	Closing status	Care Coor. 1= yes 2 = no	Offered appt. days	Accepted appt. days	Method of appt. set (SS1)	Ease of setting (SS1)	Level of progress at closing	Number Sessions	Refer to therapist (SS2) 1= yes 2 = no	Refer to agency (SS2), 1= yes, 2 = no
200803172			3	6	1	4		9	1	1
200803173			1	5	1	4		10	1	1
200803174			0	1	1	3		3		
200803175			2	7	3	2		3	2	1
200803176			4	4	1	4		24		
200803177			3	3	3	2		1		
200803178			2	3	1	3		2	1	1
200803179			5	6	3	1		3	2	2
			2.2	4.4				6.9		

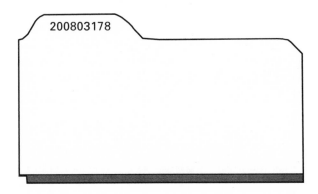

er having the separate spreadsheet file with just client ID and name. Despite being a redundant step to add client ID to the Business Profile spreadsheet, it is worth the extra few seconds and key strokes to protect client data.

Your next step is to create the client's electronic file. The name of each file will be the client ID. You have now protected your client list with a password-protected spreadsheet file, and each client chart is also password protected. You will need to create your own unique password system for easy recollection to open each unique client file.

After creating an electronic client file, you will need to create the paper file. The paper file will inevitably have forms that indicate client names because signatures are needed. On the tab, the label is the case number you assigned. You are the only one privy to whose chart this is (Figure 5.4). This system helps protect client privacy as the client name is not in the open.

E-mail Appointment Reminders

E-mail is expeditious, easy, inexpensive, and now an accepted form of communication. Our Web site has converted a number of potential clients to clients because of our e-mail reminder system. Potential clients, under distress and seeking services, feel reassurance and safety when they learn about e-mail reminders. In an era of over-commitments, e-mail reminders provide an extra bit of customer service that can pay big dividends with loyalty and lifelong customer building.

Whenever I discuss this customer service variable with therapists, the feedback I receive is that I am taking too much responsibility for my clients. E-mail reminders represent an interesting intersection of clinical work with business principles with best practice standards. Clinically, e-mail reminders might be taking too much responsibility for clients. Yet, e-mail reminders are great business interventions to increase revenue and satisfaction, and they certainly assist

BOX 5.2
Unrealized Revenue: Preventing No Shows
Conservatively estimating that e-mail reminders prevent two no-show sessions per week results in saving $7,040 per year (2 sessions per week x 4 = 8 per month x 11 months = 88 per year x $80 per session = $7,040.00).

in meeting practice standards. The bottom line, like so many practice-building interventions, is that many dynamics may need clinical attention. If you believe that sending e-mail reminders is taking too much responsibility for clients, my suggestion is to consider how to incorporate the use of reminders into a clinical discussion. E-mail reminders have far more benefits than risks if simple steps are being taken to protect privacy and avoid clinical complications.

E-mail reminders create an enormous win-win situation, providing convenience for clients and reducing income lost from no-show and late cancellations (Box 5.2). With more than 30 clients per week, it only takes a few minutes on Monday morning to send out all e-mail reminders. These few minutes greatly reduce the no-show or late cancellation rates, thereby increasing revenue. Furthermore, this process helps achieve a best practice standard by increasing client participation in care. From the client's perspective, this simple reminder demonstrates customer service. Although this reminder may not instantly build loyalty, it will create satisfaction.

Client permission. Clients are quick to say something like, "Just e-mail it to me" without considering the consequences of the action. When reminded that family members or coworkers might easily access e-mails, they often change their mind or want e-mail reminders sent to a private or unknown account. It is important to discuss this situation prior to sending e-mails. It is your responsibility to outline the possible adverse consequences and seek their written permission to allow you to send e-mails. We use an online scheduling system, and new intakes, even when scheduling their first appointment, must give permission for us to send a confirmation e-mail.

Create a simple form for clients outlining the type of system your practice uses for receiving and sending e-mails, remind them that they will be receiving e-mails that others might be able to access, and specifically ask for their permission to send to an identified e-mail account (Form 5.5).

Sanitizing E-mails. If you are using e-mails to remind clients of their appointments, it is important to "sanitize" the e-mail. Sanitizing e-mails is the process of minimizing information in the event an unanticipated party receives

Tracy Todd, PhD, LMFT
7800 South Elati Drive, #230
Littleton, CO 80120
www.btid.com

E-MAIL APPOINTMENT REMINDERS

The [your name or practice name] offers free-of-charge e-mail appointment reminders. If you would like to receive e-mail appointment reminders, please read and sign below.

I understand that [your name or practice name] uses a secure e-mail server to send and receive e-mails from clients. I understand that I am solely responsible for the security of e-mails that I send/receive and that [your name or practice name] is not responsible for a breech of privacy, confidentiality, or security for e-mails that I send/receive.

I understand that if [your name or practice name] fails to remind me of an appointment, I am still responsible for the late cancellation or no show fee agreed to at intake.

The e-mail system is solely used for appointment reminders.

The e-mail address at which I wish to receive reminders is:

_____

_____   _____
Signature   Date

_____
Print Name

or reads the e-mail. Compare the two examples of unsanitized and sanitized e-mail (Form 5.6 and Form 5.7), respectively. Sanitizing helps protect privacy in the event that an unintended party receives the e-mail. For the example, if the sanitized e-mail is read by someone other than Cindy, her privacy is still protected. It also contains a statement at the bottom of the e-mail message about legally protecting the information.

Security

Security is a fundamental necessity for the infrastructure of your business. In 20 years of practice, I have known four practices that have had client files stolen. In each situation, the therapists had appropriate security measures implemented. Techniques in *Practice-Building 2.0* actually allow much greater practice protection. For example, a client chart 2 years old is probably safer on a flash drive stored in a safe deposit box than a paper file in a file cabinet in your office.

To: Jane Doe
From: Cindy Smith, PhD, LMFT
Re: Psychotherapy appointment

Dear Jane,

This is a reminder of your family therapy session this Thursday at 4:00 P.M. As a reminder, we will be addressing the history of substance abuse in your family so that we can better discuss the issues still challenging your son William.

Sincerely,
Cindy Smith, PhD, LMFT
Do Well Therapy Center

To: Jane Doe
From: Cindy Smith
Re: Appointment reminder

Dear Jane,

I just wanted to drop a note as a reminder of your appointment this Thursday at 4:00 P.M.

Thank you,
Cindy

The information contained in this transmission is legally privileged and confidential information intended only for the use of the individual or entity named above. If the reader of this transmission is not the intended recipient, you are hereby notified that any dissemination, distribution, or duplication of this transmission is strictly prohibited. If you have received this transmission in error, please immediately notify us by telephone xxx.xxx.xxxx or via the U.S. Postal Service at [practice address here].

Infrastructure

The significant difference in infrastructure is of course the necessity to understand electronic security. Your computer needs security features that prohibit access to client information or the files within a program from storing client information. When asked, "Can someone access your computer and then access client information without a password?" your answer must be *no*.

With electronic file management, e-mail reminders, e-mail, and online scheduling, your computer will become the repository of client information. You must ensure that the computer has prudent security measures in the event of theft. Most computers have locking functions that require passwords to unlock the computer (basic and necessary), while newer computers have fingerprint identification to access. Because you are storing client information, use the most advanced security you can afford. For an extra $200, the protection is worth it. Finally, make sure your software allows password protection. Virtually all MSOffice products (i.e., Word, Excel) needed for *Practice-Building 2.0* strategies allow you to password protect each file, thereby adding another layer of privacy protection. Even the screen saver can be password protected so that once it turns on, you need a password to turn it off. Security is simply part of all newer computer systems and is easy to integrate into data protection.

Free Services

There are many free or nearly free services on the Internet, and many psychotherapy business owners, trying to cut costs, understandably enroll and use these services. Some commonly used services include Google's Gmail, Yahoo! Mail, MSN Hotmail. Associated with these systems are other functions such as data storage, Web sites, calendars, instant messaging, and CMS. These systems often advertise that you can manage all your affairs, including a business, within their environment.

Although their claims are accurate, there are some important hidden "costs." Conti (2009) provided a great discussion of the security compromises when using the Internet, particularly free services such as Google and Gmail. There are a few important considerations as they pertain to your incorporation of technology into your business. First, your computer is exposed to numerous vulnerabilities, or areas of data leakage, including such areas as e-mail, people, wired or wireless connections, peripherals (smart phones), and devices such as USB flash drives. When using free services, any and all data on your computer are vulnerable to compromises. Through various technologies, your data become a rich source of information for harvesting to serve advertising and possibly malicious actions.

Psychotherapy business owners probably face the greatest vulnerability when using free e-mail services personally and professionally. Using a free e-mail service for personal use on the same computer you store any client information exposes all client information to possible compromise. Using a free service to communicate with clients does expose all client information. For example, all e-mail sent via Gmail is read by machine. Even though claims are made that humans will not read the e-mail does not mean that humans cannot access or read e-mail (i.e., for information needed for a subpoena). Typically, machines that read your e-mail are looking for key words for advertising purposes. For those using Google or Gmail, have you ever noticed that something you are searching for or writing about suddenly appears as an advertisement on your screen? That is not an accident. Now, imagine sending an e-mail, unsanitized, to a client with the word "depression" in the content from your Gmail account. Also, it so happens that your client has a Gmail account. Guess what? It is likely that sometime in the near future, while your client is checking the Gmail account, the client will see an advertisement for an anti-depressant. Here is the kicker: *you* provided Google and the anti-depressant company with the ability to advertise to your client.

Pushing the envelope a bit further, Conti (2009) reported that one possible reason these companies offer large storage capacity for documents and e-mail is to provide the company with data for mining. Old e-mails and documents are machine scanned to provide valuable information about you.

Google is not the only company engaging in data mining. Therefore, it is important that you understand the services you are using. E-mail, Web sites, and online scheduling all offer hosting companies the opportunity to place your computer's data in a position for data mining. You should give careful consideration to the services your professional computer is using (e.g., personal e-mails via free e-mail accounts) and the services you wish to add to your business. These risks should not deter you from implementing technology. However, like anything else, be a smart shopper. If something is offered for free, it usually is not.

On a practical level, what does this information mean to your business-building efforts? First, keep your business computer free from services that can potentially scan your computer. If you are using a laptop at work for business and personal matters, discontinue the free services or transfer them to a personal computer on which you conduct only personal affairs. Second, understand what and how information is stored with an online scheduling system. Systems that have customers register to use the scheduling function with auto-syncing to your personal digital assistant (PDA) or Smart Phone boast many technological advantages. However, once your client has registered to use the system, his or her registration information (e.g., name, date of birth, phone number, and so on) are potentially part of a database that can be data mined and possibly never permanently deleted. Similarly, if choosing to use a free Web site service or shared service, understand whether the service is data mining the visitors to your Web site. Finally, try to keep your links away from your Web site minimal. For example, if you decide to participate in the Amazon Associates Program, recognize that Amazon tracks the origination of each referral. This means that a visitor to your Web Site who clicks a link to a specific book on Amazon and subsequently purchasing that book has left a footprint showing that he or she came from a psychotherapy Web Site. Is this a confidentiality breach? It is not, because there is no way Amazon can determine if the person was visiting your site or actually a client. However, if you are using Gmail to communicate to your clients, then it is quite easy for the search engine functions associated with Google and the direct referral to Amazon to create a conclusion that the person purchasing a book from Amazon is also a client.

In the end, security and privacy matters regarding technology are a matter of prudence and comfort. Allowing complications to paralyze your business-building efforts will compromise your business potential. At the same time, being careless or inconsiderate of basic Internet privacy and safety protocols will jeopardize trust among your clients, future clients, and treatment stakeholders. Fox (2008) reported that users of the Internet are less worried about privacy issues, accepting that life on the Internet does compromise privacy. Therefore, it is incumbent on therapists to take the necessary steps to either protect or warn customers of privacy risks.

Infrastructure Technology Options

E-Newsletters

Newsletters are radically changing. Creating paper newsletters, especially with color print, is quite expensive. Add postage costs and envelopes, and these great ideas quickly fade into another good idea never implemented. With technology, newsletters take on an entirely new dimension. First, they are affordable. There are no printing or distribution costs. Second, they can become interactive. Third, your creativity is limitless because you are not constrained by paper printing limitations.

E-newsletters can be distributed basically two ways. First, you can create your newsletter and directly send it to subscribers (remember CAN-SPAM). Second, you can send e-mails to your subscribers to highlight the contents of the newsletter, including a link in the body of the e-mail to take the reader directly to the newsletter on your Web Site. If you send the newsletter via an attachment to e-mail, be sure to include in the newsletter a link to your Web Site.

Regardless of distribution, your newsletter can be colorful, graphical, include links to resources, and if posted on your Web Site, even include audio and video. Newsletters become fun to create and read.

Finally, e-news is free to deliver. With your e-mail merge program, you can deliver newsletters as frequently as your subscribers will tolerate. Gone are the barriers of postage and labor associated with stamping, labeling, and stuffing envelopes. Over the course of nearly 10 years of sending paper newsletters, I consistently had 3–5% of those receiving the newsletter call for additional appointments. Keep in mind, as your distribution list grows, so does the number of referrals resulting from your newsletter (Box 5.3).

BOX 5.3
Unrealized Revenue: Quarterly Newsletter

Assume you send quarterly newsletters (200) and conservatively each distribution results in a 3% return rate (6 per quarterly distribution or 24 per year) of clients returning for a "reality check" or "tune up." Estimating fewer sessions because of the prevention focus, use three sessions; the resulting referrals yield $5,760.00 per year (24 referrals x 3 sessions = 72 sessions per year since they are more likely to be prevention services x $80 per session = $5,760.00).

Online Therapy Strategies

Online therapy is receiving a great deal of attention, and there is significant debate regarding effectiveness, ethics, and legal issues surrounding it. Online therapy can range from simple e-mail exchanges to more complicated and elaborate interfacing with clients. Regardless of one's position concerning online therapy, it is here stay.

All online therapy methods provide convenience while presenting serious security issues and risks that each therapist must assess. Despite your comfort with using the Internet for therapy purposes, you need to provide adequate discussion about risks to privacy to your clients. Help them make informed decisions.

E-mail Exchange Therapy. Some important variables include your agreement and disclosures, finances, billing, and privacy policies (Form 5.8). Your agreement and disclosures need to identify your basic policies and procedures when conducting e-mail exchange. For example, how often will e-mails get responses? Clear agreements are necessary prior to engaging in therapeutic e-mail exchanges with clients.

Unlike sanitized e-mail reminders that protect confidentiality, e-mail exchange therapy cannot be sanitized. Therefore, choosing to use e-mail exchange therapy requires a secure and encrypted e-mail account with security and protections.

Another consideration is storage of clinical e-mail. Will each e-mail be printed on paper and placed in a hardcopy file? Will the e-mail be copied and stored in your electronic file management system? When will you delete and then permanently delete the e-mail from your computer? Deleting typically involves moving a document or file to "trash" but not permanently deleting it from the computer. You will need a system that "empties the trash" to ensure your e-mail exchanges are deleted. Again, these important questions must be addressed with clients before engaging in regular e-mail exchanges.

Tracy Todd, PhD, LMFT
7800 S. Elati Drive, #230
Littleton, CO 80120

**BRIEF THERAPY
INSTITUTE
OF DENVER**
www.btid.com

The Brief Therapy Institute of Denver, Inc. offers online supportive therapy. If you are interested in participating in online supportive therapy, please complete this form.

I understand the Brief Therapy Institute of Denver Inc. uses a secure e-mail server to send and receive e-mails from clients. My therapist will make every effort to respond to any e-mails I may send the following morning.

I understand that I am solely responsible for the security of e-mails that I send/receive and the Brief Therapy Institute of Denver Inc. is not responsible for a breech of privacy, confidentiality, or security for e-mails that I send or receive.

I understand and agree that I will **not** use the online supportive therapy system for emergencies or critical situations needing immediate responses. I understand that emergencies and critical situations will be addressed telephonically, through a pager system, or by voice mail.
I understand that the charge for online supportive therapy services are

> $50.00 per 30 minutes
> $90.00 per 60 minutes
> $120.00 per 90 minutes

payable prior to starting online supportive therapy.

My therapist will indicate at the end of each e-mail the time spent for responding to my e-mail, the total charge for the e-mail exchange, and my remaining balance. When I have a balance of less than $5.00. I will either purchase more online supportive therapy services *or* my therapist will refund any remaining balance and online supportive therapy services will be terminated.

Payment for services can be made via cash, check, Visa/MasterCard.

By signing below, I have read and agreed to these terms and conditions. I want to purchase the $_____ per _____ minute plan. The e-mail address I wish to use for conducting online therapy support is: _____

_____   _____
                Signature   Date

_____
              Print Name

You may fax this form to [fax number here].

Billing for e-mail exchange is another area that needs careful attention to policy and procedures. When clients send questions, they usually do not consider your thought process prior to sending a response. They might ask questions discussed in a previous session that requires research and a review of notes. Your research time needs reimbursement. However, the actual typing time of a response might only be for two or three sentences and may create some customer distress when they realize a bill for $40.00 (30 minutes worth of work). Understandably, clients question how a few sentences can cost so much. The difficulty with e-mail exchange, unlike therapeutic conversation, is that clients are not present for the actual processing time. Therefore, clients believe they are being billed for the typing of the response (two or three sentences), not the research or thought behind the message.

Another area requiring careful thought involves the billing model. Will clients receive monthly bills for e-mail exchanges? Is a retainer system preferred? Sending a monthly statement to bill clients for services rendered "fits" with how therapists typically conduct business. However, because this method may create collection problems, a retainer system might require clients to pay $100 in advance. When the retainer is depleted, another $100 is collected. This method requires less worry about collections.

Instant or Text Messaging. Clients and former clients have varying demographics, with clients under 35 years old more comfortable interacting with e-mail and instant messaging. There are numerous occasions when working with adolescents that they ask if we could use text messages. They are surprised, given the other technological components of the practice, that I decline. Yet, I am certain there are brave and innovative therapists engaging in this form of client–therapist interaction. *Psychotherapy Finances* ("Technology," 2006) reported how two therapists use chat rooms to provide therapy services.

E-mail therapy and possibly text messaging, however, do seem to have a time and place:

- Business professionals traveling a great deal.
- Your schedule has no immediate openings.
- Clients live in rural settings and travel may not be easily conducted.
- Mother nature (snowstorms, hurricanes, and so on) limits face-to-face interactions.

E-mail exchanges and online therapy forums become the ideal solution to such complications. Boundaries play into conducting e-mail exchanges. Clients clearly need to know when you will respond so they are not filling your e-mail box because they have not heard from you in the last 15 minutes. E-mail exchanges can quickly become unmanageable.

Clients and former clients do appreciate having the opportunity to ask "quick questions" rather than needing to schedule an appointment. This connection is convenient, creates satisfaction, and over time will build loyalty. Clients appreciate the opportunity to ask clarifying questions about homework tasks or to get a note of reassurance.

Potential clients, knowing of the availability of e-mail therapy, may schedule with you for this very reason. For example, during an intake appointment one of my clients explained that she scheduled her appointment while in Hong Kong, downloaded and printed her paperwork in Los Angeles, and arrived in Denver 2 days prior, and would be in town for another 5 days before going back on the road. Her company, every month, gave the sales representatives travel itineraries, often taking her out of town for weeks. Not believing her problem was "too serious," she felt having e-mail exchanges might be good for "reality checks." She appreciated both the online scheduling and the opportunity for e-mail exchange.

Skyping. Another method of delivering online therapy services is through the Web site Skype (www.skype.com). The *only* tools needed to use Skype are a high-speed internet connection and Webcam. A Skype account allows two people to converse via the Internet and Web cam. One criticism of e-mail exchange therapy is that a therapist cannot see a client. With Skype, you are able to see your client while conversing. Again, however, you need to give careful consideration to privacy and security issues when discussing sensitive issues via the Internet. Skype is not a secured connection, and it is possible that your interactions are not private.

With returning military personnel, accustomed to using Skype for family interactions, there will be increasing demand for this method of service delivery. Skype is free and easy to set up, and face-to-face interactions take on new meaning. I have my reservations about this form of interaction and have only one experience, therefore I cannot speak from the expert perspective. However, when a family I was seeing for some common adolescent challenges arrived with a computer in my office so they could "include mom" in the session, I was curious. I clarified whether security or privacy was a concern, and they stated they felt her input was more important, so we proceeded. Five minutes later, mom was in my office while serving in Iraq. I admit that after a few minutes of adjusting to the new medium, I became comfortable, and the family—including mom—was extremely appreciative of the opportunity. Reflecting on the interaction later in the day, I found myself surprised at the high quality of the session, and the lack of the mother's physical presence did not have a significant impact on the therapy process. Furthermore, the family was grateful for my participation in this form of therapy interaction. The risk–reward ratio is something every therapist needs to consider. After taking the proper security precautions, Skype provides another practice-building tool.

Online Environment Therapy. Mytherapynet.net (www.mytherapynet.com) virtually eliminates the complications and challenges of e-mail exchange and Skype methods of online therapy. This environment allows teleconference, Webcams, instant messaging, and much more. Billing is handled by the service, thereby keeping reimbursement issues minimal.

Practicing psychotherapy over the Internet has many controversial issues. There is no set of rules and regulations, and each therapist should inquire with their professional association and state regulatory boards about ethics and standards of online therapy.

Derrig-Palumbo and Zeine (2005) did a great job of explaining how to run an online therapy practice. Their online therapy environment Mytherapynet advertises privacy compliance. Mytherapynet.com is a good example of a fully contained service environment that provides a forum for online therapy. They claim to have created a secure environment that allows therapists and clients to interact through multiple methods: Webcam, chat, audio, telephone. They also provide the billing mechanism and other useful tools to conduct online therapy. Such an environment eliminates the privacy concerns of using an online therapy mechanism such as Skype.

There is enormous potential for conducting online therapy in such self-contained environments. Users need to worry less about having technology and security measures and can focus on performing therapy. Understandably, the potential for practice growth is impressive. Therapists, minimally, need to examine this option closely before ruling it out. It provides the advantages of providing your practice with self-pay clients, convenience to both therapist and client, and a growing demographic in which this form of service delivery is extremely marketable.

Listed are some resources for further exploration regarding online therapy:

- The American Association of Online Psychotherapists: www.aaop.com
- PsychCentral, online therapy information: http://psychcentral.com/resources/
- Ask The Internet Therapist: www.asktheinternettherapist.com
- Therapist Online: Private Healthcare: www.therapistonline.org
- Guidelines for Mental Health and Healthcare Practice Online: www.ethicscode.com

Online Seminars/Webinars/Teleclasses. Online education can range from a simple podcast and PDF (portable document file) to an elaborate PowerPoint with video integration and voice narration. The technology for creating good online seminars is most likely already on your computer. You simply need to create a PowerPoint presentation with voice narration and accompanying handouts (PDF format). Keep in mind that your PowerPoint presentation will record in .wav file format, taking up space, so you will need to either keep the presentation shorter or use a flash converter. Another method is not to include voice narration but set up a conference call with participants. By creating a hidden Web page, not accessible to the public, they can follow your presentation and ask you questions while you are presenting.

Importantly, offering a simple class provides many advantages to practice building, and these classes are easy to create. For these two reasons, every practice should consider some form of online seminar format to increase revenues. Online educational forums have a good potential for becoming supportive aides to your practice or revenue generators. Monitoring treatment trends provides clues for potential classes. For example, over the last 18 months you notice that you are treating a number of individuals adjusting to divorce. Predicting some normative emotional challenges related to the holiday season, a seminar is created: "Your First *Single* Holiday Season." Depending on your energy level and time, you could create a "miniclass" consisting of tips and suggestions. The entire presentation could be 8 to 10 minutes, done in PowerPoint with voice narration and an accompanying one-page sheet of tips and strategies. Then, send a quick e-mail to all your clients, former clients, and treatment stakeholders (who have given permission for such e-mails), and you are finished. Although you noticed this trend among current clients, sending to your entire distribution list is advantageous because those who are lifelong customers, or soon to be, will advertise the class for you without asking.

Choosing to create a more expansive seminar to generate income might result in creating more comprehensive materials and then scheduling a 90-minute teleconference. Participants could dial in to a conference calling system and begin working with you as the seminar leader. They would have the opportunity to ask questions and discuss important issues.

Smart Phones

Raising the bar of technological sophistication requires raising the bar on your own personal access to your practice/business. Smart phones (e.g., Blackberry, Treo, iPhone) are devices that allow access to calendars, e-mail, and the Internet as well as make routine telephone calls. Each feature becomes increasingly important as upgrades are made to a business. A smart phone is a fundamental infrastructure tool. Privacy regulations require secure, backup copies of all personal health information. Almost everyone using paper scheduling systems has client names, phone numbers, and maybe even a scribble or two about individuals. Guess what? You are carrying around a document that now is subject to privacy regulations. Do you have a backup copy of your planner? Is it under lock and key? These are two fundamental privacy standards for the protection of personal health information. With a smart phone, you can store all the same information, have backups made daily, and use passwords to protect any personal health information. It scares me to observe therapists using a paper scheduling system. The information is never backed up. Further, it is easily deduced by finding a therapist's day planner what all those names stand for . . . clients. There is *no* privacy protection or security with a paper planner.

When engaging in e-mail exchange therapy, it is good to know someone has e-mailed and awaits a response. Smart phones are more than simply fun or cool to own; they are highly functional tools for practice building and management.

Keeping in mind that a private practice is also a small business, psychotherapists tend to forget that image is important, particularly to the more hip and technologically sophisticated millennial population born between 1977 and 1998. This demographic not only uses technology but also demands technology. Furthermore, 44% of 18 to 29-year-olds and 41% of 30- to 49-year-olds use mobile devices to stay connected (Horrigan, 2008). After scheduling her first appointment online, a young lady (under 30 years old) arrived for her appointment and soon into the session asked if I used a paper scheduling system or a gadget. I found this to be an interesting question and informed her I use a smart phone. I then asked why this information was important to her. Stating that she had seen two "older" therapists, she elaborated that their advice seemed parental, and they were old fashioned because of paper scheduling. Chuckling, I asked if she really thought I would use a paper scheduling system since we offer online scheduling and video introductions. Although this example is exceptional, clients are becoming more sophisticated and are evaluating therapists based on tools and practice patterns.

Summary

Practice-building encompasses more than simple strategies to increase referrals. Practice-*Building* includes utilizing technology as the backbone for your business to reduce labor, increase cost efficiencies, and thereby allow more time to focus on strategies that result in increased profit margin endeavors. Although not glamorous, integrating Web Site functionality with a CMS and electronic file management results in substantial gains in revenue and savings in labor costs.

The planning of these steps is critical. Building a practice in a flattening world with consumers with greater expectations requires forethought. Plan, organize, and invest in your business as though it is what it is, a *business*. All businesses need investment in their operations, psychotherapy practices are no different. Fortunately, in today's technological world; the investments for a solid private practice are inexpensive, requiring more time than money.

Key Points

1. Technology results in both increased direct revenues and decreased labor costs, resulting in substantial positive revenue.
2. Immediately implementing infrastructure technology is a critically important practice. Avoid the trap of "I only have 5 clients so I don't need it," or when you have 25 clients this becomes "I have 25 clients and I don't have the time."
3. E-mail is necessary for strategies given in *Practice-Building 2.0.*
4. With e-mail comes security and privacy considerations: encryption, storage, addresses.
5. Understand the CAN-SPAM law as it applies to your business.
6. An electronic file management system is vital for streamlining your infra structure.
7. Remember to sanitize all e-mail appointment reminders.
8. E-newsletters are vital for practice building.
9. Online therapy can take many forms and is here to stay. Consider the option and your risk tolerance.

Action List

1. Purchase a CMS if you do not have one.
2. Create an intake system that allows you to capture and enter necessary data into your CMS.
3. Purchase a dedicated business e-mail account. Avoid public accounts such as Hotmail, Gmail, AOL, and the like.
4. Within your e-mail program, create separate folders for sending and receiving e-mails to keep personal and professional e-mails separate.
5. Purchase an e-mail merge program so you can engage in confidential e-mail distributions.
6. Convert all forms, letters, and documents to a template system with form fields, drop-down menus, and prepopulated fields.
7. Create a client identification system.
8. Create password-protected files for client identification and client files.
9. Create a unique method for recalling passwords for client files.
10. Create client authorization forms for e-mail reminders and, if you choose, online therapy.
11. Weigh online therapy risks and decide whether this is an option you will pursue.
12. Possibly purchase a smart phone.

CHAPTER SIX

Purposefully Building Loyalty and Lifelong Customers

You are well on your way to building and sustaining a practice for the new millennium:

- You are aware of the myths of practice building.
- You understand the importance of satisfaction, loyalty, and lifelong customers.
- You can differentiate and prioritize referral pools.
- You understand the necessary technologies needed for strategies in *Practice-Building 2.0*.
- You can strategize and apply those technologies to various referral pools.
- You recognize how implementing technology creates positive revenue opportunities.

In Chapter 5 I outlined how *Practice-Building 2.0* technological strategies increase revenue, reduce labor, and create positive revenue opportunities. *Practice-Building 2.0* strategies involve taking these applied strategies and tools one step further. It is important that you give purposeful thought to specific loyalty-building activities along the treatment continuum. These loyalty building activities vary between therapists and practices, allowing accentuation of those strategies that ensure the greatest potential for both high-quality care and advertising. This chapter focuses on pulling the strategies and technologies together, thereby maximizing all practice-building efforts.

Flagship Services

What services are you offering that clients, former clients, and treatment stake-holders find extraordinary? One or two select extraordinary loyalty-building services should represent your practice and demonstrate your commitment to high-quality services. Most companies consider these services or products as their "flagship" services. These flagship services have the sole purpose of carry-ing a reputation and creating lifelong, loyal, customers.

For example, a dentist may have a full range of dental services but have the flagship service of helping high-anxiety patients. Automobile manufacturers will have a flagship car. Before the Internet, the Brief Therapy Institute of Den-ver Inc. (BTID) flagship service was orientation paperwork sent prior to the first appointment. Immediately upon scheduling an appointment clients were sent orientation material. However, this service changed with our first Web site because we could upload paperwork, thereby allowing new clients the lux-ury of downloading and completing it before their first appointment. Now, with an increasing number of providers building Web sites and offering orien-tation information on them, this service is no longer our flagship service. Although we continue to offer paperwork downloads and orientation infor-mation, our flagship service has changed. Understanding that our competitors lack online scheduling services, we now promote online scheduling as our flagship service.

Care variables should be integrated at all steps of the treatment process. If, however, you were to choose a flagship service variable, the one you want everyone to mention when they talk about your practice, what would it be? There is no correct or incorrect answer, rather just the answer that makes for great advertising. Importantly, choose a service variable you believe will create lifelong customers. Pay attention to your data. Quite possibly, clients indicate on satisfaction surveys that they appreciate your e-mail reminder system. Maybe e-mail reminders become your flagship service.

Another consideration are your competitors. Do your homework. Do they have Web sites? If so, what type of functionality do the sites have? These com-petitors are accessing the same treatment stakeholders and referral sources. What will you offer that draws business away from your competitors? After learning about their services, consider a flagship service to create a competitive advantage. Some possible flagship services include:

- Intake paperwork download
- Online scheduling
- E-mail appointment reminders using a secure, encrypted system
- Self-help handouts

TABLE 6.1: LOYALTY BUILDING MATRIX

Service variable	Satisfaction	Loyalty	Lifelong customer
Web site	x	x	x
E-mail reminders	x	x	x
Paperwork download	x		
Online scheduling	x	x	
Podcast	x	x	x
Contact management system	x		

Keep in mind that your services do not need to be entirely different from those of a competitor to achieve a competitive advantage. For example, a competitor might advertise offering e-mail appointment reminders to customers, but does the competitor advertise "secure and encrypted" e-mail? With privacy being a major concern, this simple and inexpensive difference could be the difference in customer choice when comparing therapists.

Why are specific loyalty-building activities and flagship services so important? Simply put, they become the highlights when advertising your practice. Integrating the many strategies and activities found in *Practice-Building 2.0* will fortunately create a situation in which you cannot fully describe your practice to others in a simple brochure or in 30 seconds. Certain loyalty-building services should be so powerful that they grab the attention of your clients and treatment stakeholders, thereby becoming your flagship services. As you develop your practice and adapt to future unknown additions to practice patterns, your flagship services and customer service and loyalty-building points will change.

Creating a matrix is your next step (Table 6.1). Take some time to list all the service variables your practice offers treatment stakeholders, clients, and former clients. At least start with those you plan to implement within the next 12 months. This matrix assists in identifying whether you have ample tools and strategies to create satisfaction, loyalty, and lifelong customers. Although the distinction between these three areas is not always clear, keep in mind that satisfying events over time create loyalty, and the stronger the loyalty bond is the greater the likelihood you are creating a lifelong customer. There is no right or wrong about whether a strategy creates satisfaction or loyalty. More important, however, is that throughout the treatment continuum you are highlighting your services, to develop satisfaction and loyalty. After listing your current services, you may find it helpful to organize all these services in a timeline. Your timeline begins prior to treatment and ends 1 year posttreatment.

When developing the matrix, keep in mind that variables can be duplicated. For example, e-mail reminders might be a satisfying reason for a new referral to schedule an appointment. However, over the course of treatment and numerous unknown (to you) times the reminders served the purpose, and your client did not forget an appointment, thereby avoiding the late cancellation or no show fee. Because the client consistently attended therapy, your services were more effective, leading to a higher-quality therapy experience, and it is hoped resulting in loyalty and a lifelong customer. Such subtleties, unrecognized by those not using a reminder system, clearly need strategizing for implementation to create production.

Example Worksheets

Starting an e-mail reminder system involves a bit more than waking up on Monday morning and starting to send e-mails to clients. Worksheet 6.1 is an example of the steps involved to start e-mail reminders. The steps are simple,

WORKSHEET 6.1: STRATEGY FOR E-MAIL REMINDERS

Strategy or Tool: E-mail Reminders

Technology needed: E-mail, preferably with secure Web site connection

	Strategy tasks	Target date	Helpful person?
1	Obtain an e-mail account from my Web-hosting company; consider whether I may do e-mail exchange therapy and need a secure e-mail account (Chapter 4)	Next 30 days	My neighbor works for a tech company, I will ask; if yes, problem solved
2	Create an e-mail reminder agreement (Chapter 5)	Next 30 days	I can do
3	Create a form/template e-mail reminder letter (Chapter 5)	Next 30 days	Still a bit fuzzy on forms. Sister is great with word processing I will ask her to teach me
4	Have a disclosure statement concluding the e-mail reminder	Next 30 days	I can do
5	Sanitized e-mail reminder	Next 30 days	I can do
6	Create an announcement to post in the waiting room	Days 30–45	I can do
7	Create an announcement for the Web site	Days 30–45	I can do
8	Send announcement to all treatment stakeholders and former clients	Day 45	I can do
9	Begin with all current clients; start with any new intakes	Day 45	Done

take minimal time to complete, but when thought of as a whole, easily overwhelm many. If someone is technologically savvy, then let that person look into secure Web mail. Someone who is a privacy expert can write the agreement. If you are a solo practitioner, maybe you can seek help from a family member or friend to find the SSL (secure sockets layer) and secure Web mail system. That is worth a nice lunch for the helper, and from there you can easily complete the process.

Video technology is now common, no longer requiring expensive specialty services or equipment. Remember, if you are a solo practitioner or practice in a small group, there is a "good enough" level of quality. Importantly, do not become intimidated by this endeavor. Most families now have digital camcorders, nearly all computers have some sort of video-editing software preinstalled, and the only technical piece needed is a microphone. Make a recording and do some edits and the video is ready to be published. Assuming your Web site can accommodate a 3- to 5-minute video, publishing the video is the final step. I know: You are thinking I make it sound too easy. Candidly, the most challenging aspect of publishing a video to your Web site is getting out of your own way. You will need to resist the temptation to make many recordings because this or that was not perfect (Worksheet 6.2).

If you are in a group practice, these worksheets help with coordinating tasks as responsibility can be shared in creating the system. These two examples demonstrate that breaking down tasks creates manageability. Rather than considering the overwhelming nature of each, it is important to take your time and schedule each project. Seek help where you needed.

Task

At this point, you have a matrix of service variables to enhance satisfaction, loyalty, and potential for lifelong customers. After creating the matrix, develop your worksheet for each variable and begin scheduling the projects. Consider how your services can be satisfaction- and loyalty-building opportunities.

Satisfaction- and Loyalty-Building Points

Practice-building opportunities are those natural or automatic points along the treatment continuum at which a client or another professional experience services so great that they become loyal to you and your treatment agency. These opportunities *do not* stop when you secure a new referral. It is a rare therapist that (a) has identified opportunities for building loyalty, (b) has tools for maintaining loyalty, and (c) continues emphasizing loyalty following treatment. Ask yourself, "How does your clinical and administrative system build and sustain satisfaction and loyalty before, during, and after treatment?"

WORKSHEET 6.2: STRATEGY FOR VIDEO INTRODUCTION

Strategy or Tool: Video Introduction on Web Site

Technology needed: Digital video camera, good microphone for camera

	Strategy tasks	Target date	Helpful person?
1	Practice creating good enough video with sound using camera and editing system, I'm going to be a talking head, so I should look good chest up; no bright colors and an acceptable back drop	Next 45 days	My spouse enjoys this activity, seek assistance
2	Contact Web hosting company and inquire about process to post a video.	Next 20 days	I can do
3	Create a 3-minute script introducing myself and services	Next 30 days	Friend writes advertise-ments, get her help
4	Read my script to family, friends, colleagues	Days 30–45	I can do
5	Modify script to create right "tone" for my personality and professional style	Days 30–45	Validate via family and friends
6	Memorize my 3-minute introduction	Days 45–60	I can do
7	Create usable video; this may take a few hours to capture it "just right"	Day 60+	My spouse can play producer
8	Submit the video file to web hosting com-pany or publish the video myself	Day 60+	I can do
9	Done	Day 60+	Call my friends and have them watch the video

Developing Loyalty Before Therapy

Loyalty starts *before* a person or family becomes a client. For example, when accessing your services, is there something so impressive that a potential client, who has never met you, has an overwhelming positive reaction? There are numerous service variables that can begin to create satisfaction and loyalty prior to therapy:

- Video introduction
- Self-help handouts
- Self-help readings
- Online scheduling
- Paperwork download
- Podcasts

Potential new clients and treatment stakeholders who make referrals find these services helpful. These are services all practices should be offering, but intentionally accentuating a specific service (flagship) such as online scheduling, sets a positive first impression. Compare the following two conversations.

Nakita, referred by her primary care physician, listens to Bill's (therapist) voice mail and leaves the following message, "Hi, my name is Nakita and I would like to schedule an appointment. My doctor has referred me to you."

A few hours later, Bill calls Nakita and after some small talk asks:

BILL: I have a 7:00 P.M. open on Thursday. Will that work?
NAKITA: Yes, and I would like to ask you some basic questions about your qualifications.
BILL: No problem. What would you like me to answer?

Nakita and Bill spend a few minutes reviewing his qualifications.

BILL: Do you have any other questions?
NAKITA: No, I think that covers it all.
BILL: Can I get some basic information from you?

Bill then collects his basic client information. Variations of this conversation are common between a client and therapist when scheduling an initial appointment. The client is satisfied making personal contact with the therapist, and the therapist is satisfied a new client is scheduled. Neither knows that a different exchange potentially exists.

In this scenario, Nakita, referred by her primary care physician to both Bill's voice mail and Web site, calls and listens to Bill's voice mail, which includes the phrase, "If you would like to learn more about me or schedule an appointment online, please visit our Web site at www.btid.com." Nakita does not leave a message. About 30 minutes later, Bill receives a text message on his cell phone indicating that someone has scheduled an appointment for 7:00 P.M. Thursday. Bill accesses the online scheduling system and collects the information Nakita provided. Bill calls her to confirm the appointment.

BILL: Hello Nakita. I noticed you scheduled an appointment with me this Thursday at 7:00 p.m.. Do you have any questions that I can answer?
NAKITA: No everything was self-explanatory. I think my husband is going to like you, your style, and your qualifications. We also appreciated scheduling an appointment at our convenience. I called my husband and read him your available times, and I did not need to guess when he could make it. That is so cool.
BILL: Thank you. Did you have any problems downloading the paperwork?
NAKITA: No. We will have it done before we get there. We will start

reading one of the books you recommend for couples, and we want
to listen to your communication podcast before our appointment.

BILL: Great. Do you have any questions?

NAKITA: Well, I noticed one of the forms I downloaded asked us to list
our goals for therapy. Should we do those together or separately?

BILL: Do them separately, and we will compare notes during the session.

NAKITA: Okay.

BILL: See you Thursday.

The second conversation has a higher likelihood of creating *loyalty*. From
Bill's Web site, Nakita reviewed his professional biography, scheduled an
appointment and examined the paperwork. The "tone" involves more "personality," allowing Nakita, her husband, and Bill to start the joining process prior
to therapy. Nakita and Bill bypassed having a conversation about his professional qualifications and delved into questions about the therapy process.
Although this may seem subtle, consider some additional benefits of this simple process:

- Nakita visited Bill's Web site because her primary care physician and Bill's
  voice mail indicated he had a Web site. Bill has done a nice job of
  driving traffic to his Web site to enhance a potential client's experience
  and save him labor. A customer's visit to your Web site is a process for
  which you need complete understanding. As you gain knowledge of
  what drives traffic to your Web site, you can develop strategies to drive
  more traffic and convert visitors to customers.
- Nakita and her husband found the process convenient and "cool." The
  cool factor cannot be overlooked. Of the process, what was it that they
  found cool (video, paperwork download capabilities), and why did they
  think these service variables were cool? Understanding this information
  places Bill in an advantageous position over competition. Also,under-
  standing what is cool helps him identify his flagship service if he has
  not already.
- Nakita has a higher potential of accessing Bill's Web site for future
  services. Bill has laid the foundation for creating a lifelong customer.
  Assuming Nakita and her husband find additional information on the
  Web site helpful they will continue to access the Web site as long as Bill
  keeps the Web site updated.
- Nakita can easily refer family and friends. This dynamic may be the most
  important. If she relies on Bill's Web site for high quality information,
  she is likely to pass on the Web address to others.
- Bill's Web site has an interactive component (self-help handouts, pod-

Purposefully Building Loyalty and Lifelong Customers   167

casts, and more) that Nakita and potential clients can access. Podcasts or simple audio file postings create interaction and connection to Bill even without his knowledge. Nakita may refer a friend to the Web site; the friend listens to a podcast and becomes comfortable with Bill's style and demeanor. Now, the foundation is laid for turning a visitor into a customer.

- Nakita can access information long after therapy ends. She is in a position, say 3 years later, to access Bill for additional services if needed.

The difference between the two scenarios is that the Web presence and high technology of the second scenario are powerful practice-building tools. They are not simply nice features of a practice located on a Web site.

Unlike the 1990s and early 2000s, when information was the commodity, today the commodity is the *conduit* to the information. The Internet has fundamentally changed the value of information—there is no value. Information is abundantly prevalent. Perform a quick Google search and information on nearly every subject is on your computer in seconds. Keep in mind that this is not just didactic information. Rather, it will be likely that videos, podcasts, discussion forums, blogs, and polls are just seconds away. The reliability and validity of the information are suspect. As a trusted provider of health care services, your treatment stakeholders, clients, former clients, and visitors should trust the information on your site. It is your responsibility to ensure links and resources are credible, high-quality pieces. Compiling these resources and publishing your own information provides a great service and advertising opportunity for your practice.

Becoming a community resource to all three rings of referrals is a primary objective of your Web site. Keep in mind your practice demographics. For example, if your practice is primarily children and teenagers, then your Web site needs to be geared toward the parents of this population as well as the kids. Today's teenagers may use your Web site more than ever. If your practice is primarily couples, then your Web site needs to cater to their specific needs.

Resources are limitless. If your local paper posts information on summer day camps in early spring, you can add this link to your resource sections. Other ideas for resources include

- Symptom-tracking tools
- Job classified ads
- Financial counseling services
- Bookstores
- Family vacation-planning guides
- Self-help guides and podcasts

- Web sites specifically addressing treatment populations
- Services such as WebMD
- Career counseling Web sites

When creating a community resource linking to other sites, never lead a viewer away from your Web site. Always have new links open in new windows.

I often hear therapists state, "I feel like I'm giving away information that they should pay for," or "Why do they need to see me if I'm giving them this information?" Really, are your skills and knowledge so limited that short bits of information on a Web site can replace you? Ironically, you will actually gain more business by having information available. Think about it for a moment. Any time you access and utilize a company's information, you are placing trust in that company. This trust potentially leads to loyalty and potentially lifelong customers. So, although you may lose a session or two because some former clients accessed information, thereby not needing your face-to-face services, you are developing trust and loyalty. Remember, information on your Web site is not the same as having a therapy session. True, former clients may not need an immediate session, but you are providing them with convenient, reliable information. Whatever information you consider costing you a session or two is already on the Web. There is no such thing as secret information—especially in mental health. Keep your clients and stakeholders loyal to your Web site by providing high-quality information and resources.

Developing Loyalty During Therapy

Good clinical services should develop satisfied and loyal clients. Take a moment and consider what makes you a loyal customer to a dentist, primary care physician, plumber, or auto mechanic. There are many professionals delivering your needed services, but why do you keep going back to the same professional?

After moving into a house, the swamp cooler needed service. I never owned a swamp cooler and lacked knowledge about starting it. After receiving a mailer (pre-service) from the Heat Guy offering "spring hookup," I called and scheduled an appointment. Jim, the serviceman, showed up on time (+). Before entering the house, Jim put on some slippers to keep the floors clean (+). As Jim hooked up the unit, he explained each step of the process (+) and showed me where someone had "cheated," causing some water damage (+). After completing the service, Jim walked me through how to operate and troubleshoot the system (+). He accepted my mailer coupon (+). During the entire process, Jim was exceptionally polite, kept me informed, answered questions, and constantly offered tips and ideas (+). I am now loyal to the Heat Guy and never shop around for these services.

Compare the Heat Guy to my former primary care physician. After two appointments with a new physician, I discontinued the relationship. Why? The first appointment started over 90 minutes late with no explanation, not even a weak excuse. The second appointment, which I scheduled so it was the first of the day, started 45 minutes late. Why? Because I helped an elderly couple through the main door, and they signed in before me. They were seen first, and I waited. When I was seen, the physician acted like the receptionist, as though I was a burden.

Quality services are critical for practice-building success. For example, Jennifer and her husband, Bill, bring their son in for an evaluation for attention deficit hyperactivity disorder (ADHD). They are upset with this diagnosis because they report feeling it was imposed on them and never really evaluated. During the assessment process, you give them some informational handouts and a tracking log for ADHD behaviors. As you are talking, you are also discussing options with them. You give them the opportunity to provide feedback and explore ideas. Because they are a busy family, you have implemented e-mail appointment reminders. You also have a podcast with some basic information about ADHD. After a few sessions, you conclude that the diagnosis of ADHD is correct and begin working with their pediatrician. You engage in some high-quality care coordination, and you keep the parents informed of what you and the pediatrician are considering for treatment. When you make your recommendation to the parents, they are satisfied because they feel well informed, kept in the information loop, and that their son is receiving high-quality care. The use of podcasts and e-mail appointment reminders has enhanced the care, while care coordination with the pediatrician provided high-quality services. Following treatment, the parents receive a satisfaction survey, and they request electronic newsletters. You now have a lifelong client.

Web site. Although many advantages of a Web site seemingly benefit pretreatment and post-treatment clients, review your Web site design to ensure that there are services available to current clients and treatment stakeholders. Current clients might benefit from an online symptom inventory, a clinical feedback form, blog, or a handout of self-help skills. Treatment stakeholders, sharing a current client, can benefit from a symptom inventory or podcasts about specific self-help strategies, to help them stay on the "same page" as your treatment philosophy.

E-News. Providing treatment stakeholders with news about your practice will have unrecognizable or unpredictable gains. We live in a busy environment, and good providers, regardless of services—mental health, medical, financial planning, legal—are always looking for tips, strategies, and tools to become more effective. By providing news to your treatment stakeholders, you keep them abreast of the happenings in your practice and quality resources, saving them time searching for information. You never know what they might find helpful. For example, a human resource director with whom you coordinated care on numerous occasions receives a newsletter from you highlighting summer vacation resources for children. The director posts these resources for the employees of the corporation. This information helps employees and enhances the reputation of the human resource director. Furthermore, you are receiving free advertising from the posting.

Whether your newsletter is sent to clients or former clients or simply posted on your Web site, it provides fresh information. You are able to stay connected, provide useful information, and engage in a positive form of advertisement.

Unknown potential referrals who visit your Web site and read a current newsletter or a historical newsletter experience a sense of connection. You are indirectly stating that you are not forgetting your clients when therapy is over. You are demonstrating comprehensive services as well as developing a sense of community.

Treatment Feedback From Clients. Another important customer service variable is treatment feedback from clients. This variable should include regular feedback about their therapy experience. Try to create a system that allows your clients to give feedback without intimidation or fear of reprisal while in therapy. For over 10 years, we have used what we call the "half sheet" (Form 6.1).

This half sheet gives clients the opportunity to complete at the beginning of each session to give us feedback about how they perceive the therapy process and stimulates excellent conversation not about the therapy topic but about the actual process. Clients appreciate the opportunity to inform their therapist that they are on track, would like more homework, would like less homework, and more.

Depending on your treatment population, you should look for or create a system for clients to give you feedback. Consider yourself when interacting with other professionals; sometimes you might be assertive and tell them that you need more of this or less of that. Given that we work in mental health, clients may be leery or suspicious of expressing such information. However, in written format they might feel safer, validated, and in partnership with you as a treatment provider. This partnership is a critical variable in any business trying to create a lifelong customer.

Practice Feedback from Clients. Every so often, collecting feedback about potential new services from current clients helps to guide your strategies and create loyalty (Form 6.2).

FORM 6.1: HALF SHEET

Tracy Todd, PhD, LMFT
7800 S. Elati Drive, #230
Littleton, CO 80120

BRIEF THERAPY
INSTITUTE
OF DENVER
www.btid.com

Name:_____   Date:_____

Is the problem you sought counseling for
___ better
___ same
___ worse

What do you feel about your level of
progress
1   2   3   4   5
none   excellent

Have you attempted the homework task
assigned?
___ yes
___ no

What would help to better achieve those
therapy goals?

How close do you feel you are to
completing therapy?

Was the homework helpful?
1   2   3   4   5

1   2   3   4   5
Not at   nearly
all   completed

Are you having thoughts of wanting to
harm yourself or others? ___ yes ___ no

Have you changed your medications?
If yes, what has changed?

_____
         Signature

You might be considering a new service or service variable to enhance your practice. Get input from current clients and assess if the idea is feasible. While we felt clients would welcome an e-mail reminder system, we were uncertain if enough clients actually used e-mail at the time. Therefore, we spent about two months collecting information before implementation. We initially intended to spend three months collecting data, but the idea was so overwhelmingly favorable that we cut the data collection process short.

E-mail Reminders. The powerful loyalty-building service component of e-mail reminders must be well maintained. Simply sending e-mail reminders now and then will potentially do more harm than good. Clients experiencing inconsistency will view this as an unreliable and untrustworthy technological advancement. Maintaining consistency demonstrates your high-quality services and certainly helps to build a trusting lifelong client.

Administrative Satisfaction Survey. Satisfaction surveys are critical for practice building. A customer receiving a satisfaction survey feels that his or her opinion does matter and that the customer can positively contribute to the agency.

Tracy Todd, PhD, LMFT
7800 South Elati Drive, #230
Littleton, CO 80120

BRIEF THERAPY
INSTITUTE
OF DENVER
www.btid.com

WE NEED YOUR HELP AND FEEDBACK

As you may know, the Brief Therapy Institute of Denver Inc. has received many awards over the last 10 years, has been highlighted in publications such as the *Wall Street Journal* and *Glamour* magazine, and continues to make adaptations to provide more effective services. Last fall, we launched an exciting new service for our clients, online appointment setting. This system has been an overwhelming success, and we will continue to try to improve access to services. To this end, we would like your thoughts about a new system we are considering implementing, e-mail appointment reminders. Due to HIPAA regulations, sending e-mail appointment reminders is a complicated process. However, it can be done. We would like your feedback on the following questions:

1. Would you like to receive e-mail appointment reminders?
    ____ Yes   ___ No

2. Would you like e-mail appointment reminders for all appointments or only those that are more than
    ___ all   ___ 2+ weeks away   ___ 3+ weeks away

3. The only information you would receive would be your therapist's name, and date and time of appointment. No information about this agency would be listed, further protecting your privacy. How comfortable would you be with this minimal information being sent to you?
    ___ Not comfortable   ___ Comfortable

4. Would you be able to give an e-mail address at which you feel relatively safe accepting these reminders?
    ___ Yes   ___ No

Please make any suggestions you feel would help us to determine if we should initiate an e-mail appointment reminder system:

Thank you for taking the time to give us feedback. Please give this form to your therapist.

Cultural Sensitivity. Achieving satisfaction with your services might occur, but loyalty is unlikely if cultural sensitivity is lacking in your practice. Are you expected to understand all nuances of all cultures represented in your practice? No. Are you expected to have enough awareness and sensitivity with culturally diverse populations that you can ask questions and interact in a respectful manner? Yes. It is vitally important to receive training in cultural sensitivity to place yourself in a position to treat clients from diverse cultures respectfully. Such respect also increases the potential for loyalty and lifelong customers.

From a business perspective, cultural sensitivity extends to micro-cultures or, in business language, trend analyses among subpopulations. Subcultures such as "affluent teens," "singles over 30," "computer users over 65 years old," "metrosexuals," or "emos" may need attention depending on your practice location and specialty. Most therapists give little attention to diverse subcultures. For example, if a primary treatment demographic is those over 65 years old, are you on a second floor with no elevator? Do you have automatic doors that open into the building? Does your main office door allow for the use of walkers? Or, what if you have a practice specializing in adolescent issues? Do you understand the expectations and interactional styles of emos? What about resource links on your Web site that can offer support to this population?

Paying attention to trends, cultural diversity, and subculture changes helps to create a practice that meets the varying demands and expectations of each group. Hence, the more practice-building tools that develop satisfaction and loyalty throughout treatment, the more likely you can develop a diverse lifelong customer base.

Treatment Options. Treatment options are empowering because clients are influencing treatment direction. Everyone expects customization. Walk into any coffee shop and you can hear every customer ordering a specific type of coffee. I recently ordered sneakers from a shoe company to customize a pair of shoes for my beloved Wisconsin Badgers. Customers expect options.

How do you customize care for your client? Do you offer education? Do you assign specific worksheets or readings? As I mentioned concerning cultural diversity, clients are becoming increasingly diverse in their expectations of treatment and treatment processes. Is your treatment one dimensional? In other words, do you have a conversation with your client and treatment ends with the session? Or, do you have multiple treatment options: handouts, Web site bookmarks, podcasts, and treatment symptom diaries?

Care Coordination. Although care coordination is a fundamental practice-building strategy, it is also a crucial variable for clients to experience. Most therapists have seen and heard the expression of exasperated clients when they dejectedly state, "My physician told me she did not receive your report." You know that you sent the report during the session. Clients feel reassured when they perceive a sense of unity or collaboration. In contrast, we all have been in situations in which a client or former client receives differing information from multiple providers. This mixed-message situation understandably creates distress among all members of the treatment system.

Therapists who engage in comprehensive treatment collaboration not only benefit clients directly but also assist treatment stakeholders in delivering higher-quality services. Confusion is reduced because routine communication keeps issues clarified and roles distinct but complementary. Treatment stakeholders and therapists can reinforce collaborated messages and interventions. Clients, definitely sensing a team and coordinated approach, feel high-quality care is being delivered.

Unlike clients and former clients, who may feel embarrassed to acknowledge being in therapy and unable to refer family and friends, treatment stakeholders enhance their own reputation and effectiveness by making high-quality referrals and participating in coordinated care.

Symptom Inventories. Symptom inventories serve two important purposes. First, as a treatment provider they provide assistance with gains and current symptoms. Second, inventories communicate to clients that you are a thorough provider. Administering symptom inventories over the course of treatment facilitates communication between client and therapist. Despite one's theoretical or therapeutic approach, a symptom inventory creates a talking point to assess treatment gains or lack of them. Symptom inventories also provide great communication among client, therapist, and treatment stakeholders. For example, one of my clients was struggling with symptoms of anxiety and depression. I administered a symptom inventory, which indicated a significant degree of symptomology. He reported that he was seeing the psychiatrist immediately after our session (the psychiatrist was two buildings away), so I gave him a copy of the inventory. He took the inventory to the psychiatrist; they discussed the situation and modified his medications. Both the client and the psychiatrist were extremely complimentary of my strategy to give the completed inventory to the client. In this example, the client felt confident and reassured about the treatment coordination, and the psychiatrist was appreciative that he could see the inventory and use it for further assessment. Not only was care enhanced, but also the secondary "side effect" was great practice advertising.

Symptom inventories and trackers are readily available on the Internet. Using Google, search "mental health symptom checker" and "mental health symptom tracker" to review sites and tools. For example, WebMD provides numerous quality symptom inventories, and myPsychtracker (www.psych-tracker.com) provides a private environment to log symptoms and track. If the user is uncomfortable doing so online, symptom trackers can be purchased.

Developing Loyalty After Therapy

The Institute of Medicine (2001) strongly advocated that patients should expect interaction with health care providers following treatment, and health care professionals should anticipate client needs. Clinically, posttherapy strategies such as psychoeducation newsletters, clinically relevant podcasts, and self-help tips posted on your Web site can help fulfill the best practice standard of anticipating client needs. Anticipating client needs begins the prevention process for future mental health issues. From a practice-building perspective, these strategies prevent the "out of sight, out of mind" process from occurring.

Technology clearly is creating a situation by which contact with a client can remain in effect well after concluding treatment. Such contact may prevent decompensation at predictable times. For example, Harry visits his primary care physician for depression that is having an adverse impact on his work performance. The primary care physician's office, recognizing the need for counseling, refers Harry to your Web site, where he reviews your biography and is happy to learn that you encourage family members to attend sessions. Harry downloads the initial paperwork and immediately schedules an appointment using your online scheduling system, thereby increasing his convenience and reducing your overhead costs. During the intake, Harry gives you permission to coordinate care with the primary care physician and human resource director monitoring his performance. You learn from Harry's wife that he is irritable and creating relationship problems (atypical of him), and that the primary care physician started him on an antidepressant. After a few sessions, a symptom inventory combined with clinical interviews indicates depression continues. You fax your care coordination form and symptom inventory to the primary care physician, who adjusts the antidepressant. Harry and his wife work on some family dynamics contributing to the depression. As therapy progresses, Harry's wife and human resource director report that Harry is returning to his "old self," and feel satisfied with treatment. Concluding therapy, Harry and his wife receive a satisfaction survey, and you inform the human resource director and primary care physician of the case status. As his therapist, you are aware that Harry has difficulty with extended family members during the holidays. Since this is a common situation, in November you send a newsletter to Harry, current and former clients experiencing similar clinical issues, and treatment stakeholders. The newsletter includes self-help and prevention strategies informing the reader that your Web site also includes a 10-minute podcast, "Managing Your Mood During the Holidays."

This example demonstrates the possible range of services that create satisfaction and loyalty throughout treatment as well as help stay connected post-treatment. Furthermore, the connection certainly accommodates the health care expectation of anticipating client need (Institute of Medicine, 2001).

Clinical Satisfaction Survey. Of course, the clinical satisfaction survey not only provides you with useful information about your practice but also provides your customers an opportunity to give feedback. Whether positive or negative, providing feedback helps customers feel valued on a business level.

Posttreatment Follow-Up. Six months after purchasing my most recent vehicle, I received not only a survey asking me about the vehicle but also a telephone call from the dealership inquiring about the vehicle. They asked about the automobile, the financing, if I was happy with the purchase I made, and more. The dealer also offered resources, gave me helpful reminders about shuttle service when the car needed servicing, and encouraged me to contact the dealer with any questions or concerns. Follow-up after a purchase of a product or service feels good. Customers feel valued and not like "just another customer." Do you engage in any posttreatment follow-up beyond satisfaction surveys? Posttreatment follow-up can take many forms:

- Letter
- E-mail
- Newsletter
- Symptom inventory
- A reading list of interesting books for that particular customer

Importantly, with technology, these strategies are simple point-and-click opportunities that can enhance loyalty and perpetuate the lifelong customer relationship.

Measuring Perceived Progress and Status of Closing. You will pay attention to what to you measure. Specifically, using a treatment summary for every client forces you to pay attention to those variables you feel are critical for understanding your business (Form 6.3). This treatment summary assesses the therapist's perception of level of progress before closing as well as case status at closing. Information on each variable is completed by the therapist, and it is important that the information is completed honestly. There is a tendency, of course, to skew our perceptions to more favorable indicators. As with all forms, create drop-down menus to eliminate steps for completion (Figures 6.1 and Figure 6.2). If you chose to monitor this information over the course of treatment, you would enter it into your Business Profile (Table 6.2).

Paying Attention to Treatment Stakeholders

Obviously, a necessary variable in creating loyal treatment stakeholders is quality clinical services. In understanding that good clinical services, however, may

FORM. 6.3: TREATMENT SUMMARY INDICATING PROGRESS

Tracy Todd, PhD, LMFT
7800 South Elati Drive, #230
Littleton, CO 80120
www.btid.com

TREATMENT SUMMARY

Client Name: Case #:
ID: DOB:
Working diagnosis:Axis I
Axis II
Axis III
Axis IV
Axis V

Threat of Self-Harm:
Threat, Harm Others:

Substance Abuse:
Child Abuse:
Care Coordination: *2 = NO*   *If yes 0 = None*
If other:

Number of sessions:
Last appointment, date:
If needed, date follow-up letter sent?

Level of Progress:
3 = Goals met, motivated

Status at closing—please circle appropriate number:
1 = Mutually agreed, goals mostly met

_____
electronic signature

Notes:

FIG.6.1: LEVEL OF PROGRESS DROP-DOWN MENUS

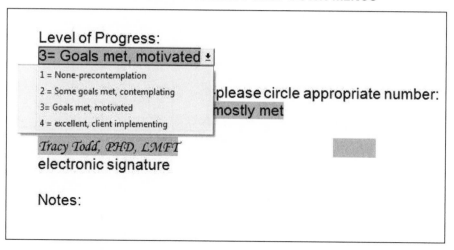

FIG.6.2: CASE CLOSING DROP-DOWN MENU

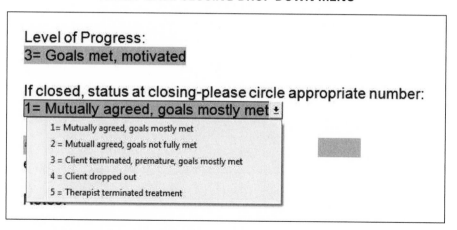

not achieve a loyal and lifelong treatment stakeholder, it is important that you assess your entire treatment continuum for loyalty-building activities and services. It is vitally important that the information most often accessed is kept up to date. For example, the Insurance Matrix must be updated at least quarterly. The smallest changes need immediate changing on your Web site. If a new employer contracts with an atypical new insurance company and you accept that insurance, immediately update your matrix. Those employees will need medical care (treatment stakeholders), and these stakeholders need to know if you are eligible to accept referrals.

A second service component that needs consistent attention is your care coordination notification. Similar to e-mail reminders with clients, treatment

TABLE 6.2: BUSINESS PROFILE WITH CLOSING INFORMATION

Client ID	Closing status	Care Coor. 1= yes 2 = no	Offered appt. days	Accepted appt. days	Method of appt. set (SS1)	Ease of setting (SS1)	Level of progress at closing	Number Sessions	Refer to therapist (SS2) 1= yes 2 = no	Refer to agency (SS2) 1= yes 2 = no
200803172	1		3	6	1	4	3	9	1	1
200803173	1		1	5	1	4	4	10	1	1
200803174	2		0	1	1	3	2	3		
200803175	3		2	7	3	2	2	3	2	1
200803176	2		4	4	1	4	2	24		
200803177	3		3	3	3	2	1	1		
200803178	3		2	3	1	3	2	2	1	1
200803179	4		5	6	3	1	2	3	2	2
			2.2	4.4				6.9		

FORM 6.4: TREATMENT SUMMARY INDICATING CARE COORDINATION

Treatment Summary

Client Name: Case #:
ID: DOB:
Working diagnosis:Axis I
Axis II
Axis III
Axis IV
Axis V

Threat of Self-Harm: No
Threat, Harm Others: No

Substance Abuse:
Child Abuse:
Care Coordination: 2 = No   If yes 0 = None   If other:

Number of sessions:
Last appointment, date:
If needed, date follow-up letter sent?

Level of Progress:
3 = Goals met, motivated

If closed, status at closing-please circle appropriate number:
1 = Mutually agreed, goals mostly met

_____

electronic signature

Notes:

stakeholders consistently receiving a care coordination form will find this service process reliable and trustworthy. Inconsistency will not build a lifelong referral base. One method of monitoring is by entering closing data information about care coordination at closing (Form 6.4 and Figure 6.3). If you believe this information is important to your Business Profile, enter it into your Business Profile spreadsheet (Table 6.3). Another service component important for treatment stakeholders is access to appointments. They require an easy method for scheduling appointments (online), always wanting fast and easy access to your services.

Finally, try to consider some inexpensive opportunities to connect with your

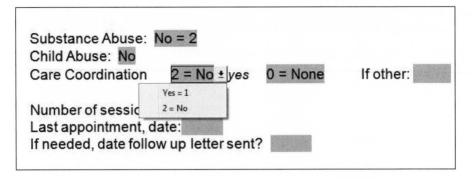

best referral sources, possibly taking them each to lunch or dropping off a small, inexpensive gift. We identify treatment stakeholders who work cooperatively and share referrals then each holiday deliver a basket of pleasantries. Keep in mind that food is great, but once it is gone, so is your name. Despite this drawback, one year we delivered customized M&Ms. Each M&M was stamped on one side with the initials BTID (Brief Therapy Institute of Denver) and the other side was stamped with the word "solutions." We received plenty of fun and playful remarks. Typically, however, you should deliver gifts that have more permanency, such as

- Motivational pictures with your name engraved on the frame.
- Post-it notes or pens with your name printed on each.
- Pads of paper with your name as a watermark.

Often, therapists inquire about how we afford such "expensive" gifts. We are sensitive to business ethics, and these gifts never cost more than $25 each. Although increasingly difficult, try to maintain this dollar amount ceiling. The second part of managing these gifts is limiting the number of treatment stakeholders receiving them to fewer than 20. As a group, determine your highest-referring treatment stakeholders. Many treatment stakeholders do not, or because of their position cannot, make referrals. For those who regularly refer, acknowledge with a gift or thank you gesture.

Rather than attending a networking function that is likely to attract competitors and place you in a position of gripping and grinning with unknown potential referral pools, host your own networking function. For example, inviting high-referral treatment stakeholders to a luncheon has a potentially investment high return on investment (ROI). You already have a great working relationship with these stakeholders, now is the time to solidify this and thank them for the collaboration and cross referring.

TABLE 6.3: BUSINESS PROFILE WITH CARE COORDINATION

Client ID	Closing status	Care Coor. 1= yes 2 = no	Offered appt. days	Accepted appt. days	Method of appt. set (SS1)	Ease of setting (SS1)	Level of progress at closing	Number Sessions	Refer to therapist (SS2) 1= yes 2 = no	Refer to agency (SS2) 1= yes 2 = no
200803172	1	1	3	6	1	4	3	9	1	1
200803173	1	1	1	5	1	4	4	10	1	1
200803174	2	2		1	1	3	2	3		
200803175	3	2	3	7	3	2	2	3	2	
200803176	2	2	4	4	1	4	2	24		
200803177	3	1	3	3	3	2	1	1		
200803178	3	2	2	3	1	3	2	2	1	1
200803179	4	1	5	6	3	1	2	3	2	2
			2.2	4.4				6.9		

Begin by assessing the projected ROI. For example, for a group of four clinicians and five treatment stakeholders attending the lunch, assess a projection of 30 days postlunch. Understanding that you are receiving referrals from these sources (3 per month per clinician, equal to 12 referrals per month as a baseline), you receive an additional 2 referrals per clinician, for an added 8 new referrals equaling 56 sessions (8 referrals x 7 average session per client).

$$\frac{\text{(Total sessions generated)} \times \text{Average reimbursement rate}}{\text{Average reimbursement rate} \times \text{Number of sessions lost for project} + \text{Cost of supplies}}$$

Sessions generated: 56

Average reimbursement rate: $80.00

Sessions lost per project: 13 (3 sessions to attend the lunch x 4 providers, 1 session lost for creating the invitation and faxing to the offices, no postage costs)

Supplies: $180 ($20 per lunch, nine lunches)

$$\frac{56 \times \$80.00 = 4{,}480.00}{(\$80.00 \times 13) + \$180 = 1{,}220.00}$$

$$\frac{\$4{,}480.00}{\$1{,}220.00} = 3.67$$

A 3.67 ROI is outstanding, and the luncheon provided personal contact with your treatment stakeholders. One commonly asked question is, "What is the decision-making process to determine who to invite?" My suggestion is to pick a referral number that you find outstanding. For example, among your treatment stakeholders you will have some who do not make any referrals, others who refer once per quarter, others who make one referral per month. You might decide that you want to invite only treatment stakeholders who have referred a minimum of 10 clients in the last 6 months.

Summary

Providing good clinical services does not automatically convert to building satisfaction and loyalty among your treatment stakeholders, clients, and former clients. Satisfaction and loyalty require purposeful attention and strategizing. There are multiple opportunities along the treatment continuum when you can deliver high-quality services that also enhance your reputation. Accentuate these areas. Get noticed and build a reputation that creates lifelong customers and referral sources.

Technology provides many strategies and activities to enhance satisfaction and loyalty building. Use of inexpensive technological interventions can significantly enhance your connection to treatment stakeholders, clients, and former clients. These connections, combined with your clinical services, will provide your practice the mechanisms to create lifelong loyal customers.

Key Points

1. Define your flagship services.
2. Create a matrix of all your customer service variables (outside-the-room services) and identify whether these variables build success, loyalty, and lifelong customers.
3. Create specific strategy worksheets for each customer service variable, that needs development.
4. Identify pretreatment, during treatment and posttreatment customer service variables to ensure that your customers are continuously receiving high-quality care.
5. Identify special events that acknowledge those treatment stakeholders who actively help build your practice.

Action List

1. Choose a flagship service that promotes satisfaction and loyalty. It should be a service that your competitors lack or have with an inferior quality.
2. Complete your service-building worksheets to begin purposefully building your flagship services.
3. Examine your pretherapy process: Do you have services available that draw customers to your business because of satisfaction?
4. Implement strategies that build satisfaction and loyalty during therapy, and beyond clinical service.
5. Offer online resources for customers.
6. Create feedback mechanisms for customers to comment on (a) therapy and (b) any possible service delivery component you are considering to enhance your business.
7. Create services that maintain connection and loyalty following therapy.
8. Be creative and find methods both to thank and to provide service to your treatment stakeholders.

CHAPTER SEVEN

Accessing and Building Referrals from Ring 3

In the introduction to this book, I suggested creating benchmarks and goals relating to diversity of referrals and the direct referral rate. Once these goals are accomplished, representing a self-defined balanced and strong practice, it is time to explore accessing and developing Ring 3 referrals.

If, for example, you defined a successful practice as achieving an 80% direct referral rate represented by diverse reimbursement systems, then it is time to mine that last 20% purposefully. What is the current demographic of this indirect referral pool? Continuing with our example, you find that this 20% is a diverse pool of clientele from a variety of random referral sources, such as insurance and online directories. The concerning aspect of this referral pool is that the reimbursement rate is nearly 33% less than that of the 80% direct referral pool.

Consider the situation. Of your practice, 80% is generating the income you want and providing a continuously stable referral flow. Although the last 20% is random but at a lower reimbursement rate, your practice is still theoretically "full." Now is the time to start experimenting with Ring 3 referrals. However, it would be perfectly natural to decide to increase the 80% to 100% and choose *not* to engage in any Ring 3 strategies. The decision is yours; neither is right or wrong. This chapter is for those who choose to explore, experiment, and take risks associated with Ring 3 referral development.

Web Presence

One important consideration when developing Ring 3 referrals is speed of conversion from potential customer to customer. Follow a business example from a customer service perspective. Have you ever purchased a book from Amazon?

If yes, how easy was that purchase? My Amazon account is set up in such a manner that I can engage in "1-Click Ordering." The ease of becoming a customer is of paramount importance in business. This emphasis on converting and capturing customers is a gaping hole for most practice-building therapists. Clients referred by treatment stakeholders and former clients might have some tolerance for inefficiencies in your practice, but unknown referral potentials are most likely looking for reasons *not* to access your services. Ease and speed of converting them to customers is paramount as you consider the strategies described next.

Paid Online Directory Exposure

In addition to the free online therapy directories available on the Internet, there are some affordable directories that require little labor to participate. Yet, many therapists simply do not take advantage of these directories. *Psychotherapy Finances* ("Mini-Survey," 2008) reported that only about 30% of the respondents of a survey indicated that they use Web site directories.

A quick Google search for therapist directories results in many possibilities for therapists:

- Psychology Today (therapists.psychologytoday.com/rms/prof_search.php)
- Finding Stone (www.findingstone.com) (a directory of directories)
- Find-a-Therapist (www.find-a-therapist.com/)
- Network Therapy.com (www.networktherapy.com)
- 4Therapy.com (www.4therapy.com)

Begin to compare the directories in terms of cost and features and how they are marketed. A simple method to assess marketing is to pretend you are a client searching for a therapist. Using multiple search words such as "psychotherapist," "counselor," "family therapist," and multiple search engines (Yahoo, BananaSlug, Dog Pile, and the like), assess which psychotherapist directories are continuously listed on your first page of search results. These directories are investing in tools to create prominence. Subscribe to these directories as they have a higher likelihood of increasing your return on investment (ROI).

There are a few qualities to assess when determining in which therapy directories you will financially invest for subscriptions. First, can you post your picture? Shy away from those not allowing you to post a picture. Photos sell. Second, can you describe your service components, or will they only allow you to list your clinical specialties? You are working hard to develop service variables that create satisfaction and loyalty. Can you advertise these services? *Psychotherapy Finances* ("Tips for Getting," 2006) reported that good directory listings include a photo and a list of your specializations and focus on what you can do for clients rather than your credentials. Third, examine how the search results are posted. When you conducted your searches while assessing the directory, are therapist names listed randomly, in alphabetical order, or by some sort of ranking system? A directory is of little use if it gives search results in alphabetical order and your name does not begin with A. Being located on the second page of any search result is wasted money. Some therapy directories use ranking systems. If they do, how will your listing rank? For example, not too long ago one directory ranked therapists based on information from an insurance company. What if that insurance company is not prominent in your geographical area? Your ranking may be poor for an invalid reason, resulting in a poor ROI. Fourth, as directories become more sophisticated, can you add an audio or video introduction? Stay ahead of the competition. Finally, does the directory allow you to link to your Web site? Someone reviewing your directory listing should be able to click a link to your Web site and go directly to it. Without this feature, the odds of converting a potential customer to a customer diminish. Give each question careful attention.

Web Advertising: Click-Through Campaigns

Click through campaigns are advertising campaigns that create traffic to your Web site. To explain, log on to your computer and, using Google, search for "marriage family therapist [your town name]." The right margin should list "sponsored links" with the names and Web site addresses of marriage and family therapists in your area. If you did not get any results, for our purposes, try the search again using a more general term, such as "psychotherapist." Eventually, you should see a "sponsored links" section on your screen.

The sponsored links are to individuals and companies paying for the listing and are specifically designed to generate Web site traffic. Each major search engine has such marketing campaigns:

Google	AdWords
Yahoo	Search Marketing (http://sem.smallbusiness.yahoo.com/searchenginemarketing/)
MSN	Adcenter

The Google AdWords function is a good starting point as Google garnishes over 50% of search traffic, while Yahoo and MSN respectively receive 25% and 12% of the search traffic ("Yahoo, MSN Fight for a Share," 2007).

Basics of Web Marketing. All three systems work basically the same way. For example, you are a family therapist and want to generate traffic to your Web site. Your first step is to create a list of words that describe your practice:

psychotherapy, family, therapy, counseling, child, adolescent, teen. The search system will then provide the cost to list your advertisement. The more expensive the quote, the greater the potential your sponsored link appears on the first page of a search. For example, if the search system indicates that for $3.00 per click you will hold the number one position (top of the list, first page), you can choose if you want to pay $3.00 or not. When someone clicks on your sponsored link, they are then taken to your Web site. The cost of that "click" was $3.00. If you set a monthly budget of $30 for advertising, your campaign will terminate after ten users click to your Web site. Make sure to monitor the effectiveness at least weekly.

It is critically important to use the Analytics program when investing in a Web marketing campaign. You need to assess your ad placement position, click-through rate, and conversion rate. If your ad placement is consistently outside the top six or seven, you will need to increase your bidding price. If your ad placement is in the top six or seven but your click-through rate (how often viewers are clicking to your Web site) is low, then you need to modify your advertisement to be more alluring. Finally, if you are getting a high click-through rate, thereby increasing the number of visitors to your landing page, and these visitors are not scheduling services, begin experimenting with the landing page. Try altering the format, adding graphics, maybe posting an audio file. If you are driving traffic to the landing page but not converting customers, you are halfway there, but the landing page clearly needs some work to convert.

The beauty of these campaigns is that you set your monthly budget and guarantee Web traffic. These campaigns are easy to create. In addition, depending on your geography, you may consistently be in the top position of sponsored links. However, you need some minimal components on your Web site for these campaigns to be effective.

Landing Page. A common mistake is linking your sponsored link to your home page. While this step seems logical, it will lack effectiveness. Those clicking on sponsored links are looking for the specific information you are advertising, and they will decide in seconds whether they will further investigate your site. You need a Web page specifically for these campaigns, usually referred to as a *landing page*. The page must quickly highlight your practice and flagship/signature services and have enough appeal to engage the visitor into reading more. From the landing page, provide links to take the visitor to your home or other Web pages.

Online Scheduling. A visitor is using the Internet to find a family therapist, is visiting Web sites, and probably is more inclined to use online scheduling than to make a phone call. Although your advertising campaign might be successful without online scheduling, maximize your dollars and eliminate all barriers to services. Advertise your online scheduling on the landing page.

Video Introduction. On the landing page, indicating that you have a video introduction is highly advantageous. However, you may not want to place the video on the landing page. Unless your Internet service provider can reasonably guarantee that your video will be immediately available to a visitor on your landing page, by the time it streams enough information to the landing page, the visitor may be gone. Consider providing the visitor with information to indicate the visitor can watch your video introduction on your Web site. Having a video introduction will give you a competitive advantage which needs to be a goal when spending money for a higher-risk advertising strategy.

These campaigns can serve many purposes. First, you can test market the possibility of new services. For example, your practice data indicate that you have been assisting single people with becoming more assertive, dating, and improving interaction skills in groups. You feel a seminar would be a nice additional service. One practice-building strategy is to engage Google AdWords to offer a seminar for shy singles. Cautiously experiment with testing this practice building idea. *Psychotherapy Finances* ("Special report," 2007) reported that you need to control your budget as these campaigns can get expensive, and that it is important you have a specific landing page for this strategy. Also, use the Google Analytics program to monitor patterns, thereby enhancing the ROI as you learn the migration patterns of visitors on your Web site. A second purpose is to take advantage of current events locally and nationally. For example, assuming you take insurance, during financially challenging times you may choose to increase your treatment population of couples dealing with financial stress. It is possible, due to a weak economy, that your own self-pay cash clientele is paying less than usual, and you want to recession-proof your practice. If you are competent in dealing with financial stressors and have an excellent working relationship with a financial planner treatment stakeholder, you may test to see if the key words "family," "couples," "financial," "money," "management," and "stress," drive traffic to your landing page, resulting in customers.

Seminars

Well-strategized seminars can provide many advantages to your practice. Anytime my practice was full and my appointment time offered to new clients was greater than 5 days, I would consider offering a seminar. My first step was to examine my caseload and evaluate what treatment population was most represented. Since I usually did relationship counseling, I would have many couples trying to improve their communication skills, and I also dealt with men's issues. Therefore, I would offer a seminar, "Communication Skills 101 for

Men." I would put the couples sessions on hold until the men finished the seminar, resulting in more appointment times becoming available and allowing me to increase my caseload.

If you are thinking, "Tracy, this is not Ring 3, rather this strategy focuses on current clients," you have been paying attention. Opening the seminar to current clients seeded the group so that I would have the minimum to hold such a seminar. It is devastating to your practice-building efforts to offer a seminar, knowing you need a minimum of, say, four participants, get three enrollees, and then cancel. You effectively lost three new clients who may never return for any type of services. Seeding the group provides some insurance for not losing Ring 3 enrollees.

Advertising for Ring 3 participants then included a flyer that many women on my caseload would distribute to family and friends, publishing the flyer on the Web site, creating a landing page to describe the seminar, and then conducting an AdWords campaign to advertise the seminar.

Seminars also increase reimbursement rates. Charging slightly more than your average copayment is a good strategy. If the average copayment for your practice is $30, then charge $35 per couple or participant in a seminar. Seven attendees at a 90-minute seminar produce $245 or just over $163 per hour.

Finally, seminars are an excellent strategy for creating outstanding advertising representatives for your practice. Those attending leave with handouts, brochures, reading materials, and personal experience. On numerous occasions I gained referrals from a seminar participant who passed along materials to neighbors, friends, or family members.

Webinars/Teleclasses

Webinars or teleclasses can either be referral or income-generating mechanisms. *Psychotherapy Finances* ("Marketing: Free," 2008b) reported that a therapist used a free 90-minute teleclass as an introduction to a full 5-week teleclass costing $197.00. The therapist reported that 15% of those taking the free class signed up for the full class. An inexpensive Webinar may be an excellent income generator if the quality and pricing are competitive with the free information sources you can find in many other locations (i.e., YouTube). Before going the route of investing in the development of an online class, scour the Internet to assess if the same information is available for free. If you do find the information for free, you need strategies to exploit the weaknesses of the free information (e.g., quality of information) to compete.

Publishing

Writing a book is always helpful in generating clients. However, this is a time-consuming and risky endeavor. You could spend many hours writing and editing a book and then not find a publisher. One way to hedge the risk of not finding a publisher is to consider self-publishing. *Psychotherapy Finances* ("Publishing," 2008) reported on therapists using self-publishing to various degrees of success. Yet, once published, you become an authority, which leads to speaking engagements and training and consulting gigs. There are self-publishing companies that help minimize the costs of large print runs by offering print-on-demand services (e.g., www.lulu.com).

Rather than print publishing, another option to consider is online publishing. *Psychotherapy Finances* ("Online Publishing," 2005) reported that a therapist wrote an e-book selling for $49.95 and sold over 6,400 e-copies ($319,680). Although the therapist had varying resale agreements and did not pocket that entire amount, even at a 50% take-home rate, he did quite well. Furthermore, he reported that he built his practice on clients who desired additional coaching after reading his book.

Podcasting

Rather than allowing your podcasts to get picked up randomly and accidently by podcasting directories as discussed in Chapter 5, become aggressive with getting your podcasts distributed. Before starting a distribution project, ensure that your podcasts are completely tagged and labeled: singer (therapist name), song title (subject title), and album (your name or logo).

Similar to therapist directories, look for directories to get your podcasts listed. Some directories include iTunes, Podcast Alley, Yahoo Podcasts, and Podcastdirectory.com. Using podcasts to increase your Ring 3 referral rate requires two considerations. First, because anyone in the world can listen to your podcast, you should have the opportunity to convert anyone in the world to a customer. What revenue-producing services will you have available on your Web site? This situation is perfect for a Webinar or teleclass. Second, look for mechanisms in the directory listing to give your podcasts a local presence. Doing so provides you the opportunity to convert listeners into psychotherapy customers. Typically, directories will ask some form of the question, "Do you want your listing to have a global, national, regional, or local presence?" Give careful thought to this question and how you can maximize the ROI.

Podcasts resulting in visits to your Web site but not converting visitors to customers may still be successful. Even if the visitor does not schedule an appointment, do you offer the visitor something that keeps him or her connected to your practice? Podcasts, whether subscribed to or not, give the visitor a reason either to come back to your practice or to have your self-help audio files sent directly to the visitor's computer. When the visitor is motivated or after reaching a comfort level with your style by listening to your podcasts, your practice is in the prime position of gaining a referral. The visitor has been connected to your practice and is gaining loyalty.

Web Banner Advertising

Web banner advertising is risky and challenging. Essentially, you are trying to create a Web-based billboard that drives traffic to your Web site. The risk is selecting the correct Web sites for placement. For example, do a Google search on "depression." Many of the predominant sites listed in the results section are sponsored by pharmaceutical companies. For obvious reasons, you will have no luck getting a psychotherapy banner ad placed on these sites.

More challenging is that the Web sites, such as those for depression, are designed for global viewership. Purchasing banner advertisement for your practice in, say, Oconomowoc, Wisconsin, is simply not going to generate customers viewing the depression site outside a 30-mile radius. A company seeking your advertising dollars will most likely make statements such as, "The Web page where your banner ad will be placed is viewed 10,000 times per month." That may sound great, but how many of those viewers were within 30 miles of Oconomowoc? Even if the banner advertising is situated for local viewership (meaning only those in the Oconomowoc area will see your advertisement), will there be enough viewers to create a healthy ROI?

Accidental Free Advertising

Significantly overlooked and virtually impossible to plan are the numerous accidentally free advertising opportunities on the Internet. The Internet is literally alive with programs that seek out information. For example, if you start a blog, eventually the Google search programs will find that information and begin listing your blog in search results. A blog on say, communicating with your teenager, will undoubtedly get listed in a search result of someone searching "talking to my teen."

Likewise, posting a podcast (remember podcasts include RSS [Really Simple Syndication]) will eventually get discovered by search engines specifically looking for RSS feeds. Suddenly, you get an e-mail from someone 1,000 miles away thanking you for the information and asking for more (it happened to me). Such contacts may not necessarily lead to customers, but they may open up other opportunities: Webinars, teleclasses, online therapy, consulting, and training. Sometimes good, sometimes bad, your practice information is listed and present in many areas on the Internet unknown to you. Because you cannot stop it, capitalize on this phenomenon.

Locally, Internet opportunities combined with customer service strategies that heighten satisfaction and loyalty among clients, former clients, and treatment stakeholders will result in surprisingly numerous Ring 3 opportunities. The ripple effect of outstanding services results in offers to conduct trainings and provide consultations and even offers of academic positions. Everyone is different in treatment settings, and there is no guarantee that you will receive such offerings, but the odds certainly improve. I know of providers who, because of outstanding customer service, were offered to provide consultation services for attorneys (rate of reimbursement in excess of $200 per hour) and training opportunities (often exceeding $1,500 per day).

Human Presence

New Specialty Service
Because it is inevitable that someone will want to develop a new clinical service to increase referrals, this new service needs strategizing. A new specialty service requires time and money. Training costs are incurred, marketing materials need developing, and advertising the new service becomes imperative. Before engaging in such labor- and cost-intensive activities, consider some basic steps.

Step 1. Trust your data when developing a new service. What are your most common clinical populations served? For example, if your data indicate that you have a heavy caseload with work performance problems, and your satisfaction survey data suggest you deliver high-quality services, then it is time to get creative and begin developing this area of your practice. Examine your data carefully, even if this means spending some time reviewing your charts. Look for trends such as:

- Type of occupation or employment setting
- Type of work performance problem
- Average number of sessions within this subpopulation of your practice
- Interventions typically used when assisting your clients
- Distance clients are traveling to your office

These trends provide a great deal of information. For example, knowing the average number of sessions provides a cost comparison point. Whatever type of service you offer, you will need to ensure that the cost is less or the quality is significantly greater than what you currently offer. The distance clients are traveling to your office provides you some information about how much time is being spent either away from work or home, thereby providing additional information about the type of service you need to offer.

Step 2. From the data trends, determine if face-to-face service delivery is the primary method to deal with the specialty. Possibly, face-to-face services are offered because that is the only service available. Yet, you may determine that a different delivery method could be more effective as a primary delivery method. Some possible delivery options include:

- Live classroom seminar
- Webinars
- Online therapy via online therapy environment or e-mail exchange

It is also possible that any of these mechanisms could complement your current face-to-face expertise. As a supplement, maybe you can help reduce the cost to the payer while decreasing your labor. For example, you might create a simple PowerPoint presentation on communication skills and, using the employers' conference call system, provide a didactic seminar on healthy communication skills. Although you may charge for 45 minutes of time, if it has the potential to decrease the average number of sessions by one session per employee, you will be saving the third-party payer a significant amount of money.

Step 3. After determining the best delivery method for your new service, you need to do some research and development, research to see if the product is already created and if you can license the mechanism. Why reinvent the wheel? For example, why create a communication skills video when there may be one available on YouTube?

Developing the final product is important. Avoid going off on fun tangents; remain focused. Remember, your data informed you about the specialty, and it should also inform you about delivery. There is so much creativity involved when the world of technology is at your fingertips that it is often difficult to remain true to your project.

Step 4. Part of the research is calculating finances. Is the new service going to result in a satisfactory ROI? You should conduct a projected cost analysis and then a worst-case analysis. Determine if you are embarking on a project that under the best scenarios may have only a negligible ROI and under the worst scenarios create financial disaster.

Completing these four simple steps allows you to more objectively make decisions about creating a new clinical specialty for the purpose of building a practice. There are many other more affordable and less labor-intensive options for developing this 20% referral base, so be sure about engaging in this pursuit.

30-Second Commercial

By now, you should clearly get the message that *everything* you do in your practice, from in-the-room service delivery to simple administrative tasks, should double as advertising. The final component of adequate preparation to capitalize on the remaining 20% indirect referral rate is your ability to confidently and comfortably deliver your "30-second commercial." Everyone attending a small business seminar has heard of the "30-second commercial." The objective is to deliver information to a listener about your company and services so compelling that they want to use your services. With *Practice-Building 2.0* strategies, the commercial should have only one goal: get the listener to visit your Web site.

What should your "30-second commercial" include?

- Your name
- Your license type
- Practice name
- What types of problems you treat (in-the-room services)
- Your flagship, outside-the-room services
- How you can help the listener

You may have multiple 30-second commercials for different groups. For example, a commercial for human resource directors will be different from a commercial for introducing yourself to a primary care physician. The important feature of the commercial is your confidence. No one respects an impotent introduction to a new service provider.

EXAMPLE—EMPLOYER-RELATED EMPHASIS

"Hi, my name is Chester Smith. I'm a licensed marriage and family therapist and president of the Therapy Center 3. My area of expertise is improving relationship and communication skills between people, regardless of context. I have extensive experience with employee assistance programs, particularly enhancing communication skills among coworkers. I believe that I can certainly assist your business, and if you would like to schedule a meeting, we can do so at this time." If they choose not to schedule the meeting, then complete the commercial with, "Okay, then here is my brochure with my Web site listed, and you can always feel free to use the online scheduling function to schedule a meeting."

In this example, skills and areas of expertise are highlighted, and if they decline a meeting then the Web site and online scheduling feature (flagship) are mentioned. It is important to have different commercials for varying circumstances. Memorize and deliver confidently when the introduction is on you.

Effective Networking

In Chapter 6, I discussed hosting a lunch for treatment stakeholders who have referred you a predetermined number of referrals. Execute the same strategy with treatment stakeholders not referring to your practice. Begin by creating a list of names and the frequency of treatment involvement. You are trying to sort treatment stakeholders who interact frequently with your practice but fail to make referrals. After creating your list, then sort those treatment stakeholders to whom you can refer and those you cannot. For example, a school counselor can refer to you, but you cannot return the favor. A psychiatrist can refer to you, and you can reciprocate. Of those with whom you share a reciprocal relationship, identify how many referrals *you have made* in the last year. There is nothing more embarrassing than asking, "Why aren't you referring to me?" when the person in question could ask the same of you. Assessing your list, you notice that Mr. F requires a conversation about how he can earn referrals and you can earn his referrals. You choose not to invite Mr. F but make a concerted effort to refer clients over the next 12 months in an attempt to create a reciprocal relationship. Next year, Mr. F will be invited to lunch, either with those who refer or with those for whom you are trying to assess why they are not referring.

Your invitation list indicates a few primary targets. The psychiatrist and psychiatric nurse are the two you need to spend some time with in this nonthreatening format. Alarming is the psychiatrist who referred one client and never made another referral. Why? Did the psychiatrist get bad feedback, dislike your approach, or simply forget about you? The psychiatric nurse, despite receiving 3 referrals, has not made any. Why? We once had this situation occur, and we asked. We were informed that the psychiatric nurse had a "loose agreement" with another group practice never to refer to another group. Therefore, regardless of the number of referrals we made, we were never going to get referrals from this nurse. Although Mr. S (school counselor) has not made referrals and despite the fact you cannot refer to him, your clients have teenagers predominantly attending the high school where Mr. S is a counselor. Mr. S is going to remain a frequent treatment stakeholder, and it is incumbent on you to discover why he is not referring. Do not be shy; during the lunch, directly ask each attendee, "What do I need to do to earn referrals from you?" These treatment stakeholders are coordinating care with you but for some reason hedging when making a referral. This luncheon, unlike the luncheon with treatment stakeholders who do share referrals, is really a combination of an infomercial and a fact-finding mission.

Summary

Importantly, before implementing any strategy to increase referrals from the unknown referral pool, Ring 3, achieve your predetermined goal of direct referrals. Implementing these strategies prior to accomplishing a solid foundation of referrals from clients, former clients, and treatment stakeholders only perpetuates a risky referral stream not easily influenced by any efforts you make.

Increasing Ring 3 referrals also requires a new paradigm. Technology provides, and users of technology require, opportunities to gain valuable information about your practice without any personal interaction. This referral pool will quickly compare health care providers, typically seeking out specific pieces of information important to them. Lack of access to your information is an automatic loss of business.

Key Points

1. Achieve the direct referral percentage you predetermined before starting any of these strategies.
2. Pay attention to online directories, especially free ones; get yourself listed. Take full advantage of free advertising.
3. Ring 3 referrals require planning on how to drive them to your Web site. Plan your campaigns.
4. Create a separate landing page for AdWords campaigns. They will seek different information than Rings 1 and 2.
5. Have multiple 30-second commercials ready for any situation.
6. Host networking events for treatment stakeholders who are not referring to you. Find out why they are not and what you can do to earn their trust and loyalty.

Action List

1. Before engaging in any of the Ring 3 strategies assess your goals and ensure you are purposefully, not desperately, using these strategies.
2. List all possible online directories available to you. These can include professional association, insurance, proprietary, and free directories. Get yourself listed on free directories. Prioritize and select if you will participate in any directories requiring you to pay a fee.
3. Consider Ring 3 strategies that "fit" your practice patterns and personality. Choose those that have the highest potential ROI; be realistic.
4. Develop, memorize, and rehearse your 30-second commercial.

CHAPTER EIGHT

Hard Realities of Maintaining Your Business

Face it: a full-time, income-sustaining career in private practice has unique and intense challenges. The purpose of this chapter is to acknowledge openly and directly the pressures and ongoing hard realities of small business ownership. I feel it is important that when building a business we account for challenges as well as unforeseen circumstances and disasters. Unlike barriers to building and growing your business, these hard realities are ever present and challenging to your ongoing success.

Emotional

The emotional drain of more than 30 clients per week requires playtime, rest, and relaxation. There are failed sessions and failed services. It is important to recognize that regardless of our level of professional development, the emotional drain of working with others is quite high. This emotional drain needs relief. The less you need to worry about building your practice, the more you can deal with the emotional investment needed to provide psychotherapy services. It is imperative to begin streamlining your services through technology.

Throughout this work I have highlighted the importance of having an administrative system that works for you rather then you working for it. Technology becomes a useful coping strategy for battling the emotional drain of administrative and clinical services. While this may seem a bit odd, please give it careful consideration. If paperwork demands occupy a huge chunk of your time, leading to frustration and resentment, implementation of electronic forms and templates saves labor and frustration. If you are uncomfortable attending networking functions, maybe hosting your own luncheon will prove to be more profitable and comfortable. When you are experiencing emotional drain clinically or from business processes, it is critically important to assess the source of distress. If necessary, seek supervision or consultation to identify the source and appropriate corrective action. Often, sources of clinician burnout are tracked back to administrative or business development issues. Use technology to make your life easier. If you are frustrated with the high cost of postage when offering seminars, then develop and implement an e-mail database so you can decrease this cost and increase the frequency of your seminars. These types of strategies will decrease the emotional drain and create a more fulfilling practice, thereby allowing you to do what you do best: provide clinical service.

During the streamlining of your practice and stabilization of your referral flow, you can diminish many ongoing hard realities. While unpleasant, they are simply part of owning a business.

Failed strategies

My business partner and I can easily write a book, "100 Unsuccessful Strategies of Psychotherapy Practice-Building." We have experienced far more failures than successes. However, we have learned how to minimize the adverse impact of the failure and maximize the impact of success. Because you experience failure does not mean you should quit. Although failure hurts and creates feelings of frustration and resentment, it is important to assess and seek consult regarding why a strategy failed. Learn from it. See it as an opportunity to capitalize on your time and investment, thereby enhancing your potential for success with future strategies. Technology allows you to take more risks without the immense loss of time and money. A simple e-mail merge program allows you to send out many announcements for a seminar, and the only time that you have truly spent on the seminar is the development of the brochure. With a point-and-click system you have eliminated the postage and supply costs. If this endeavor fails, your investment is minimal, and the failure is much easier to digest. Without technology, failure is like salt on an open wound. It truly hurts because there has been a great deal of money and labor invested.

Confusion

What strategy should I use? How do I increase revenues? This software or that shareware? Can I do this or that? Confusion will reign. With every strategy, there is the thought that a differing strategy will work more cost-effectively. It is important for you to set annual benchmarks, create a plan, and steadily work the plan. Similar to sports, stick to the game plan and keep your eye on the ball.

In my opinion, confusion is the most paralyzing force when it comes to a psychotherapist engaging in practice-building strategies. What is the reason? Simply, therapists tend to have a great deal of difficulty taking risks or minimizing risks. I have met with therapists who had great ideas that never were implemented because of perceived risks. Risk is part of building and owning a business. Doing nothing is often a greater risk than being aggressive and calculating your risk. I once met with a practice group of four who were avoiding the risk of spending $10.00 per person, per month for online scheduling. Talk about risk adverse! The group acknowledged that $10.00 per month was not cost prohibitive, but they just did not want to take the risk. I had to ask the clichéd phrase, "What do you have to lose?" before they would engage in being proactive and more open to the idea of spending $10 per month (www.healthescheduler.com). Remember, using the return-on-investment (ROI) formula helps with risk assessment. In this case, we calculated that if each person spent 2 hours ($160 of labor) to investigate the service and then to purchase to purchase the service ($30 set-up fee plus $120 at $10 per month) would cost $150 per person for implementing online scheduling service:

$$\frac{\text{4 referrals of 7 sessions} = \text{28 sessions at \$80 per session} = \$2,240}{\$80 \times 2 \text{ hours educating about the service} = \$160 + \$150 \text{ (set-up of \$30} + \$10 \text{ per month)}} = \$310$$

$$= 7.22$$

Estimating one referral per quarter or four per year results in an ROI of 7.22 per person. Do not let confusion and risk paralyze you. Know your risks, manage your risks, and then go for it.

Comparison to Others

When therapists do well, they let everyone know, which I encourage. Success is exciting and feels good. However, reports of success can be deceiving. Therapists will get three referrals for a new service and begin boasting of their new practice-building strategy. Be careful not to compare yourself to others.

Comparison to other therapists is a natural tendency, especially when trying to determine how to build your practice. Will an AdWords campaign work for you as well as it did for someone else? Did your seminar have as many attendees as someone else doing a similar seminar? When it comes to comparing, it is important to compare apples to apples and oranges to oranges. If you are part of a group and a colleague decides to initiate an AdWords campaign that results in great success, how can you replicate it? Now, compare the results. Use your technology for data collection so you know what is effective, and you can stick to your game plan. I have met many therapists without a plan of action, simply copying every good idea they hear. If you are going to compare, make sure you are doing so in a manner that is realistic.

Hobby Practices

There is a significant difference between hobbyists and full-time owners of private practices. I consider hobbyists to be those clinicians who have a second source of income considered "primary income." These psychotherapists might have a full-time job in an agency or university or maybe a spouse who is the primary income producer. Hobbyists see clients for *additional* income. Contrast this situation with full-time business owners. These are clinicians whose practice must pay all the practice bills and also contribute at least 50% or more of the household income.

Hobbyists provide interesting lessons and challenges to full-time owners of private practices. Many hobbyists may see up to 10 self-paying clients per week. Often, these clients are not crisis oriented, are high functioning, and are motivated. To me, that sounds like a dream caseload. How do they do it? Although I have not seen research on this genre of psychotherapists, I hear my hobbyist colleagues make statements such as, "I only accept clients by referral" (meaning Ring 1 or 2) or "I tell potential new clients I cannot adequately deal with crises, and I have no emergency system." Both statements indicate that these practitioners have networks of colleagues and former clients (Rings 1 and 2) directly referring to them a self-selected population, often more oriented toward personal growth issues than mental illness situations. The fact is that their reputations for high-quality care gain them referrals, *not* networking events, advertising, and so on. Although there are lessons to be learned from these therapists, it is also important to recognize the hard reality that there are many hobbyists. You can probably easily think of a dozen colleagues with hobby practices. Another hard reality is that these hobbyists are drawing self-pay clients away from your practice. These types of clients would be excellent for diversifying your referral pool and revenue stream. You need business strategies that effectively compete with these practices. Generally, hobby practice therapists fall into four categories.

The first group of hobbyists are those who hold positions of prestige or high visibility in the community. For example, professors and directors of treatment centers have natural connections throughout the community that can generate referrals. The second group of hobbyists includes those who have spouses with prestige, high-income, or high-profile positions. For example, physicians and attorneys in the community, via their networks, bring attention to their spouse's business. The third group is those therapists who have national or international reputations. Typically, however, clients lack awareness of such prestige, but the local professional community is aware. Those in the community then refer the appropriate clientele. Finally, there are the hobbyists who will only work with a specific niche population, so specific that they cannot generate enough business to operate a full-time business. Therefore, they rely on other sources of income (e.g., spouse, full-time job, and so on).

The first three hobby groups basically come down to visibility of the therapist among treatment stakeholders. By now, you should have full confidence and ability to gain referrals from similar treatment stakeholders. The challenge is getting these stakeholders to know you. With aggressive care coordination, you will develop a similar network thereby allowing you to compete with those operating a hobby practice. You really cannot compete with the fourth group. This group is financially subsidized to engage in delivering services they fully enjoy. You can add a niche market, but if the referral possibilities are too small to maintain a full-time practice, you may simply serve this population as part of your business rather than making it your business.

Regulations and Liabilities

Regulations and liabilities take an enormous emotional toll. It does not seem like a month passes without a third-party payer or referral source informing private practitioners of a new policy and procedure. In addition, there are new federal and state regulations that need constant attention. For example, trying to stay abreast of the changes in privacy regulations can be more emotionally exhausting than worrying about the next referral. Plans for increasing referrals are limited only by creativity. However, transgressing a federal privacy law that results in the potential of an attorney holding up a manual and stating, "You should have known this!" is simply overwhelming.

New legislation will begin dealing with areas such as telehealth, online therapy, and even simple e-mail interactions. Privacy laws will need modification as technology allows professionals to deal increasingly with clients and customers via the Internet. What will the insurance industry do, and how will it respond to psychotherapy delivered without in-person, face-to-face services? Furthermore, when there is a federal initiative requiring the expansion of services beyond face-to-face delivery, how will these services be reimbursed or covered by the insurance industry? Already, there are therapists who engage in private practice-building efforts in foreign legal and ethical territory. For example, there is currently no uniform legislation offered by governments or associations to guide online therapy.

Streamlining a practice with technology frees up time and your ability to pay attention to things that can potentially result in disastrous effects on your practice. Use some of those 249 free hours resulting from improved efficiencies for continuing education on legal, ethical, and regulatory issues.

Business Processes

Rapidly Expanding Technology Culture

While writing this book, there have been numerous technological changes in a short period of time. At times it was like describing moving targets. For example, when I started writing, I reported on personal digital assistants (PDAs). Now PDAs are nearly extinct as they are being replaced by smart phones.

Technology evolves quickly. Do you need to be up to date with the fanciest or newest gizmo? No. Do need you to keep abreast of changes that may enhance your practice? Yes. The rapid change of technology, particularly as it applies to business settings and privacy, can easily lead to overwhelming feelings of frustration. Remember, immediate changes are not necessary. Simply educate yourself regarding changes that can benefit your practice and then set some priorities. For example, say you just threw away your Day-Timer and replaced it with a PDA. You also added an online scheduling function that sends e-mail notifications when appointments are scheduled. You wake up one day and wish you had a smart phone to allow you the capability of accessing the Internet, getting your e-mail, and still include your beloved PDA functions. Do you throw up your hands and ask, "Do I need to implement an entirely new system?" When you reach this point, compliment yourself for staying informed about the technological possibilities benefitting your practice. It is important to keep yourself informed and purposely plan when you want to make changes.

Flat Business Model

Flattening will continue. Putting aside legal and ethical matters, it is easy to envision delivering a significant amount of psychotherapy by Webcam. Imagine no need for clients or yourself to travel, hardly a need for a business office, and working from anywhere you choose. Removing such barriers and creating a flatter relationship with clients is happening.

As flattening occurs, we need to keep abreast of how we can continue to build our services to provide a more profitable and enjoyable private practice. Competing with, and adapting to, these changes will probably be the single greatest challenge to our field in the next 20 years. It is important that you calculate exactly how long you plan to be in the field. If you think you are going to retire in 5 years, *Practice-Building 2.0* strategies are probably unnecessary. If, on the other hand, your career could extend beyond 5 years, it is important to start making plans, getting educated, and conducting your own analysis so that you can commit to a plan of action that accounts for this changing process.

Business and Market Changes

Historically, business and market changes were responses to regulation and the insurance industry (e.g., Health Insurance Portability and Accountability Act, managed health care). Over the next 10 years, the impact will most likely come from flattening, allowing the client or customer to participate and guide some aspects of treatment. This shift in the business climate, unlike historic shifts, will place therapists in a position to need to adapt much more quickly to meet market demands.

Consumerism

Although consumerism can create an incredibly positive opportunistic position for psychotherapists, it also creates challenges. For example, your office is near numerous employers of high-technology sales representatives or possibly pharmaceutical representatives. These are potential clients with a high likelihood of needing some additional contact via some form of Internet-based service. Are you prepared to make this adaptation? Or, do you shift your demographic? Possibly, for the first time in the history of modern-day psychotherapy, consumers are shaping service delivery. They have more access to providers than ever before. With the Internet, it is irrelevant if they use insurance or cash pay; they can comparison shop, and they will. Even superficially, while photos and videos knowingly increase sales, consumers may start choosing providers partially based on physical attractiveness. Never before have therapists been placed in a situation in which they need to account for the numerous demands, needs, preferences, and expectations from treatment stakeholders, third-party payers, and referral sources, clients, and former clients.

Clients will increasingly gain power in determining the type of services offered by psychotherapists. As the millennial population matures and seeks services, there will be a significant proportion who will demand electronic interaction as part of the treatment process. It is unlikely that they will want electronic interaction to replace the treatment process completely. However, the use of electronic interaction as a supplement to the treatment is going to alter the financial implications for psychotherapists significantly. This market change is only one example of consumers' increasing power to determine the look of psychotherapy. As you continue to evolve and build your private practice, consumerism should be the number one priority in guiding what you will be implementing.

It is important that as a practice-building therapist you associate with therapists who are maintaining a practice that meets consumer expectations. Attend forums at conferences, seek online information about best practice standards, and start your own collaborative network via e-mails or professional blogs to gain an advantageous position of consumerism and demographic trends. Satisfaction surveys as well as the monitoring of consumer expectations will also play a vital role in meeting these needs. Ensuring that you can offer a diverse range of service (podcasts, videocasts, online therapy, and more) will enable you to meet the diverse needs and expectations of today's consumer.

Health Care Cost Sharing

Already we are seen major changes in health care benefits. For example, there are many employers with health savings accounts now offering insurance policies with high deductibles and copayments. However, the deductible and copayments might have a matching system with the employer, and the deductible or copayment is paid from a health savings account. This simple example presents many challenges for a practice-building therapist. How will you more effectively monitor deductibles? Do you have the opportunity to collect payment from a health savings account (credit card)? There are many challenges looming around the corner regarding the financial obligations and reimbursement for behavioral health care services. Simply resigning and stating, "I will only see self-pay clients" may not financially be in your best interest. Again, for these reasons it is important that psychotherapists create, or associate, in a manner to keep informed about upcoming changes.

National Health Care System

Although only a conversational piece at the time of this writing, some form of national health care system will eventually emerge. Will you be prepared? Even though no one knows what it will look like, it is a safe bet that the federal practice guidelines outlined in the introduction will have influence. Creating best practice standards for your business and collecting data only seem prudent to meet whatever the expectations and requirements from a national health care system.

Stagnant Reimbursement Rates

Probably the biggest challenge for all providers who accept third-party payment will be the eventual challenge for increased reimbursement. Unless there is a major shift in the position of insurance companies to increase reimbursement rates for behavioral health care services, there could easily come a time when psychotherapy services are delivered by novice or desperate therapists. I believe there is already emerging a significant difference between those primarily accepting third-party payments and the more entrepreneurial providers. For example, online therapy providers, while it is unknown what their total population or caseload is, are certainly positioned to generate a significant amount of income as compared to those delivering services face to face, and covered by third-party payers.

Although insurance companies have improved their speed for claims, lacking are significant increases in claim reimbursement. High-quality providers cannot sustain a practice when they are paid minimum wage by a health maintenance organization (HMO) or insurance company. You will need to prepare for, plan for, your own minor skirmishes. For example, do you see clients with a specific insurance plan that pays $55.00 per session at 7:00 P.M.? Probably you do not, especially if you are building a practice in which your direct referral rate is high and you could place a $120 client at 7:00 P.M. There may come a time when you do not schedule anyone with insurance after 4:00 P.M. Are you prepared for your third-party contracts to give you grief or threaten to terminate your contract?

Technology will offer psychotherapists a legitimate opportunity to create a diversified and passive revenue stream. This opportunity is quite exciting. Depending on how insurance companies and employers deal with health savings accounts, customers may actually get some reimbursement or coverage for online or Web-based training. Through the use of technology, psychotherapists at least have the opportunity to diversify their practices and create less dependency on face-to-face services and third-party reimbursements.

Technology also allows for providers to make a good argument for increasing reimbursement services from insurance companies. By keeping some fundamental data on your practice—such as average number of sessions and access to care—providers can demonstrate their value and the necessity for increasing the reimbursement. As consumers continue to be in the power position regarding services, they will also have more input and guidance on covered benefits. Through such mechanisms as health savings or flex accounts, consumers can apply pressure to their employer and insurance companies to request varying forms of psychotherapy service delivery.

Third-Party Payer Changes

Profiling

Insurance companies and managed health care organizations have long been collecting data on practice patterns of network clinicians. For some companies, these initiatives are simplistic, while others are quite comprehensive and sophisticated. Either way, have no reservations, third-party payers are monitoring your practice patterns. Some profiling initiatives include quarterly consumer satisfaction data collection, monitoring of access to care, use and reporting of symptom inventories, reported treatment effectiveness on submitted closing reports, and claims data analysis (cost per diagnosis, cost per treatment episode, diagnostic code use). *Psychotherapy Finances* ("Managed Care Notes," 2008) reported that Wellpoint began publicly rating physicians based on such variables as availability, trust, and communication. What or how companies will use these data is still unknown. However, certain safe assumptions can be made:

1. Companies will increasingly monitor practice patterns.
2. Data points will be in line with best practice standards: access to care, client satisfaction, and treatment effectiveness.
3. Providers meeting certain "floor" benchmark data points will receive recognition, while those not meeting these benchmarks will either be offered training or lack recognition (referrals).
4. Companies will increasingly expect more from providers while not offering any significant increase in reimbursement.

Providers who want to build a practice need to recognize that their performance is being evaluated at some level by third-party payer systems. Furthermore, without a streamlined, efficient infrastructure, the lack of significant increases in reimbursement will threaten the existence of keeping the private practice doors open. Therapists need to start becoming more efficient to maximize every dollar spent on their business.

Online Directories
Online directories will continue to offer a wonderful convenience to potential customers and clients. The challenge for practitioners is keeping their online directories current with information that sells their business. If a directory implements a rating system, how will you rate within their system? Can you influence the rating? Even the greatest therapists may have low ratings based on uncontrollable variables (e.g., use, feedback from clients, and the like).

As therapists continue to have an online directory presence, online directories will experience bloat. You will need countering strategies so your listing is not entirely lost in the mass.

Convenience Store Mentality
Insurance companies will continue their convenience store mentality when it comes to behavioral health care. At one time, third-party payers referred poten-

tial clients to "preferred providers" because they trusted certain psychotherapists would provide high-quality services. Interestingly, now third-party payer and referral systems are less interested in using quality care clinicians and more interested in providing clients convenient access to care through online directories with zip code search functions. The self-service online directories reduce labor at the expense of directing clients to high-quality providers.

If you conduct a simple search of an insurance company's online directory, you will notice that virtually all zip codes have many therapists. Insurance companies have committed to having a network in which clients can choose therapists within a close driving distance—not quality of service. Such a convenience store mentality creates a competitive situation among therapists within a small geographical area.

As long as third-party referral sources maintain the position that there must be a provider on every street corner, high-quality providers will lack recognition. Without publicly announcing how they define high-quality service and allowing network providers to achieve the standards, quality providers will continue to be included with providers who lack even the basic forms of customer service.

It is important that your direct referral rate maintains a high percentage, and that those making referrals have the necessary tools to continue to make referrals. It is important that you keep your Web site up to date and attractive. Keep yourself current with technology so that you are not adversely impacted by bloating insurance directories.

Summary

Recognize that there are many hard realities working against your business. You need mechanisms of support, education, and consultation. The *Monthly Labor Review* ("Survival and Longevity," 2005) reported that approximately 66% of new companies will survive at least 2 years, diminishing to 44% at the 4 year mark, and 31% will survive seven years. Examined from another perspective, these statistics indicate that one third of new companies will close their doors in the first 2 years, and over half will close up shop within 4 years. The business of psychotherapy is not immune. Manage your business for success.

Key Points

1. There are emotional challenges to owning your own business. Prepare and expect these challenges. Owning a small business is risky and requires long hours and attention. Do not go into practice building with the mindset that a few folders, some business cards, and attendance at a networking function now and then will result in success.

2. Hobby practices are significantly different from an owner-operated full-time practice. There is much to learn from hobbyists. At the same time, hobby practices siphon off higher-paying clientele. Create strategies to capture these clients.
3. Regardless of how many clients you have and revenue streams involved, reimbursement will always present challenges. Manage your time and scheduling wisely. There is absolutely no reason a client with insurance paying $55 per session should be seen in a primetime slot, costing you the loss of a client paying the full fee.
4. If you provide services for third-party payers, prepare for profiling of your practice. Unless these companies inform you of exactly what they will profile, you will need to develop your own profile and keep the data fresh on your Web site.
5. There is no indication that third-party payment systems are interested in recognizing high-quality providers. Therefore, you must have a referral system to capitalize on your direct contact with treatment stakeholders, clients, and former clients.

Action List

1. Identify and begin associating with successful psychotherapists throughout the U.S. Use e-mail, participate in discussion groups, or even create your own Facebook group to share ideas and strategies.
2. If a practice-building strategy fails, learn from it. Get outside consult and opinion. It may still be a potentially successful strategy, but something that was overlooked doomed the possibility.
3. If you have a low direct referral rate or believe that a hobby practice is securing referrals that should be coming to your practice, make changes to enhance your attractiveness to these clients and the associated referral source. Examine your relationship with treatment stakeholders. Are you engaging in sufficient advertising via collaboration?
4. Know your reputation or profile within a third-party payer system. Call the provider relations specialist and ask about your status within their company.

CHAPTER NINE

Concluding Our Business Profile

Simply put: numbers talk! Throughout this book, I have highlighted "unrealized revenue" in boxes. This unrealized revenue is money lost, money lost due to inefficiencies in a treatment system, excessive labor and supplies, or lost opportunities. Importantly, more than money is lost; time is lost which could be spent building your business, playing with your kids, or just having fun.

Unrealized Revenue

Although the numbers speak loudly, it is important to note two significant numbers: 66 and 183. These are the number of hours saved per year by *not* engaging in returning phone calls to reschedule appointments and hand-written charting, respectively. Stop and think about these savings: 249 hours per year. Let me contextualize 249 hours:

- 249 hours/40 hour work week = 6.2 weeks of vacation time gained
- 249 hours/11 months = 22 hours per month of time to engage in practice-building tasks
- 249 hours/44 (weeks per working months) = 5.7 hours per work week of self-care time

I must emphasize that these numbers are conservative, and there are many other time savings realized when implementing technology in a private practice. Choosing *not* to implement technology costs your practice in terms of positive revenue and your self-care.

TABLE 9.1: UNREALIZED REVENUE

Strategy	Revenue
Revenue savings	
Collections from no shows and late cancellations (Box 4.5)	$7,040.00
Paperwork download savings (Box 4.2)	$124.00
E-mail reminders saving loss of income (Box 5.3)	$7,040.00
Online scheduling current clients saving call-back time for rescheduling, 66 hours per year saved (Box 4.4)	$5,280.00
Documentation and charting time savings with electronic format, 183 hours per year saved (Box 5.1)	$14,080.00
Total	**$33,564.00**
Revenue income	
Resulting from Web site (Box 4.1)	$18,480.00
Amazon revenues (Box 4.7)	$60.00
Newsletter (Box 5.3)	$5,760.00
Referrals resulting from directories (Box 4.6)	$12,320.00
New referrals resulting from using the online scheduling system (Box 4.3)	$12,320.00
Total	$85,900.00
Grand total of positive revenue	**$119,464**

Table 9.1 exemplifies a few things:

- How much revenue is gained with having an online payment system to increase collections related to no show and late cancellations.
- Time costs that are saved when *not* needing to return calls to reschedule appointments with an online scheduling system.
- Increased revenues with an e-mail reminder system.
- How much documentation time is costing your practice in money and time and how an electronic forms system can reduce this loss.
- How much a Web site can generate income.
- Increased revenues with online directories.
- Substantial income and time savings resulting from online scheduling.

Remember, practice building is more than referral generating. Focusing on streamlining and reducing inefficiencies is as important as how you will get the next referral. These are simple tools that use conservative estimates and result in positive revenues. How can a practice afford to be without them?

Business Profile

We began building a practice by collecting and evaluating some specific data points. Now, our Business Profile is complete (Table 9.2).

Analysis

Examining the data from any single client may not produce useful results because there are many variables associated with satisfaction, loyalty, and outcome. Also, we are not keeping data for pure scientific purposes but rather to spot trends and clues that will assist in delivering higher-quality services inside and outside the therapy room.

In summarizing the data, we find:

Closing status:
63% of clients' termination was mutually agreed on.
25% of clients terminated treatment prematurely.
12% of clients dropped out.
Care coordination:
50% of cases involved care coordination.
50% of cases did not involve care coordination.
Appointments:
Appointments were offered 2.2 days from initial contact.
Appointments were accepted 4.4 days from initial contact.
Scheduling appointments:
63% of clients scheduled online.
37% of clients used voice mail.
Ease of scheduling appointments:
63% reported it was easy or very easy to schedule an appointment.
37% reported it was difficult to schedule an appointment.
Level of progress during treatment:
75% clients had little progress or were contemplating change.
25% of clients were more motivated.
Average number of sessions: 6.9.
Refer to therapist:
There was a 40% return rate, which indicated 60% of clients chose not to complete Satisfaction Survey 2 at the completion of treatment.
60% of clients indicated that they would refer to their therapist.

TABLE 9.2: BUSINESS PROFILE ANALYSIS

Client ID	Closing status	Care Coor. 1= yes 2 = no	Offered appt. days	Accepted appt. days	Method of appt. set (SS1)	Ease of setting (SS1)	Level of progress at closing	Number Sessions	Refer to therapist (SS2) 1= yes 2 = no	Refer to agency (SS2) 1= yes 2 = no
200803172	1	1	3	6	1	4	3	9	1	1
200803173	1	1	1	5	1	4	4	10	1	1
200803174	2	2		1	1	3	2	3		
200803175	3	2	3	7	3	2	2	3	2	1
200803176	2	2	4	4	1	4	2	24		
200803177	3	1	3	3	3	2	1	1		
200803178	3	2	2	3	1	3	2	2	1	1
200803179	4	1	5	6	3	1	2	3	2	2
			2.2	4.4				6.9		

LEGEND

CLOSING STATUS
1 = Mutually agreed, goals mostly met
2 = Mutually agreed, goals not fully met
3 = Client terminated, premature, some goals met
4 = Client dropped out
5 = Therapist terminated treatment

EASE OF SETTING APPOINTMENT

1	2	3	4
Not			Very

METHOD OF APPOINTMENT
1. Online
2. Voice Mail

LEVEL OF PROGRESS AT CLOSING
1 = None contemplating
2 = Contemplating, some goals met
3 = Motivated, goals met
4 = Excellent, client integrating interventions

40% of clients indicated that they would not refer to their therapist.

80% of clients indicated that they would refer to the agency.

20% of client indicated that they would not refer to the agency.

Of course, you will use your spreadsheet formula functions to keep your data as fresh as the last data entry point.

Discussion

When you look at the snapshot of eight clients, shown in Table 9.2, what strikes you about the data? For me, there are three concerning data points that suggest possible compromises in treatment and development of the reputation as high-quality service providers. First, only 50% of the cases involved care coordination. Best practice standards suggest that this data point should be around 66%. It is also alarming that half of the cases lacked generation of information about your treatment abilities. The second data point causing concern is that in 75% of the closed cases the therapist indicated no progress or the client was only contemplating treatment. Why is this percentage so high? Finally, only 60% of the clients who returned Satisfaction Survey 2 indicated that they would refer to their therapist, and only 80% would refer to the agency. These three data points suggest a clinician who is not aggressively involving treatment stakeholders in treatment, poor treatment progress, and understandably a referral rate too low to sustain a practice. This practice is seemingly in trouble.

Now, examine the data by clusters. Notice that those who scheduled their appointments via voice mail also reported difficulty scheduling their appointment, the therapists noted lack of progress during treatment, and clients dropped out or terminated prematurely and indicated that they would not necessarily refer to the therapist or agency. Although not favorable, examination of these data suggests that those clients encountering a rough start to therapy do not necessarily recover. I no longer believe this practice is in trouble because the situation is correctable. Notice that in the first two cases for which there was both care coordination and online scheduling, the results were all favorable for the therapist and agency. Knowing these data, what suggestions might you have for this practice-building therapist?

First, I would want to begin examining the referral sources for this therapist. Who is referring, and are they referring to voice mail or a Web site? If they are referring to voice mail, does the therapist's voice-mail suggest going to the Web site and using the online scheduling? How can the therapist help the referral sources refer to the Web site? Does the therapist need to send letters, visit personally, or create a quick-and-easy brochure highlighting the Web site? The second area I would want to collect more information about involves care coordination. Is the therapist even considering treatment stakeholders in the greater picture of service delivery? What if some of these clients are referred by a local primary care physician who is prescribing psychotropic medication and the therapist is not coordinating care? Not only is this situation bad treatment, but also it creates negative advertisement for the therapist and agency—a bad reputation.

Regardless of how these data are examined, generating more referrals will not solve the practice-building challenges. More referrals have the potential of accelerating a bad reputation. This data set indicates that without correction the practice and therapist are in for a long struggle to maintain the practice, and growing it is out of the question. When a practice struggles, clever ideas for generating more referrals are *not* the answer. The answer involves *knowing* that high-quality services are being delivered and advertising of those services is ongoing before, during, and after treatment.

You may look at the data differently, and that is okay. Most important, however, is that with eight simple cases we are beginning to see a practice pattern. None of these data are difficult to collect or store once you have a streamlined system. Furthermore, the information you will gain about your practice is invaluable.

Developing your Business Profile results in more efficiently advertising and observing trends. You can choose any data points for monitoring. What is important is that you are paying attention to your practice patterns. Knowing your patterns will help you reduce labor, correct bad trends, take advantage of positive trends, and advertise your practice more effectively.

Final Thoughts

As a business owner who prides himself as quickly adapting and adopting to technology, I am excited and encouraged by the seemingly endless possibilities awaiting the psychotherapy field. Yet, I understand the majority of psychotherapists, and the field as a whole, will certainly wake up one day asking, "What just happened?" Therapists were shocked at the speed and decimation of managed behavioral health care, but there were trend signs long before practices were adversely impacted.

The trend signs for a new era of psychotherapy exist today. Unfortunately, credentialing bodies, associations, regulatory boards, and universities continue to pay little attention to customer service, flattening, and technology. Training continues to focus on traditional face-to-face services, thereby setting up new professionals for failure. Regulatory boards and credentialing bodies enable experienced clinicians to ignore trends with an adverse impact on their careers and businesses.

This situation will lead the unaware group of psychotherapists further down a path of unknown outcome. I have mixed feelings about this dynamic. Although failure and possible exiting from the field are painful to those experiencing them, culling of providers not keeping up with consumer expectations and technological trends helps provide a healthier field.

Despite a few gloom-and-doom thoughts, I believe the psychotherapy field is on the precipice of amazing opportunities. Therapists who examine their infrastructures and practice-building patterns can begin maximizing profit margins, reducing labor, and providing a multitude of services that generate income.

Integrating technology to meet practice standard expectations provides business owners exciting opportunities. Diverse revenue streams will emerge as will diverse service delivery methods. Businesses that deliver psychotherapy can evolve into highly profitable ventures for those with the risk-taking business owner mentality. Those exploring the numerous new possibilities will experience success and failure. However, the energy and rewards will certainly be at levels never before possible for owners of psychotherapy businesses.

Practices that eliminate desperate random acts of practice building such as networking, developing specialty niches, and other strategies trying to gain unknown referrals (Ring 3) through cold-calling efforts will prosper. Focusing on improving infrastructure efficiencies, thereby reducing labor and increasing profit margins, will result in more time available for self-care or business caretaking activities. Those practices offering technology and high-quality customer service to treatment stakeholders, clients, and former clients will create a sound business built on a reputation of trust and quality. Trust and quality always have been, always will be, the two most important components for providing psychotherapy services.

Appendix A

Starting Your Business

This book focused on helping those already owning a private practice. For those who are interested in starting their own business, I created a checklist of priorities and activities to increase the potential for a successful startup. These items should be done prior to scheduling your first client (up to 1 year before).

Start Up

____Determine a name for your corporation. Keep in mind that your treatment stakeholders, clients, and former clients need an easy name to remember and for referal.

____Seek accounting assistance. Determine what type of corporation you will create (e.g., limited liability corporation [LLC], professional corporation [PC], and so on). Understand the quarterly tax payment system versus employee payment structure.

____Seek legal services to ensure that the proper forms and documents are created and filed.

____Get yourself an NPI (National Provider Identifier) number: https://nppes.cms.hhs.gov/NPPES/Welcome.do

____Purchase a computer that can create and edit sound and video.

____Purchase/obtain software that allows you to e-mail, word process, create spreadsheets, convert sound files to MP3.

____Create an electronic filing and charting system, including all forms and letters you will use when charting your sessions. See Appendix B, Forms.

____Create a data collection system.

  ____Client and treatment-identifying stakeholder information.

  ____Access to care measures.

____Referral tracking.

____Average number of sessions (although you have not yet seen a client, what will be the method to collect this information?)

____direct vs .indirect referral rates

____Implement a contact management system (CMS) minimally allows you to sort clients, former clients, and treatment stakeholders.

____Create and implement a security system on your computer and within your computer files.

____Get a Web site. Make sure the company offers secure Web-based mail, not standard Web mail.

____Design the Web site to reduce labor and increase revenue.

____Clinical intake paperwork is uploaded so new clients can download the necessary forms.

____Insurance and treatment population matrices are posted.

____Create an audio or video file introducing yourself. If you use an audio file, have a picture of yourself posted on the Web site.

____Sign up for the Amazon Associates Program or a similar program with another retailer.

____Create a reading list that links to Amazon.

____Identify the online scheduling system you feel most comfortable using.

____Integrate an online payment system into your Web site. Although some feel PayPal is a bit expensive, literally within a few minutes the entire system is set up.

____Outline or write your next 12 months of e-newsletters or Web site updates.

____Set your goals.

____Direct referral rates

____Reimbursement diversity

____Referral diversity

____Definition of success for your first 12 months

____Create a brochure outlining not only the client populations served but also your flagship customer service variables (e.g., online scheduling, aggressive care coordination).

____Develop at least one "teaser" Webinar on a clinical topic using Power-Point and a voice-over narration.

____Develop at least six podcasts on self help issues. Get these podcasts listed in some podcast directories.

____Create an AdWords campaign landing page for your eventual AdWords campaign.

____Immediately before opening up for business, get a telephone system with voice mail and your online scheduling system. You do not want to pay for such services until you need the services.

____Order 500 business cards, maximum, prominently displaying your name and Web site address.

Now, it is time to get clients calling and using your online scheduling system. Because you have not seen a client, you will need to engage in cold calling, Ring 3 strategies.

____Identify and enter into your CMS all primary care physician offices within a certain radius of your office. This distance varies by practice location; urban practices may set a distance of less than a mile, while those in the suburbs or rural settings may have a greater distance.

____Identify and enter into your CMS all psychiatrists within a certain radius of your office. This distance varies by practice location; urban practices may set a distance of less than a mile, while those in the suburbs or rural settings may have a greater distance.

____Identify and enter into your CMS any hospitals providing psychiatric services.

____Schedule time to meet the identified psychiatrists, and individuals primary care offices and hospitals. Deliver your brochure and business cards. Highlight your flagship services.

____Talk to every friend, family member, and acquaintance about your practice in an attempt to identify a few referral sources who will begin immediately referring to you because they trust the mutual introduction.

____Meet with these potential referral sources and highlight your flagship services.

____Start a Google AdWords campaign. Spend the extra money to ensure that you are on the top list of the sponsored links.

____Get yourself listed on every possible psychotherapist directory that is affordable and allows the listing of your Web site.

You have covered some of the basics for generating your first few referrals. Now, you need to capitalize on every single referral you get. Your first 10 referrals should receive extra care and attention as they may make or break your practice. It is absolutely imperative to accomplish the following:

____Engage in aggressive care coordination with all appropriate treatment stakeholders. Send the care coordination notice, make follow-up phone calls, and leave messages inquiring if the treatment stakeholder would like any additional information.

_____Educate your clients about all of your services (e.g., online scheduling to reschedule appointments, online payment system, podcasts, tips and strategies on the Web site).

_____Each client should receive an administrative satisfaction survey at the completion of the first session.

_____Inform your new clients that you are accepting referrals and they should feel free to have potential new clients call you or visit your Web site.

_____Each client should receive a clinical administrative survey at the completion of treatment.

_____You inquired, and for those saying "yes," start an e-mail reminder system.

_____You inquired and for those saying "yes", enter each e-mail address in a distribution list for future e-newsletters.

_____Following treatment, and for those saying "yes," you send a 3-, 6- and 12-month follow-up letters.

While not exhaustive, these strategies should result in some clients in your smart phone and using your online scheduling services. Do not get discouraged or give up. Keep your eyes open for opportunity. Remember, however, that you want your reputation to build loyalty with your treatment stakeholder and clients. Focusing on providing high-quality services accomplishes this goal.

Appendix B

Biased Resources

Admittedly, I am biased concerning the recommended resources. As I have repeatedly emphasized throughout this project, your practice should focus on building satisfaction and loyalty. The same is true for the resources I am recommending. I trust and am loyal to these tools and agencies. Provided they stay in business, I will continue to refer to these resources.

Online Scheduling

As a previous owner of Healthe-scheduler.com (www.healthe-scheduler.com), I can attest to the ease and satisfaction of both subscribers/therapists and users/clients. This is a simplistic system, requiring you to print the receipt, then manually transfer the information into your contact mamagement system (CMS). However, by now, it should be apparent why there is a manual function: privacy protection. With this system, there is little chance of clients leaving "footprints" that can potentially compromise their privacy. The receipt allows you to record your data relating to days offered and days accepted for an appointment, thereby beginning your data collection process. After 5 years, the customer satisfaction rate is outstanding. Clients continuously comment on the ease and efficiency of using the scheduling system.

Mytherapynet.com

A forerunner in online therapy service environments, Kathleen Derrig-Palumbo and Foojan Zeine wrote a definitive book regarding online therapy. Mytherapynet.com continues to upgrade and keep pace with the many changes concerning online therapy. This business is generous with advice and assistance to help you achieve success with your online therapy endeavors.

Forms

The American Association for Marriage and Family Therapy (AAMFT) has created an outstanding tool, *Practice Management Forms*, available in the publications area of their online store at www.aamft.org. Use these forms to get you started and modify or add as you feel is appropriate. There is no need to guess which forms you need. Your first task is to convert these forms into your electronic filing system by creating default answers, drop-down menus, and form fields for data entry.

Practice-Building Resource

Beyond a doubt, *Psychotherapy Finances* is a must-have subscription. Every month new ideas, strategies, and industry trends are highlighted. You can subscribe at www.psyfin.com.

Sound Editing

As mentioned in Chapter 4, *Audacity* is simple and free sound-editing software. Converting audio files to MP3 is easy. As you become more comfortable with the software, you can enhance your audio files to the point of sounding almost professionally created. Audacity can be found at http://audacity.sourceforge.net.

E-mail Merge

Addins4Outlook is an extremely simple software tool for e-mail merges (available at http://www.addins4outlook.com). For about $40.00, you can make the e-mail merge a simple and fast process.

References

Amazon Associates Program. (2008) *Make money advertising Amazon products.* Retrieved November, 2008 from https://affiliate-program.amazon.com

American Association for Marriage and Family Therapy. (2001). *Code of ethics.* Alexandria, VA: Author.

American Counseling Association. (2005). *Code of ethics.* Alexandria, VA: Author.

American Psychiatric Association. (2001). *The principles of medical ethics with annotations especially applicable to psychiatry.* Arlington, VA: Author.

American Psychological Association. (2003). *Ethical principles of psychologists and code of Conduct.* Washington DC: Author.

Conti, G. (2009). *Googling security: How much does Google know about you?* New York: Addison-Wesley.

Derrig-Palumbo, K., & Zeine, F. (2005). *Online therapy: A therapist's guide to expanding your practice.* New York: Norton.

Federal Trade Commission: Protecting America's Consumers. (2003). *Facts for business: The CAN-SPAM Act: Requirements for commercial emailers.* Retrieved November 28, 2008 from http://www.ftc.gov/bcp/edu/pubs/business/ecommerce/bus61.shtm

Fox, S., & Rainie, L. (2000). *The online health revolution: How the web helps Americans take better care of themselves.* Pew Internet & American Life Project. Retrieved November 28, 2008 from http://www.pewinternet.org/report_display.asp?r=26

Fox, S. (2008). *Report public policy: Privacy implications of fast, mobile Internet access.* Pew Internet & American Life Project. Retrieved November 28, 2008 from http://www.pewinternet.org/PPF/r/238/report_display.asp

Friedman, T. (2006). *The world is flat: A brief history of the twenty-first history.* New York: Farrar, Straus and Giroux.

Gitomer, J. (1998). *Customer satisfaction is worthless, customer loyalty is priceless: How to make them love you, keep you coming back, and tell everyone they know.* Austin: Bard Press.

Google. (2008) *Google analytics.* Retrieved November 28, 2008 from http://www.google.com/analytics/

Horrigan, J. (2008). *Mobile access to data and information.* Pew Internet and American Life Project. Retrieved November 28, 2008 from http://www.pewinternet.org/pdfs/PIP_Mobile.Data.Access.pdf

Horrigan, J., & Rainie, L., (2002). *Counting on their Internet.* Pew Internet & American Life Project. Retrieved November 28, 2008 from http://www.pewinternet.org/PPF/r/80/report_display.asp.

Ice cream versus therapy. (2008). *Psychotherapy Finances, 34*(10), 7.

Institute of Medicine, (2001). *Crossing the quality chasm: A new health system for the 21st century.* Washington DC: National Academies Press.

Latest trends: Who's online. Pew Internet and American Life Project. Retrieved November 28, 2008 from http://www.pewinternet.org/trends.asp

Levesque, P. (2006). *Customer service made easy.* Irvine, CA: Entrepreneur Press.

Mackay, H. (1997). *Dig your well before you're thirsty: The only networking book you'll ever need.* New York: Doubleday Business.

Madden, M. (2003). *America's online pursuits: The changing picture of who's online and what they do.* Pew Internet & American Life Project. Retrieved November 28, 2008 from http://www.pewinternet.org/report_display.asp?r=106

Making web marketing more effective by tracking visitors. (2008). *Psychotherapy Finances, 32*(7), 8.

Managed care notes: Wellpoint members have begun publicly rating their health care provides. (2008). *Psychotherapy Finances, 34*(1), 11.

Marketing: A creative practice name can boost your professional profile. (2008). *Psychotherapy Finances, 34*(10), 1

Marketing: Free tele-class attracts clients. (2008b). *Psychotherapy Finances, 34*(3), 4.

Mercer, J. (2003). *May I help you?: Great customer service for small business.* Crows Nest, Australia: Allen & Unwin.

Merriam-Webster. *Marketing.* Retrieved January 24, 2009 from http://www.merriam-webster.com/dictionary/marketing

Merriam-Webster. *Advertising.* Retrieved January 24, 2009 from http://www.merriam-webster.com/dictionary/advertising

Michelli, J. (2006). *The Starbucks experience: 5 principles for turning ordinary into extraordinary.* New York: McGraw-Hill.

Mini-survey: PsyFin readers reveal their marketing tools and strategies. (2008, June). *Psychotherapy Finances, 34*(6), 5.

Monthly Labor Review. Survival and longevity in the business employment dynamics database (2005). Retrieved November 28, 2008 from http://www.score.org/small_biz_stats.html

National Association of Social Workers. (1999). *Code of ethics.* Washington, DC: Author.

New Freedom Commission on Mental Health. (2003). *Achieving the promise: Transforming mental health care in America. Final report* DHHS Publication No. SMA-03-3832. Rockville, MD.

Online Publishing. (2005). *Psychotherapy Finances, 31*(11), 4.

Publishing: Clinician-authors discuss lessons learned on writing, publishing and self-publishing. (2008). *Psychotherapy Finances, 34*(2), 6.

Robbins, T. (1984). *Jitterbug Perfume.* New York: Bantam Books.

Special report: Strategies for improving your web marketing through Google AdWords. (2007). *Psychotherapy Finances, 33*(5), 6.

Still no Website? Here's what you need to get started. (2006). *Psychotherapy Finances*, *32*(7), 4.

Technology: Two therapists who make extra money doing "chat-room" therapy. (2006). *Psychotherapy Finances*, *34*(6), 5.

TechTerms.com. *Bit rate*. Retrieved January 24, 2009 from http://www.techterms.com/definition/bitrate

TechTerms.com. (*Certificate*. Retrieved November 28, 2008 from http://www.techterms.com/definition/certificate.

TechTerms.com. *Meta tag*. Retrieved November 28, 2008). . http://www.techterms.com/definition/metatag

TechTerms.com. *RSS*. Retrieved January 24, 2009 from http://www.techterms.com/definition/rss

TechTerms.com. *SSL (Secure Sockets Layers)*. Retrieved November 28, 2008) from http://www.techterms.com/definition/ssl

Tips for getting the most out of online therapist directories. (2006). *Psychotherapy Finances*, *32*(10), 5.

Todd, T. (2006, July–August). *Understanding and implementing best practice standards. Family Therapy Magazine*, 5(4), pp. 32–35.

U.S. Department of Health and Human Services. (1999). *Mental health: A report of the surgeon general—Executive summary*. U.S. Department of Health and Human Services, Substance Abuse and Mental Health Services Administration, Center for Mental health Services, National Institutes of Health, National Institute of Mental Health. Washington D.C.: SAMHSA's Natinal Mental Health Information Center.

Yahoo, MSN fight for a share. (2007). *Psychotherapy Finances*, *33*(5), 7.

Index

In this index, the abbreviation *f* denotes figure or form and the abbreviation *t* denotes table.

30-second commercial, 196–97

access to care, 35–36, 37*f*, 38*t*, 125*t*–26*t*, 208
    see also care coordination; online scheduling
Achieving the Promise: Transforming Mental Health Care in America, 6
adaptation, as a practice building barrier, 23–24, 42
administrative skills, *see* infrastructure technology; practice building; referral development
advertising
    blogs, 122–23, 193
    click-through campaigns, 188–90
    cold calling, 16–17, 74–75
    flagship services as, 161–64, 162*t*, 163*f*, 165*f*, 167
    free, 193–94, 196–97
    myths about, 12–13, 15–16
    seminars as, 191
    Web banner, 193
    see also care coordination; client loyalty; online directories; podcasts; videocasts
Amazon Associates Program, 124, 150–51
American Association for Marriage and Family Therapy, 113
American Association of Online Psychotherapists, 156
analytics, 95, 97, 189, 190
appointment reminders, 145–47, 147*f*, 148*f*
appointment scheduling, *see* online scheduling
attitude, as a practice building barrier, 23
audio files, 116–19
authorization to disclose form, 66*f*
automation, as a practice building barrier, 26
autoresponse, 133

best practice standards, 6–8, 57–58, 125*t*, 156, 215
    see also care coordination
billing, *see* online payment system; retainer model of billing
blogs, 122–23, 193
book publishing, 191–92

brochures, 13
burnout, *see* challenges of private practice
business acumen inventory, 40
business card myth, 13–14
business challenges, *see* challenges of private practice
business paradigm shifts, 3, 5
business plan myth, 11–12
business processes, as a practice challenge, 204–7
business profile spreadsheets
    access to care, 35–36, 38*t*
    analysis and discussion, 213–16, 214*t*
    care coordination, 180, 181*f*, 183*f*
    case closing information, 180*t*
    file management, 143, 143*t*–44*t*
    general purpose, 28, 29*t*, 213–16, 214*t*
    insurance matrix, 70*t*
    referral and revenue distribution, 30*t*, 31*t*, 33*t*, 34*t*
    satisfaction surveys, 54*t*
    treatment population matrix, 71*t*, 112*t*–13*t*
    treatment stakeholders assessment, 62*t*
    treatment summary indicating progress, 178, 180*t*

calendar, *see* online scheduling
camcorder, 122
cancellation, of appointment, 106, 107
    see also appointment reminders
CAN-SPAM Act (2003), 135
care coordination
    client loyalty and, 174–75
    contact management system (CMS), 131, 132–33
    overview of, 63–64, 65*f*, 66*f*
    podcast introduction, 114–15
    symptom inventories, 175–76, 208
    treatment stakeholders, 67–68, 70, 179–81, 181*f*, 182*f*, 183*f*
case closing information, 177–78, 178*f*, 179*f*, 180*t*, 208
case management, *see* care coordination; file management; treatment stakeholders
cash pay clients myth, 17–19
challenges of private practice
    business processes, 204–7
    emotional drain, 199–204
    third-party payer changes, 207–9
checking-in letter, 138, 139*f*
claims data analysis, 208
clicking efficiency, *see* navigation, in Web site design

uploading documents, 94
usability, of Web site design, 92–93
U.S. Department of Health and Human Services, 6, 7

videocasts
  considerations for, 119–22
  consumer expectations, 24, 55
  technology needed for, 27, 122
video introduction, 119–20, 164, 165*f*, 190

Web banner advertising, 193
Webinars, 191
Web logs, 122–23
Web marketing, 188–90
Web site functionality
  analytics, 95, 97, 189, 190
  competitive advantages, 42, 83–84, 95, 97
  design, 84, 85, 86f–88f, 88–89, 89f–91f
  drop-down menus, 42, 103
  e-mail account, 133–36, 135*f*
  information accuracy and reputation,
    168–69
  insurance matrix, 70*t*, 111
  interactivity, 94
  metatags, 99
  navigation, 92–93
  online payment system, 106–7

online scheduling, 93, 99–100, 101–4
paperwork download, 94–95
positive representation, 92, 95, 97,
  168–69
purchasing a Web site, 111
referral development and, 68–69, 84
rings of referrals, 81–82
treatment population matrix, 71*t*, 111
  see also podcasts; videocasts
Web site hosting company
  data storage, 97, 98, 104, 106
  modifying a Web site, 93–94
  purchasing a Web site, 111
  technology considerations, 114*t*
Web site technology
  data storage, 97–99, 104, 105–6
  metatags, 99
  navigation, 92–93, 94
  online payment system, 110–11
  online scheduling, 104–6
  purchasing a Web site, 111
  security, 94, 98, 104–6, 110–11, 133–34
  see also podcasts; videocasts
word of mouth referrals, 35

yellow page advertising myth, 15

Zeine, F., 156